Charles E. Henderson

YOU CAN DO IT WITH
SELF-HYPNOSIS

achieving self-improvement,
personal growth, and success

PRENTICE HALL PRESS
New York   London   Toronto   Sydney   Tokyo

Published in 1987 by Prentice Hall Press
A Division of Simon & Schuster, Inc.
Gulf + Western Building
One Gulf + Western Plaza
New York, NY 10023

Originally published by Prentice-Hall, Inc.

PRENTICE HALL PRESS is a trademark of Simon & Schuster, Inc.

Library of Congress Cataloging-in-Publication Data

Henderson, Charles E.
    You can do it with self-hypnosis.
    Bibliography: p.
Includes index.
    1. Autogenic training.   2. Success.   I. Title.
RC499.A8H46   1983   158'.1   83-11115
ISBN 0-13-976621-9
ISBN 0-13-976613-8 (pbk.)

Manufactured in the United States of America

14 13 12 11 10 9 8 7 6

to F.W. Edgelgeute and Texhoma Fats,
one and the same, alive again

Contents

Preface

This book presents a safe and powerful method for self-directed improvement and personal development. With these proven methods of self-hypnosis you will discover dynamic control of your mental forces. By learning how to communicate with the powerful, hidden part of your mind, you can succeed at anything that depends on your own efforts.

More than just self-hypnosis, this book presents a complete system of self-communication. You will learn, for example, how to develop very deep states of relaxation. Deep relaxation gives you powerful resistance to stress, anxiety, and the negative influences that surround all of us.

You will learn how to develop and use self-hypnosis. These methods of self-hypnotic induction can be safely and effectively used by anyone. All you have to do is follow the easy instructions.

You will learn the fascinating methods of autoquestioning. Autoquestioning gives you direct communication with the subconscious part of your mind. With this exciting procedure you will learn why you do what you do (or why you *don't* do what you would like to), and how to go about making desired changes.

You will learn how to formulate and apply suggestions. Suggestions are the programming part of this system. They are the vehicle that will transport you to whatever level of achievement you want.

In this book you will find specific, detailed instructions for controlling weight, quitting smoking, achieving a higher income, bettering concentration and memory, improving health, and overcoming shyness. The methods and techniques of these applications can be generalized to virtually any other area of self-mastery.

Everything you need to know is here—nothing has been held back. With this system of self-mastery you will be embarking on an exciting and rewarding journey, a journey in quest of your own potential. Whatever you want to do, you can do it with self-hypnosis.

The systematic approach to self-communication presented here is unique. It is the culmination of many years of research and experience. Over the past several years I have taught this method to more than 26,000 people from all walks of life and from every part of the United States. Many of them have participated in special research projects and provided invaluable feedback and modifications. Collectively, this is as much their book as mine, and I want to thank them all.

Introduction

Nasrudin was on his hands and knees, searching for something on the ground. A friend was passing by, saw him, and asked what he was looking for.

"My key," answered Nasrudin.

So his friend joined him on the ground to help him look for the lost key. After several minutes of fruitless searching, the friend asked Nasrudin approximately where he had dropped the key.

"In the house," said Nasrudin.

"Then why are we looking for it out here?" asked his friend.

"Because there is more light out here than in the house," was Nasrudin's reply.

This ancient anecdote from the folklore of the Middle East has a timeless appeal because it exaggerates—and, in doing so, clarifies—a typically human folly which we are all sometimes guilty of committing. We know we have committed this folly when we catch ourselves looking for solutions ("keys") in the wrong places. The light may be better, but we can never solve our problems if we are searching for solutions in the wrong places. One of these "wrong places" is economic prosperity.

New cars, bigger homes, more and more money, more appliances, and more exotic toys are fine in their place. But sometimes we lose sight of the fact that they are just *things* that cannot, in and of themselves, bring happiness. The real keys to happiness and personal fulfillment are inside of us. I believe that economic prosperity is an acceptable goal. But it can bring happiness only to the degree that our inner needs will permit.

What I am calling "inner needs" will take on more meaning (and

1

different labels) in the pages that follow. Suffice it here to say that, whatever your inner needs, you can either change them or accept them as they are. The choice is yours. I will be telling you about methods for acceptance and methods for generating change. That these methods work is beyond question. Thousands of people from every walk of life have proved their effectiveness. Most of the methods are quite easy to apply, and those that are more difficult will still be within your reach. There is only one "catch" to this: You must be willing to work at it.

I am bringing this up now so you won't later accuse me of promising you a rose garden. You have probably learned by now that anything worthwhile requires some work, and the development of self-hypnotic skill is no exception.

On the other hand, the methods you will be learning here are a lot easier than trying to use willpower to achieve anything. When it comes down to a choice between self-hypnosis and willpower for personal achievement and improvement, self-hypnosis is by far the better choice.

The myth of willpower has become a mean joke. But learning to develop and use self-hypnosis is as easy as learning to type or ride a bicycle. Just how well *you* learn to use self-hypnosis will depend on your desire and on how much you are willing to practice. Merely reading this book, without following or implementing any of the methods, will be of very little value to you. *You* are the one who must apply these methods in order for them to be effective.

In other words, you can do it if you want to. You may desperately want something that you have been unable to achieve in the past. That does not make you a failure—you don't become a failure until you give up. The main reason that most people give up is because they don't know how to achieve what they want. They have never learned how to use their mental equipment. Learn to properly use your mental forces—the ones that everyone has—and you will be able to achieve your goals.

Most of these mental forces reside in the subconscious part of your mind. It has tremendous power, but it is a power that can work against you as well as for you. The purpose of the techniques presented in this book is to get that power working for you. When you bring the subconscious part of your mind into alignment with your conscious goals and desires, you will have opened the door to virtually unlimited self-improvement.

"Self-improvement" has become a magic phrase in our society because most of us have deeply ingrained desires to better ourselves. These desires have led to a proliferation of improvement programs and schemes that too often promise more than they can deliver. Fad diets, weight-loss clubs, "effortless" exercise gadgets, and various brands of meditation are just a few examples of self-improvement programs that will be effective for some people. But most people give up in sulky dismay after trying them for a while.

It is truly unfortunate that these programs are often heralded as The Ultimate Solution because all too often they turn out to have little more punch than a Girl Scout cookie. Those who fail with such programs may be left with the conviction that improvement is for them forever beyond reach. This negative conviction is unfortunate because it is far from the truth.

Self-improvement of practically any kind is almost always possible, but it must come from within. There are no panaceas that will eliminate all work on the part of the individual. Nor are there—aside from medical applications—any pills that one can take for permanent, positive improvement. Self-improvement comes only as a result of self-initiated, internal transformation. Accept that fact, and you can begin to work in the right direction to achieve changes that are exciting and permanent.

Apply the procedures and techniques presented here and you will be able to effect changes in yourself beyond your wildest dreams. And you won't need any elaborate paraphernalia, pills, or equipment to do so. The effectiveness of these techniques has been proved in practice by thousands of people. At last estimate I had trained over 26,000 people in seminars and workshops across the United States. These were people of every age and from all segments of society who learned how to use self-hypnosis to achieve their goals. Many of them were initially reserved or even skeptical about self-hypnosis because the subject has so often been associated with weirdoes and charlatans. But everyone I know of who has honestly and sincerely tried these procedures of self-hypnosis has found them to be very helpful and far more powerful than they could have imagined. I have a large file of letters from such people. Many of the letters begin with "At first I didn't believe in it . . ." and end with ". . . I'm amazed!"

Some of the self-hypnosis procedures you will be reading about here have been known for many years—in some cases thousands of years—but they have not been put together in a systematic, simplified form that the average reader could understand and use. And some of the procedures are the results of recent scientific advances.

Some people experience seemingly miraculous changes that occur overnight, but such rapid results are not the rule. If you turn out to be one of the lucky few who achieve overnight success, well and good. But if it takes longer, don't be discouraged. The speed with which these procedures are effective will vary among individuals and cannot be predicted. The speed with which you achieve success with these methods does not indicate anything about intelligence or strength of mind. Just because your rate of achievement is faster or slower than someone else's does not mean that you are more or less intelligent or that you have a weaker or stronger mind.

Be content to work with your own rate of development, and don't concern yourself with comparative speeds of improvement. Follow the step-by-step procedures as they are presented and you will achieve your goals. The achievement of these goals will for the most part be permanent. Those achievements that are not intrinsically permanent can be made permanent with a maintenance program.

By following the directions given in this book, you will learn how to bring your subconscious mind into agreement with your conscious desires. This is the process that leads to success. Whether you want to lose weight and keep it off, stop smoking, improve your concentration and memory, increase your income, or any of the countless other possibilities, all you have to do is follow the directions.

Of the several possibilities I just mentioned in the last paragraph, the one about "increased income" often piques a special curiosity. Economic progress is a category that is often left out of self-improvement programs, yet it is very definitely dependent upon one's own efforts. Those who conclude that financial success is mostly a matter of luck are in error; when attempt after attempt has failed to yield financial improvement, it is all too easy to blame fate. Losers go through life envying winners their rapport with Lady Luck, never realizing that financial success can be generated from within the mind. Or to be more accurate, those qualities that *lead* to wealth and success must emanate from within. And anything that comes from within us can be initiated, influenced, or modified with self-hypnosis.

No matter how much of a failure one has been in the past, he or she is on the way to becoming a success with the understanding and application of the concepts presented in this book (provided that the desire is there, of course). Everyone has the same basic equipment, and anyone who has the desire to succeed can learn to use that equipment for the achievement of success. These techniques do not summon mysterious, external forces to the aid of the individual, but the ways in which winners attract success often do seem mysterious. Actually, it is a person's thinking and behavior that lead to success. You, too, can do it if you wish, and it is the purpose of this book to show you how. With correct knowledge and proper application, nothing is beyond your grasp.

THE MYTH OF WILLPOWER

When we say that a person has willpower, we usually mean that he or she has a certain strength of will, or self-control. "Good willpower" is viewed as a conscious force that makes it possible for a person to quit smoking, control eating, and generally control himself or herself in any way desired. If this concept of willpower were correct, then willpower would exist as a generalized condition of mind, and it would be present in all areas of endeavor. But this is just not the case.

One person may be able to quit smoking with ease but gain weight rapidly after doing so, while another person may have no trouble controlling weight or quitting smoking, but be unable to stop chewing fingernails. We all know someone who has quit smoking and who derides those who cannot quit smoking as having no willpower, but who has conveniently forgotten that when he quit smoking he gained twenty or thirty pounds.

To tell someone that she can overcome past failures by simply developing willpower is a cruel joke, one that invokes the typically American myth of willpower. Actually, the only time "willpower" is effective in accomplishing a goal is when the subconscious part of the mind does not oppose the goal.

So the common concept of willpower is a myth and a sham. It is shamelessly paraded around as the dominant force (read *farce*) of the mind. In reality, what appears to be the result of willpower is neither more nor less than a conscious desire which the subconscious part of the mind finds acceptable. On the other hand, if there is enough subconscious resistance present, then willpower is ineffective. This subconscious resistance is often manifested in imagination.

IMAGINATION

Many people are surprised to learn that imagination is far more powerful than willpower. We have all been taught to downgrade imagination as childish and of no practical value. Yet a healthy, well-developed and *controlled* imagination can be your most effective tool for constructive change. Out of control, it is destructive. Worrying is an example of negative imagination.

When imagination and conscious will are at war, imagination always wins. The dominance of imagination over willpower causes failure when we try to use willpower to achieve a difficult task or follow a program of self-improvement. We usually experience this authority of imagination over will when we try to *make* ourselves stop worrying about something.

The seat of imagination is the subconscious part of the mind, while willpower is a strictly conscious quality. If you try to achieve something by willpower alone, while your imagination keeps saying that you cannot succeed, you will have no chance of succeeding. The positive application of imagination is far more effective in the accomplishment of desired goals than is willpower.

Stated in other terms, the subconscious is far more powerful and potent than the conscious part of the mind. Not having learned this, many people attempt to use "willpower" to *force* their imagination to work for them. They try to will themselves into imagining that success is possible. This procedure succeeds only in setting up contradictory forces that produce failure.

As long as there is the slightest doubt about success, the imagination will enhance that doubt and make success unlikely. The imagination function of the subconscious mind is just too subtle and delicate to be dealt with in a brutish, heavy-handed manner. So the harder you try, the more likely you are to fail if there is any doubt at all about success. This is called the *Law of Reversed Effect.*

The doubt that causes failure is often not felt directly. There might be an awareness of slight doubt tugging at the edge of consciousness, or the doubt may be completely hidden from any conscious awareness. The less we are consciously aware of doubt, the more freely can that doubt work its negative effects. But whether or not one is consciously aware of doubt, its presence exerts a tremendous influence on an individual's performance.

Everyone has experienced the undesirable products of doubt and the role that uncontrolled imagination plays in failure. For instance, almost anyone can walk along a six-inch-wide plank without falling off when it is on the ground. But put that plank fifty feet (or even three feet!) in the air and try to walk it! The higher the plank, the more one's doubts are magnified.

Whether the task is walking across a plank high in the air or doing something more constructive, your imagination must work for you, not against you, if you are to be successful. The cooperation of the imagination can be achieved with the techniques presented in Chapter 4, which deals with suggestion. The importance of this cooperation is not to be underestimated to ensure success.

IMAGINATION AND THE AUTONOMIC NERVOUS SYSTEM

When considering the role of imagination in our lives, it is important to know something about the autonomic nervous system. It is one of two nervous systems in the body, the other being the central nervous system.

The central nervous system is composed of the brain and spinal cord. It controls all of the so-called "voluntary" muscles. Any muscle, or more commonly any group of muscles, that you can consciously influence is in the domain of the central nervous system. Hand and arm movement, walking or running, and pouring a cup of coffee are all examples of actions controlled through the central nervous system.

Our internal organs do their work by muscular action. Lungs, heart, stomach, even arteries and veins could not function if it were not for the activity of muscles. These "involuntary" muscles are under the control of the autonomic nervous system, joined to but lying outside the spine, and which acts independently of the central nervous system.

With a little thought you will be able to come up with examples of actions or behaviors that are sometimes consciously controlled, sometimes not. Facial expressions are a good example. If not too much emotion is involved, we can control our facial expressions; we can smile, frown, or look "neutral" at will. But stronger emotions such as fear, anger, sadness, or jealousy often completely strip us of control over our faces. It takes a very good actor to suppress the facial cues that show emotions. Thus facial expressions are an example of muscular behavior that is ordinarily controlled by the central nervous system, but which can be taken over by the autonomic nervous system under certain conditions.

It was once believed that the autonomic and central nervous systems were separate and independent of one another. That position is no longer tenable. It is now well established that autonomic (subconscious) functions can be significantly influenced by the central nervous system (conscious activities). The control of involuntary actions by voluntary means will become more apparent to you when you begin to work with the methods and techniques of self-hypnosis.

You will learn how the controlled, constructive use of imagination as a form of suggestion can influence such seemingly unrelated areas as health, concentration and memory, financial success, and interpersonal relationships. To illustrate, consider the human heart. This muscle is under the jurisdiction of the autonomic system. You may not be aware that you can affect your heartbeat by thinking about it. But it is true that the proper use of imagination—especially when applied during self-hypnosis—can change the rate at which the heart beats.

Think back to some recent incident that got you really scared or angry. If you were sufficiently aroused, you were probably aware that your heart was beating at a much faster rate than usual. Rapid pulse is normal under conditions of arousal, and the arousal can be either positive or negative. Positive arousal occurs in such circumstances as making love or learning that a distant relative has just left you a fortune in her will. Negative arousal can be the product of an argument or a near-miss auto accident. Positive or negative, arousal results in increased pulse rate.

Whatever the cause, accelerated heartbeat can be slowed by imagining calmness and tranquillity, by "relaxing," as we are often told to do. But this requires practice because we have been taught to play down our imaginations. Adults have learned to think of imagination as childish and immature. Yet it can be a powerful tool for self-control and improvement. If imagination is controlled and used constructively, we benefit from its child*like* qualities while avoiding its child*ish* liabilities.

THE PRINCIPLE
OF PASSIVE DIRECTION

Once the erroneous belief in willpower has been discarded, it must be replaced with the *Principle of Passive Direction*. This means you must learn to "let it happen." It is often one of the most difficult concepts for beginners to grasp, for a couple of reasons. For one thing, our Western culture has really done a number on most of us relative to the concept of "willpower." Virtually from birth we are taught an unhealthy respect for it. This "frontier mentality" is the belief that geographic, scientific, personal, or any other kind of frontier can only be conquered by sheer strength of will. This is the "by God" concept: If something needs doing, you just by-God do it! Hence, anything that smacks of passivity gets short shrift in Western thinking. This quasi-religious frontier mentality emphasizes aggressiveness as the only way to achieve anything.

Impatience is another reason why passive direction is often misunderstood. Many people have not experienced the gratification that comes from first setting the proper forces in action, then sitting back and observing their fruition. They want to jump in and help things along, motivated by the mistaken belief that if they keep moving they'll get faster results. How many times have you been guilty of keeping busy with unnecessary efforts just so you could feel as if you were doing something to help your project along?

The Principle of Passive Direction does not prohibit you from taking action to improve yourself, nor does it mean that you should just sit back and wait for the world to come to you. But it is vitally important to know how much and what kind of action to take, and when to let the forces you have set in motion take their own shape. Once you have set the right forces in action, you can continue to be active, but your activity will be indirect. This indirect activity is the product of the forces acting in your behalf, forces that reside within you, primarily at the subconscious level. In other words, once you get the subconscious started in the right direction, stand back and let it do its work.

Here is an example to help you understand the Principle of Passive Direction. Imagine, for the purpose of this example, that a man named John wants to improve his financial status. The first thing he does to achieve this financial improvement is learn the techniques of communicating with his subconscious mind. (All of the techniques and procedures used in this example will be presented in later sections of this book.) This is a two-way communication process. He first obtains information from his subconscious mind (through autoquestioning) about any negative viewpoints, beliefs, or attitudes relative to financial success. Bringing this subconscious information to a conscious level may eliminate it as a source of resistance. If conscious awareness is not sufficient to remove the subconscious blocks to success (also determined through autoquestioning), he will go to the second step in his self-communication procedure.

The second step entails feeding back to his subconscious (through suggestion) the information that will eliminate or correct the inhibiting subconscious factors. This feedback of correct information to his subconscious mind will continue as an ongoing process. This is the "direction" part of passive direction.

Sooner or later the directions John is applying to his subconscious mind will start taking effect. He will begin to develop new attitudes toward work, money, and whatever else is relevant to his financial success. He will discover that he is having ideas that never occurred to him before. He will stop concerning himself primarily about money per se and become more interested and active in pursuing programs or projects that result in increased income.

John will also begin to notice that people are responding more positively and supportively to him than they used to. We all transmit subtle but powerful signals that prompt others to either support or resist our efforts. These signals are nonverbal and practically impossible to identify at a conscious level. They form the subconscious-to-subconscious communication system, and they can be influenced only through the subconscious part of the mind.

Some of the "passive" part of passive direction, in this example, is the cessation of concern for money itself. Instead of forcing himself into unnatural situations and adventures—all of which look good on paper but never produce the desired results—John will allow himself to be directed by the spontaneous and natural products of his subconscious mind. He becomes generally more relaxed, which in itself contributes to better results, and he begins to realize that many of the past obstacles to success were generated by trying too hard. He gradually becomes more successful as he learns to let things happen, rather than trying to force them to happen.

Some people have spontaneously discovered how to let things happen naturally, especially in areas in which they have no subconscious resistance to success. But if they don't know how to uncover and deal with subconscious resistance, they can't apply the techniques to other areas. This explains why some people are able to amass great wealth but their personal lives are a shambles. On a smaller scale, some people are able to quit smoking, but they can't control their weight. You may be intimately familiar with examples of this patchwork pattern of success and failure. With the methods you are about to learn, you can avoid this kind of success/failure pattern. Just don't make the mistake of thinking that you are going to do it with willpower.

I keep returning to the subject of willpower because I want you to be thoroughly convinced that it is not a viable concept. Willpower is not handed out at birth to some people and withheld from others. And it cannot be developed in opposition to subconscious beliefs, attitudes, or values. All in all, "willpower" is worse than a useless concept; not only will it not contribute to the achievement of your goals, it will get in the way.

Discipline is a more valuable concept. Unlike willpower, it can be developed. Self-control and efficiency in reaching goals—discipline—is achieved by bringing the subconscious needs into alignment with conscious desires. This alignment is the product of communication between the conscious and the subconscious parts of the mind. Subconscious-to-conscious communication is developed primarily through autoquestioning (presented in Chapter 3). Conscious-to-subconscious communication is largely a matter of suggestion (Chapter 4) which is aided by self-hypnosis (Chapter 2). In order to better understand the various forms of conscious-subconscious communication, it is necessary to know something about these two major parts of the human mind.

THE SUBCONSCIOUS MIND

The subject of mind is one that has intrigued philosophers and scientists for centuries. Although scientists have begun to seriously study the human mind, there is still a great deal that is not known about it. It has long been recognized that there are at least two distinct areas of mind. The most obvious area is that of consciousness, or awareness—that area of mind which we are aware of thinking with. All remaining functions, those that are below consciousness, are in the domain of the "inner" mind.

Many terms have been used to describe this area of the inner mind and its processes. If you do much reading on the subject you will encounter terms such as *subliminal, subcortical, subconscious,* and *unconscious.* Many theorists refer to all nonconscious mentation as an unconscious process. However, "unconscious" has more than one meaning (as in the case where one is knocked unconscious by a blow to the head) so the less confusing term "subconscious" will be used in this book when referring to mental processes that go on beneath conscious awareness.

We experience awareness with our conscious mind which, as a rough estimate, probably constitutes less than 20 percent of the total mind. Although we rely greatly on the conscious mind, some of the most important and significant mental activity takes place at the subconscious level. In fact, many highly respected thinkers and researchers have theorized that *all* of our more significant mental processes originate at the subconscious level (for example, Pierre Janet, Sigmund Freud, C. G. Jung, and their precursors Josef Breuer and J.-M. Charcot).

The subconscious has many functions, one of which is the protection of the individual. It is the subconscious part of the mind that makes us respond to a dangerous or painful stimulus before we can even "think" about it. If you touch a hot stove, you don't have to stand there and burn while you think "the surface of this stove is hot and burning me, and I don't want to be burned, so I'll send a message to my arm to pull my hand away from the stove." If you have ever been burned—and who has not—you know that this sequence of thoughts is not necessary. Your subconscious reacts immediately to the stimulus of extreme heat as something to be avoided and instigates the swift withdrawal of your hand from the hot surface. You jerk your hand away from the stove without thinking about it.

With a little experience the subconscious learns that stoves can produce painful burns. Knowledge of this sort often becomes generalized to the extent that the subconscious sometimes seems over-protective. You have probably accidentally touched a stove and immediately jerked your hand away in alarm, only to test it afterward and find that it was not hot.

This protective function of the subconscious continues even while we are asleep. Our inner mind is apparently aware at all times, whether we are naturally asleep, drugged, or "knocked out." Surgeons are now beginning to be more cautious in their remarks during surgery. They have discovered that comments made by them while the patient is "out" are permanently recorded in the patient's subconscious mind. There are recorded instances of people who, when age-regressed under hypnosis back to a time of surgery, have been able to accurately report everything that was said during the surgical operation.

Scientific research indicates that the subconscious part of the mind is continually functioning to protect the individual. This tireless part of our psyche is apparently alert to what is going on around us at all times.

Everyone has experienced this protective alertness of the subconscious mind at one time or another. An example is that of a mother whose child is sleeping in another room. The mother may be sound asleep, and nonthreatening noises, some of them perhaps quite loud, will not awaken her. But the moment her baby begins to whimper she is immediately wide awake. In such cases, the subconscious mind was attuned to the environment and awakened the mother only at a sound that might indicate some danger or discomfort for her child. In like manner, many people are able to sleep soundly while members of their family are making noises around the house, but they will be immediately awakened by the sounds of a stranger.

The subconscious part of the mind is also the storehouse of memory. It is believed that everything one experiences or perceives in any way is permanently recorded in the subconscious. Some of these memories are easily recalled, while others remain elusively buried and resist being remembered without special techniques.

As a conceptual model, think of the memory as a long, narrow room with filing cabinets along both walls. At one end of this narrow room is a large window which both provides a view of the world from the inside and admits light from the outside. As one moves farther from the window it gets darker and darker until the filing room is, at some distance removed from the window, in complete darkness.

The window is one's view of the world, and the lighted end of the filing room is the conscious part of the mind. As the room gets darker we are moving farther into the mind, into the subconscious area. Note that, in this model, there is a continuum from consciousness to subconsciousness with no fixed boundary or border between them. Note also that what we often refer to as *the* subconscious mind and *the* conscious mind are really two regions of the *same* mind.

To continue with this model, assume that memories are filed in the filing cabinets. It is not difficult to find something we want to remember if it is filed in the lighted area. But those memories that are stored in the dark region are difficult, often impossible, to recall. Recent memories are in the well-lighted area and are easy to recall, whether they are important or not. You can probably remember what you had for breakfast this morning, but not what you had for breakfast on this date a year ago. You probably can't remember whether or not you even had breakfast on that date. Your memory of today's breakfast is still in the lighted area, easily accessible to conscious recall. But the memory of last year's breakfast has been moved back into the inner mind (unless there was some special reason to remember it, such as a birthday).

Events that are deemed important by the subconscious are treated in one of two ways: A sufficiently unpleasant memory is quickly buried in the subconscious, but more pleasant, important memories are filed in an area where they remain available to conscious recall. The kinds of experiences that the subconscious mind considers important vary from person to person (with lots of commonalities), and whether or not an experience will be deemed important is hard to predict on the basis of conscious logic. It is logically obvious why unpleasant or pleasant experiences might be considered important, but most people can recall isolated memories that are neither pleasant nor unpleasant. You can probably think of memories of the latter sort—memories from years ago, perhaps from childhood—that are seemingly unimportant but nonetheless quite vivid.

Using the filing room as an example of the subconscious function of memory quickly breaks down if we try to make it work for the other subconscious functions. A room is a static thing with no ability to function or act on its own. Unfortunately there is no simple example that can even come close to explaining all of the functions of the subconscious mind. Norbert Wiener was one of the first to compare the mind to a computer, and it was Wiener's mechanistic concept that Maxwell Maltz elaborated in his book *Psycho-Cybernetics*. But comparing the mind to a computer is like comparing a huge, modern printing press to a rubber stamp.

Although the conscious and subconscious are both parts of the same mind, the subconscious part of the mind can reason and function independently of the conscious mind. However, there are both quantitative and qualitative differences in the ways in which these two parts of the mind function.

One of the special characteristics of the subconscious mind is its absence of negation or doubt. What were expressed earlier as "doubts" are really absolute, negative beliefs. There is very little evidence that degrees of certainty or uncertainty exist at the subconscious level. It is probable that the subconscious deals only in absolutes. But these absolute values are by no means all negative. Ever since 1824 when J. F. Herbart first introduced the idea of conflict between the conscious and subconscious, there has been a common and persistent belief that the subconscious contains only disreputable, negative, or unsavory ideas. This belief is definitely not true.

Actually, the subconscious can host both positive and negative viewpoints simultaneously. This is another of the main characteristics of the subconscious: There is no sense of contradiction. Opposite or incompatible ideas may subconsciously exist side by side without creating any logical conflict. That is, not the kind of logical conflict, or contradiction, that would be apparent at a conscious level of reasoning.

Another important difference is the subconscious concept of time. Ideas, viewpoints, and beliefs from different ages are all telescoped together into the present, and it is only the present that exists. The subconscious does not make comparative values in the same way that the conscious does. For example, we consciously know that beliefs which were valid for us as five-year-olds are not likely to be valid for us as adults. But this "common sense" evaluation does not occur at the subconscious level. What was true for the subconscious yesterday is true today and will be true in the future unless we intervene to change such subconsciously held "truths."

Related to this "timeless" quality of the subconscious is its tendency to maintain a constancy of emotional content. An experience that frightens a child may not be frightening to an adult. But if a childhood experience occurs with enough impact on the subconscious mind, the frightening quality of the experience becomes a *fixed idea* that will in most instances persist throughout life. It is fortunate that relatively few experiences become fixed or locked into the subconscious, but those that do can really be troublesome later on. For instance, if a child gets locked in a closet and becomes frightened by that experience, he may be afraid of enclosed spaces the rest of his life. It is the *emotional quality of the generalized experience,* not the event itself, which is maintained throughout life.

So far we do not know enough about the mind to be able to predict just which experiences will become fixed by the subconscious mind. It is evident that many children get locked in dark closets or other enclosed spaces without developing unusual fears of such experiences. It is also clear that subconsciously fixed ideas can originate long after childhood. Many adults develop phobias related to frightening or painful experiences, and such phobias usually manifest themselves in ways that make it difficult to logically trace backward from the fear itself to the original event or experience that precipitated the fear.

Another quality of the subconscious mind is its tendency to take the literal meaning of language. This literality can cause complications because our speech and thinking are riddled with ambiguous terms. Take the word "mad," for instance. When you say that something "makes you mad," you are literally saying that it makes you insane. Or consider phrases and words like "pain in the neck," "heartache," and "mindless." Because of the literality of the subconscious mind, these and similar ambiguities can create problems such as imprints, which will be described later.

The administration of self-punishment for guilt feelings is another function of the subconscious part of mind. Everyone has guilt feelings in varying amounts, and the subconscious can commission behavior and emotional states that will either directly or indirectly result in punishment. An accident-prone person may be punishing herself for real or imagined transgressions by stubbing her toes, bumping her head, or having car accidents. Or she may get others to punish her with derision and scorn by being clumsy or by making slips of the tongue, or even by starting fights. Of course, not all accidents and slips of the tongue are motivated by a need for punishment, but subconscious motivation is always suspect in such cases.

As I indicated in the discussion of the autonomic nervous system, there has been ample research to show that the subconscious mind regulates the physical mechanisms of the body. The autonomic nervous system is not as autonomic as it was once thought to be, and medical research in recent years has demonstrated the ability of the mind to prevent, reduce, or sometimes even cure diseases that were formerly thought to be strictly physical in nature and cause. Newly emerging concepts of psychosomatic medicine are making inroads into the entire area of medical practice. Examples from nonmedical fields such as faith-healing and hypnosis have amply demonstrated the ability of the mind to affect the health of the body. In all cases of physical influence by the mind, *communication* is the key element. Control over many of the physical functions of the body becomes possible once the techniques of conscious-subconscious communication have been mastered.

Ill health, undesirable behavior, and blocks to success are often products of the seemingly illogical methods of the subconscious. Because the subconscious is concerned almost exclusively with immediate results, it often ignores the indirect consequences and side effects of its actions. If the subconscious has fixed on the idea that food is a substitute for affection, for example, the person will be driven to eat when an unsatisfied need for affection is felt (real hunger has nothing to do with most over-eating). Such displacement of effect leads to a condition in which the real need or desire is never effectively satisfied. Overeating just goes on and on *ad nauseam*.

Because we can never get enough of what we really don't want, the unfortunate person suffering from this subconsciously fixed idea will become, and remain, overweight. This condition will persist regardless of conscious awareness of the mental and physical discomforts of being overweight or the dangers to health. The subconscious will continue to be oblivious to the *connection* between overeating and overweight, and the unpleasant syndrome will be perpetuated as long as there exists a subconscious association between affection and food.

At this point it is appropriate to repeat a caution made earlier: Don't make the mistake of thinking of the subconscious mind as another person within you. Reference to *the* subconscious mind is simply a matter of convenience and means the subconscious *part* of your mind. The human mind is all one entity. There is no actual line that divides the conscious and subconscious parts of the mind.

Now we come to one of the most significant aspects of the sub-conscious mind: *The subconscious has no relationship to reality!* The external world is interpreted through our emotional responses to it, not through objective observation of what really "is" out there. It is our emotional responses to things, events, and experiences that form sub-conscious reality.

A chair is just a chair for most of us. But imagine what terrifying symbolism chairs might evoke in someone who has been sentenced to die in the electric chair. Or, to bring our discussion back to matters with which most of us are familiar, consider once again the subject of food and eating. From the standpoint of conscious logic, food should be eaten to satisfy hunger, and nothing else. Yet, from birth onward, we learn to associate food and eating with nonnutritional pleasures such as attention, affection, support, and reward.

As infants and young children we learned to associate mother's love and attention with food. Then, later, we received cookies or some other treat for being good (and treats, like love, were withheld when we were bad). Still later, we learned to associate food and eating with family get-togethers (can you imagine your family getting together for Sunday "fast"?), national holidays (the 4th of July = hot dogs), religious events (what do you do on Christmas day?), and so on. Ultimately, we form a subconscious view of reality as it is interpreted through our emotions. In the case of food, food-is-love-is-eating-is-reward-is-not-being-lonely is subconscious *reality*.

This aspect of the subconscious, this lack of relationship to reality, is both good and bad news. It is bad news because it is the cause or source of many of the things that we dislike about ourselves, and that usually prove so hard to change. It is good news because it means that we can restructure our subconscious reality if we go about it right. And "going about it right" is what this book is all about.

Let me make one final point before we launch into methods and techniques. With the methods presented in this book you will be embarking on a journey of learning and change. In order to get the most from your efforts it is essential that you maintain an openness to new ideas and concepts. Be assured that you will be learning things about yourself that contradict what you consciously thought were true. Many of our conscious rationalizations about why we do (or don't do) things are wrong. So remember to keep your mind and your options open. You will convince yourself of the validity of these concepts when you begin to apply them.

1

Deep relaxation

There are a couple of good reasons for choosing relaxation as the topic of the first chapter in a book on self-hypnosis. For one thing, relaxation is the first step in the induction of the hypnotic state. Stated more correctly, it is a preparatory stage in the development of good self-hypnosis. Another reason is that relaxation is extremely helpful and beneficial in its own right.

The kinds of benefits achieved through relaxation depend largely on the kind of relaxation practiced. Probably the most common concept of relaxation is what we can call recreational relaxation. Going out to a movie or a play, camping in the mountains, skiing, attending a sports event, watching television—all of these activities are considered relaxation.

There is also drug-induced relaxation. Alcohol, for example, is a common palliative for reducing the tensions generated by a frenetic lifestyle. "Unwinding" is the preferred term of those who need a couple of martinis as soon as they get home from work. An occasional drink may help but there are much better ways to relax.

Tranquilizers run a close race with alcohol for popularity in this country. These drugs have many generic labels: calmatives, mood suppressants, downers, and so on. Amazing quantities of these chemicals are prescribed and swallowed, and their use and popularity are on the increase. The annual growth of this national propensity for pill-popping is just another indication of the need for adequate and effective methods of relaxing.

Drugs, alcohol, recreation, and television viewing all have their proper place in the scheme of things. But it is important to note that none of these methods is sufficient or necessary for relaxation. In fact,

19

research and practice have amply demonstrated that deep relaxation techniques are much more effective, with less hassle and no unpleasant side effects. And the best, most effective forms of deep relaxation are those that are self-induced without the aid of drugs.

To cite an illustration, consider the drug *methohexitone*. It is an amazingly effective muscle relaxant. One dose of this drug and all physical tension disappears completely. This should be a very pleasant experience, yet those who have tried it have invariably expressed a dislike for the experience. This is interesting because the *physical* aspects of relaxation achieved with methohexitone are the same as those achieved with self-induced relaxation (which everyone likes). The logical conclusion is that there is an important mental consideration involved here, one that makes it necessary to feel in control of the relaxation process. In other words, it's better to do it yourself.

From this point on, any reference to relaxation will mean *self-induced, deep* relaxation. You won't need any drugs, chemicals, or gadgets of any kind; you'll be able to do it all yourself with the techniques you'll be reading about shortly.

Deep relaxation has many benefits. One of them is learning what it feels like to be really relaxed. Many people have never really experienced *deep* relaxation. When you learn how it feels to be deeply relaxed, and after you have had some practice at developing relaxed states, you will be able to relax anytime and wherever you want to. This is a tremendous benefit, especially at those times when you find yourself in a tension-generating situation.

The ability to relax deeply is a learned skill that improves with practice. Not only that, it also becomes longer-lasting. Practice deep relaxation on a regular basis and you will find that there is a generalized effect which makes you more relaxed at all times. This applies to both waking and sleeping states; problems with sleeping, especially insomnia, often clear up rapidly with the beginning of relaxation practice.

Tension is the opposite of relaxation. A certain amount of tension is necessary for coping and functioning on a day-to-day basis, but most people maintain a too-high state of tension. Prolonged or extreme tension is generally referred to as "stress," which impairs both mental and physical functioning. It has been established that stress takes a heavy toll on health and organic well-being. Heart problems, stomach problems such as ulcers, headaches, and even diseases such as arthritis and gout have all been found to have a relationship with stress and anxiety. In fact, some physicians estimate that as many as 80 percent of their patients are suffering from stress-related ailments.

Stress lowers resistance and makes it easier for viruses or bacteria to attack the body. Resistance to infections is lowered by stress and so is the body's ability to throw off poisons. In short, all of the bodily processes are impaired by too-high stress levels, especially if the stress is prolonged over long periods of time.

Stress is a form of arousal which is a response to the external environment. We respond to an external stimulus with stress if that stimulus is either consciously or unconsciously interpreted as threatening. The key word here is "interpret": how we mentally, emotionally evaluate a stimulus. When relaxed, we interpret fewer stimuli as threatening and it takes a higher degree of threat to produce a physiological response. Our thinking is much clearer—more logical, less emotional—when we are relaxed, so things in general are less likely to be considered serious or threatening. Thus, relaxation lowers the probability of a negative response to events that are potentially stressful.

Life is full of events with stress-generating potential. Some are obvious and easily identified, others are not. Noise is an example of a less obvious stress generator. Our modern world is filled with the cacophony of traffic sounds, airplanes, sirens, blaring TVs and stereos, barking dogs, and the subtler sounds of refrigerators, furnaces, and household appliances. People and their machines make noise. Because we do not have "earlids" with which to shut out sound like we can shut out light with our eyelids, we are more or less at the mercy of noise. "More" because noise—even those noises which we are not consciously aware are bothering us—creates stress; "less" because relaxation lowers our stressful response to noise. So an additional benefit of practicing deep relaxation is that it helps us combat those stress-generating stimuli that we are not aware of.

DEEP RELAXATION METHODS

The Tensing-Releasing Method

Some of the best research on deep relaxation was conducted in the 1930s by physiologist Edmund Jacobson of Harvard University. He worked with "progressive" relaxation, and his method was later modified by psychologist Joseph Wolpe in the late 1940s.

The essence of progressive relaxation is to tense and then release the muscles of the body in groups, moving from one group of muscles to the next. In this manner the relaxation progresses until the entire body is relaxed.

The tensing-releasing method presented here is the product of several years' experience in teaching others how to develop deep relaxation, especially as it relates to self-hypnosis. It is a process you can easily learn on your own from these printed instructions. During this process it is important to pay close attention to the feelings associated with both tension and relaxation. This way you learn to recognize tension (and relaxation) in everyday situations as well as in your practice sessions.

Developing the skill of deep relaxation is just like learning any other skill. Whether the skill is swimming, golfing, riding a bicycle, or deep relaxation, you have to practice to get better at it. These relaxation procedures will be of little use to you if you do not practice them regularly.

Why use a method of relaxing that involves tensing muscles? It may seem strange to start by producing tension when it is relaxation that is desired. The reason for this will become clear shortly.

As already mentioned, everyone maintains a certain amount of tension during waking hours. If there were not at least some tension present, one would simply slump into a puddle of self. So a certain amount of tension is necessary to function in everyday life. The actual amount of tension present under normal circumstances varies from person to person. The amount of tension under which you normally operate from day to day is called your *adaptation level*. By practicing deep relaxation you will learn to reduce the muscle tension in your body to levels that are far below your normal adaptation level. Furthermore, you will be able to do this any time you want to.

You can probably already do this to a limited extent. You just think about a particular muscle group and relax the muscles by "letting go." However, by practicing deep relaxation you will learn to produce much more noticeable reductions in tension. The best way to do this is to first generate a lot of tension in the muscles, raising the tension to well above the normal adaptation level. Then you release the tension all at once. With the release of the muscle tension you create a momentum which allows the muscles to drop well below the normal adaptation level. The effect is much like that of a pendulum: If you pull a pendulum to one side and then release it, it will swing to the opposite side, passing the vertical or "resting" position because of the momentum that has been generated.

In the same way, tensing a muscle group before letting it relax develops a "momentum" toward deeper relaxation. Once released, the muscles will relax more than they would have had they not first been tensed.

Another advantage of tensing the muscles is that it gives you an opportunity to pay attention to what tension really feels like in the various muscle groups. Because of the contrast between tension and relaxation, you will be able to compare the two states and appreciate the differences between them. This is an important part of the learning process because it develops a sensitivity to *localized* muscle tension. That is, most people can recognize the fact that they are generally tense, but they cannot identify tension in specific muscles or muscle groups. By learning to recognize tension in specific muscle areas you develop a kind of alarm system that will help you nip tension in the bud, as it were.

Tension does not occur all over the body all at once. It typically starts in one or a few localized muscle groups and spreads gradually from the point of origin. Most people don't recognize the onset of tension until it has spread to a large enough area to cause a headache, backache, overall tiredness, or some other symptom. But if you are sensitive to muscle tension in any specific part of your body your "alarm" will go off when tension starts and you can stop it before it has a chance to spread.

Now for the procedure itself. With this technique you are going to become deeply relaxed, probably more relaxed than you have ever been before. We will divide the body into fourteen muscle groups, each of which is to be tensed and then relaxed during your practice. As your skill develops you will be able to combine these fourteen muscle groups into a smaller number of larger groups and relax faster.

Begin by reading through the description that follows, trying each muscle group as it is described. Then, when you feel that you are familiar enough with the muscle groups, get comfortable and go through the process on your own. You will want to refer back to the muscle descriptions from time to time until you have the procedure down pat. After you have been practicing daily for a week or so, reread this section to make sure you are doing it right and not leaving anything out.

The first muscle group is your dominant hand and forearm. ("Dominant" means "right" if you are right-handed, "left" if you are left-handed.) Tense the muscles in your dominant hand and lower arm by making a tight fist. You should be able to feel the tension in your hand, over the knuckles, and up into your lower arm. Hold the tension for about five to seven seconds (count "One thousand, two thousand, three thousand . . . seven thousand"). Then release the tension *abruptly*. Do not release it gradually—you want to release the tension in each muscle group as quickly as you can.

During the process of tensing and then relaxing, pay close attention to the feelings associated with each state. Follow this procedure of paying attention throughout the entire fourteen-muscle-group practice. Remember that your awareness of what the tension and relaxation feels like in each muscle group is an important part of the learning process.

Now move to the muscles of the upper arm (still on the dominant side). You can tense these muscles by pushing your elbow down against the arm of your chair or bed, or against your body, or both. Do not make a fist or otherwise disturb the relaxation you have already achieved in your hand and wrist. Once you have tensed and released a muscle group, leave it as relaxed and still as possible. Hold the tension five to seven seconds, paying attention to how it feels, then quickly let go of the tension. Caution: Don't try to *make* the muscles relax when you let go. Just let the momentum carry the muscles into deeper relaxation.

The next two muscle groups are the nondominant hand and arm. This is a repeat of what you just did, except now you will do it with the non-dominant hand and wrist, followed by the nondominant upper arm.

After you have relaxed the muscles of both hands and arms, move to the face and jaw muscles. These muscles are tensed by: (1) clamping the teeth together with *moderate* force (don't try to break anything); (2) wrinkling the forehead and nose, tightly closing your eyes in the process; and (3) pulling the corners of your mouth back and up as far as you can, as if you were making a big, phony smile. Hold the tension for five to seven seconds, then release.

The next step is to relax the muscles of the neck. This area is particularly important because the neck muscles are often a repository of tension. Tense the neck muscles by pulling your chin down toward your chest. At the same time, exert force to prevent your chin from actually touching the chest. By doing this you are counterposing the muscles in the front part of your neck against those of the back of your neck. If you are doing it correctly, you should experience some trembling or shaking in the neck and head.

You will discover that the abruptness with which you can relax your muscles after tensing them takes some time to develop. (This will be particularly true of the muscles in the face and in the back of the neck.) As you continue to practice and get better at deep relaxation, you will find it easier to get the muscles quickly relaxed. So remember to keep the concept of abrupt release in mind as you practice.

The group of muscles in your chest, shoulders, and upper back is next. There are considerably more muscles in this group, and the muscles themselves are generally larger. To tense this group, pull your shoulder blades together as though you were trying to get them to touch. Whether or not they actually do touch is not important. Just push them back far enough to feel a good amount of tension in the muscles of your shoulders, chest, and upper back.

Now, a note about breathing. Deep breathing is an aid to deep relaxation. It is a good idea to take two or three deep breaths before starting your deep relaxation exercises. Do this by inhaling deeply, filling your lungs, and holding the breath momentarily. Then exhale slowly, imagining that you are exhaling tensions as you release your breath. Repeat this procedure with a single deep breath three or four times during your relaxation exercise. Some of the best times to do this are after each upper arm, after the facial muscles, after the lower torso muscle group, and after each leg and foot group.

Move now to the muscles of the lower torso. Tense these muscles by making your stomach hard, tightening the muscles of the stomach as though you were preparing to receive a blow to the midsection.

It seems natural, when tensing the stomach muscles, to hold the breath and push in what is called a "grunt" response. This tends to elevate diastolic blood pressure in some people, so try to breathe a little while you are tensing the stomach muscles. This may take some getting used to, but you will be able to do it with a little practice.

Some people experience confusion about tensing their stomach muscles. If you don't know quite how to tighten these muscles, you can achieve approximately the same results by either sucking your stomach in or pushing it out as far as you can.

Now tense the muscles of your upper leg on the dominant side. Tense this part of your leg by counterposing the large muscles on top of the leg against the smaller ones underneath. If you are doing it right the muscles on the top of your leg will feel hard and stiff. Another way to achieve this is to lie flat on your back and, keeping the leg straight, lift your foot a few inches above whatever you are lying on.

To tense the muscles of the lower dominant leg (primarily the calf muscles), pull your toes upward toward your head—that is, point your foot toward your head. Just curling your toes up is not right; the whole foot has to point upward, stretching the calf muscles between your heel and the back of your knee.

Next come the muscles of the dominant foot. Tense these muscles by (1) turning your foot inward and (2) pointing the foot downward. Don't try to get too much tension in the foot muscles, and release the tension after a couple of seconds (instead of the five to seven seconds for the other muscle groups). Tense just enough to feel the tightness in your ankle, under your arch and in the ball of your foot.

Now repeat the tensing and relaxing process with the upper leg, lower leg, and foot on your nondominant side. The instructions are the same as for those just given for the last three dominant-side muscle groups.

This completes the fourteen muscle groups. When you practice this procedure, remember to pay close attention to the feelings of tension and relaxation in each group. And be careful not to introduce tension into any muscle group that you have already relaxed. For this reason it is best not to move around after you have started your practice. You can move if you need to, of course, but avoid unnecessary movement.

It is best to be alone when you practice, and try to anticipate any possible sources of interruption (turn off the TV, take the phone off the hook, and so on). Take care of any toilet needs before starting.

Most people prefer to lie down while practicing, but this is not mandatory. You may find that sitting back in a reclining chair can be just as effective. Avoid practicing in straight-backed chairs or other less comfortable positions until you are sufficiently skilled at developing deep relaxation. The less effort you must exert to maintain your position, the better.

Whether your eyes are open or closed is not critical, but most people find it easier to concentrate on the process and avoid distractions if their eyes are closed.

How often should you practice, and when? The answer to the first part of this question depends on how tense you are to begin with, and how much time you can spend practicing. If you have a problem with lethargy you obviously won't need as much practice as someone who is wound-up most of the time. Generally speaking, once a day is adequate. Two or three times a day is probably the maximum from which you will derive benefit, and three or four times a week is a minimum.

When you practice will be determined by your own daily schedule and the time of day in which you function best. If you are a morning person—one who feels best in the early part of the day—then try to get in an early practice session to take advantage of the part of the day when you are at your best. If, on the other hand, you are sluggish during the early part of the day but get better as the day wears on (or after the sun goes down), then schedule your practice for a later time in the day. After you have developed some skill you will find that relaxing renews your energy and perks you up, so you can then use it during the "down" part of your day. But stick to the good times when you first start practicing.

Try to avoid practicing within an hour or so after eating. Metabolism changes when you eat, and this interferes with relaxation. The reverse of this is not true: You don't have to wait an hour after practicing relaxation to eat, although that might not be a bad idea if weight is a problem.

The amount of time spent in practice will vary. A practice session will take longer when you first start than it will later. Generally speaking, your practice sessions in the first few weeks should take somewhere between twenty and thirty minutes. Continue to practice and you will eventually require no more than a couple of minutes to reach deep relaxation, but that will come later.

You are now ready to practice deep relaxation. Here, in brief summary, are the things you want to keep in mind as you practice:

1. Keep your attention focused on the muscle group with which you are working.
2. Maintain tension in each group for a period of five to seven seconds except for the feet, which should be tensed for only a few seconds.
3. Tense and relax each muscle group twice before moving to the next group. This applies only to the first few times you practice, or to those times when a particular muscle group is especially tense.
4. When you release the tension in a muscle group, do it abruptly.
5. Pay close attention to the differences in feeling between tension and relaxation.

Here is a list of the fourteen muscle groups:

1. Dominant hand and forearm
2. Dominant biceps (upper arm)
3. Nondominant hand and forearm
4. Nondominant biceps (upper arm)
5. Face and jaw
6. Neck and throat
7. Chest, shoulders, and upper back
8. Abdominal or stomach region
9. Dominant upper leg
10. Dominant lower leg (calf)
11. Dominant foot
12. Nondominant upper leg
13. Nondominant lower leg (calf)
14. Nondominant foot

If you have a physical disability or some other medical reason for not tensing certain muscles, just bypass the muscles involved and go to the next group in the chain.

Once you are capable of achieving deep relaxation in tension-release cycles using the fourteen muscle groups, you can begin combining the muscle groups. By incrementally condensing the muscle groups you will ultimately decrease the amount of time needed to achieve deep relaxation, while continuing to increase the depth of relaxation you can achieve.

After you have been practicing the fourteen-muscle-groups procedure on a daily basis for at least two weeks, or at some later time when you feel confident you have mastered it, you can combine the original fourteen groups into six groups as follows:

1. Both the dominant and nondominant hand, lower arm, and upper arm muscles
2. The facial and jaw muscles
3. The neck muscles
4. The muscles of the chest, shoulders, upper back, and abdomen
5. The dominant upper leg, lower leg, and foot (Slightly lift your leg while turning the foot inward and pointing it upward.)
6. The nondominant upper leg, lower leg, and foot (The procedure is the same as for the dominant leg and foot.)

When you first make the change from fourteen to six muscle groups, you may find that your relaxation is not quite as satisfactory as it was in the more familiar fourteen-group procedure. Don't be alarmed by this. You will quickly regain the lost ground and increase your relaxation efficiency.

When you have learned to achieve deep relaxation using only six muscle groups, your practice session should take less than ten minutes. This time factor applies only to the deep relaxation practice. Later you will be adding a self-hypnotic induction procedure (it will immediately follow the deep relaxation practice). The amount of time required for the self-hypnotic induction process will be in addition to that for the deep relaxation practice.

It will probably take you two or more weeks to feel totally familiar and confident with the six-group procedure. When you do, you may wish to move on to the *recall* or *blanket* method of relaxation.

The Recall Method

The recall method of deep relaxation is quite different from the preceding tensing-and-releasing procedures. It is an advanced method of relaxation and should not be used until you have practiced for at least six weeks using the tension-and-release methods.

It is called the "recall" method because it involves remembering what the muscles feel like when they are relaxed, then "recalling" that relaxed state into existence. It does not require any tensing of the muscles, but it does require full use of your increased ability to focus on tension and relaxation.

Relaxation with the recall method makes use of the fourteen muscle groups that were used in the previous procedure. Begin by focusing your attention on the first muscle group. Don't tense it, just "feel" the muscles to become aware of any tension. Then recall the feelings associated with the release of tension. What you are doing is thinking the tension away, allowing the muscles to relax.

The recall method is a combination of sensitivity, memory, and imagination. You develop the sensitivity needed for this by practicing the tensing and releasing procedures. Imagination comes into play when you imagine tension leaving and being replaced with relaxation.

Mentally tour your body, going from muscle group to muscle group, repeating this procedure with each one. With continued practice you will soon be able to achieve very deep states of relaxation in only a few minutes. This is where all of the previous practice pays off. Without it, you cannot achieve such pleasant states of deep relaxation.

If you have trouble getting a particular muscle group to relax with the recall procedure, go ahead and tense-release the muscles of that group to get them to relax.

How pleasant *is* deep relaxation, and what does it feel like? It is normal to wonder just what you should be looking for, and to wonder how you will know when you have achieved *deep* relaxation.

These questions are very difficult to answer. For one thing, everyone has a slightly different response to deep relaxation. (We'll encounter this same problem of description when we get to the subject of self-hypnosis and what it feels like.) For another thing, trying to describe internal experiences is like trying to describe a taste or color or fragrance. Several pages could be devoted to trying to describe deep relaxation and still not get it quite right for you.

If something were mentioned that you do not experience, or if something were left out that you do happen to experience, you might be misled into thinking that you are not doing it right. So let me suggest that you try the relaxation procedures for a while. You will know you are developing deep relaxation when you like it and it feels good. If, after several practice sessions, you are not noticing any difference, reread the instructions (and make sure you are not trying to take any shortcuts).

The Blanket Method

The blanket method has always been a popular relaxation technique. It is closely related to the recall method, except you imagine a blanket that moves slowly upward over your body, starting at your feet. You imagine that as the blanket progresses upward, every muscle that it covers becomes completely relaxed.

As in the recall method, remember what it feels like to relax and let the muscles go limp as they are covered by the blanket. Imagine the blanket moving upward to your knees, resulting in relaxation of everything from the knees down. Then move the blanket up to your waist and let the muscles in your lower abdomen, hips, legs, and feet become completely relaxed. When all of those muscles feel nicely limp and relaxed, move the blanket up to your shoulders and relax all muscles from the shoulders down.

When the entire trunk of your body feels completely, deeply relaxed, imagine the relaxation flowing out into your arms and down to your hands and fingers. Allow these muscles to become limp and loose. Then imagine the relaxation flowing up into your neck and facial muscles. Allow these muscles to relax the same way you would with the recall method.

If, in continuing to use the recall and/or blanket method of relaxation you do not feel that you are achieving the deepest relaxation of which you are capable, try imagining a heaviness in your muscles. Use the same muscle groups and imagine that each group is becoming very heavy, as if it were made of lead. Imagine the muscles being so heavy you could hardly move them if you tried. Learn to use your imagination to achieve the results you want, and resist any temptation to try "making" yourself relax.

A Note About Headaches

Headaches are most often caused by contraction or expansion of the walls of the blood vessels that supply the brain and head with blood. The walls of these vessels contain nerve nets that are very sensitive to changes in blood flow. Many things can change the size or shape of blood vessels—chemicals in food and drink, alcohol, smoke-filled rooms that deprive one of oxygen, and sleeping in a stuffy room, to name a few—but it has been estimated that at least half of all headaches are caused by muscle tension.

The pressures of modern living, emotional crises, and other forms of personal conflict can cause an unconscious tightening of muscles. Tense muscles need more oxygen than do relaxed muscles. This increased demand creates an oxygen shortage that expands the blood vessels. And it is this expansion that causes the pain of tension headache.

Deep relaxation, when practiced on a regular basis, will decrease the frequency, duration, and severity of tension headaches. Remember that regular practice of deep relaxation becomes generalized, so you can remain more relaxed even when you are not actually practicing deep relaxation.

If you should happen to experience a mild headache during or immediately after practicing deep relaxation, it is caused by the same mechanisms in reverse. Post-relaxation headaches are an indication that you are maintaining a generally high adaptation level of tension most of the time. When you relax you change the blood flow (primarily the rate of flow and the oxygen content of the blood), and this results in a headache. Post-relaxation headaches quickly clear up with continued practice of relaxation.

If you continue to have headaches that are not helped by relaxation practice, you would be well advised to consult your physician for a medical checkup.

2
Self-hypnosis

The historical roots of hypnosis extend far back into antiquity. The early Greeks and Romans are known to have used hypnosis, and the priests of Egyptian sleep temples used a hypnotic induction process remarkably similar to modern induction methods. The history of virtually every culture, some dating as far back as 5,000 years, shows a knowledge and use of some form of hypnosis.

The modern history of hypnosis started with Franz Anton Mesmer (1734–1815). Prior to Mesmer, the dominant method of treating aberrant behavior was the religious rite of exorcism. All forms of what we would today label as mental illness were believed to be caused by demonic possession and, although the Catholic Church never fully sanctioned such rites, exorcism was the main mode of treatment.

Mesmer, a Viennese physician, gained a great deal of attention with his theory and practice of animal magnetism in 1775. He believed that there was a mysterious fluid which he called "animal magnetism," and which he imagined to have qualities similar to those of electricity. His *baquet*, an instrument that was supposed to concentrate the fluid of animal magnetism, was the means by which he recharged the fluid of his patients, thereby "curing" them.

We now know, in the light of today's knowledge about the human mind, that Mesmer's theories were wrong. But it cannot be denied that he did effect many cures, some of them of a near-miraculous nature, and his work marked the dramatic turning point from religious exorcism to what we would now call dynamic psychotherapy.

Although Mesmer's theories were wrong, his successes in treating patients stimulated a good deal of interest and research, often by men of outstanding scientific ability. By the nineteenth century it had been discovered that hypnosis—or animal magnetism, as some still called it—could reduce or eliminate pain. Until the discovery of chloroform and ether, numerous surgical operations were performed using hypnosis as anesthesia. The medical use of hypnosis diminished rapidly after the chemical anesthetics were discovered because ether was much faster and easier to administer. It was the discovery of chemical anesthetics, coupled with late-nineteenth and early-twentieth-century preoccupation with physical science, that served to dampen much of the interest in hypnosis.

During World War II, hypnosis again emerged as an area of scientific interest. Military therapists were searching for a faster, more effective way of treating combat neurosis (sometimes referred to as "battle fatigue"). They discovered that hypnosis could be a quick and effective form of therapy so its use became widespread in military hospitals. Impressed with the results they had achieved with hypnosis, many of the wartime therapists returned after the war to university and research positions where they began to delve into hypnosis with modern research methods.

Since 1945, research has grown by leaps and bounds in universities and clinics all over the world. As a result we now know a great deal about hypnosis, but there is still much to be learned. It is safe to say that we know as much about hypnosis today as we knew about electricity a few decades ago: We know that it exists, we know how to generate and use it, but we still don't know exactly what it is. More about this later.

SOME APPLICATIONS OF HYPNOSIS

Hypnosis and Medicine

The field of psychosomatic medicine is concerned with those maladies that result from the interaction and interdependence of psychological and somatic (body) factors. It is becoming more and more difficult to distinguish between what is and what is not psychosomatic in origin. Medical researchers are constantly discovering new uses of suggestion and hypnosis with disorders that were previously believed to be purely physical. Ailments such as atopic asthma, many allergic forms of dermatitis, some urticarias (raised patches of skin with intense itching), angioneurotic edema (watery swelling), many eczemas (redness and itching of the skin), and in fact all of the nonorganic itching-skin diseases have been shown to respond in some cases to hypnotic suggestion.

33

Many dermatologists have reported the successful treatment of conditions such as warts and psoriasis (red patches of skin covered with white scales) using direct hypnotic suggestion. Warts in particular respond remarkably well, sometimes in cases where all other treatments have been unsuccessful.

Bodily dysfunctions from one end of the alimentary tract to the other—such as functional dysphagia (difficulty in swallowing), peptic ulcer, colonic spasticity, and ulcerative colitis—have at times responded positively to hypnotic suggestion.

There are numerous scientific reports of phenomena which are effected through what is probably autonomic nervous control. The calcium content of the blood has been reduced by hypnotic command and blood sugar has been both depressed and elevated by suggestions of starvation and eating, respectively. Enzyme secretions of the gut have been manipulated by the suggestion that certain foods were being eaten, and the volume of urinary output has been increased by suggestions that the patient was drinking large quantities of water.

In the cardiovascular system, many hypnotized patients have demonstrated an ability to elevate or depress pulse rate and blood pressure as a response to direct suggestion. There is a good deal of evidence that the lumen (the inner open space) of cutaneous blood vessels can be manipulated by direct suggestion, and surgery patients who have been given appropriate suggestions usually bleed far less than patients who have not received such suggestions.

Cancer, too, has in some cases responded to hypnotic suggestion. A number of striking results have been reported in a variety of cancer cases. Benign tumors have disappeared completely, and malignant tumors have been known to shrink to less than a quarter of their original size. Patients who refused surgery have shown significant improvement in carcinoma of the cervix as a result of hypnotic suggestion. In addition to the suggestions for calmness, relaxation, and increased feelings of confidence and security, such patients are given suggestions to increase their healing power and rapid tissue repair with normal cell replacement and function.

In the treatment of disease we are probably dealing with a pathological continuum in which illness is a matter of degree of involvement within a mind–body interaction. This emerging fact is still difficult for some people to accept because the old Cartesian dichotomy of mind and matter has left an indelible mark on Western thinking. This mind–matter (or mind–body) schism has been around for 300 years and, like weeds in a garden, is difficult to get rid of.

Hypnosis and Dentistry

Dentistry was one of the first applied health sciences to recognize the benefits of using hypnosis. Although it is unfortunately true that some dentists have tried to use hypnosis without adequate training or knowledge of the subject, there are many practicing dentists who achieve remarkable results through hypnotic suggestion.

There is a widespread (and unjustified) belief that all dental treatment is painful. Many people just will not go to a dentist if they can avoid it. Thoughts of needles, knives, picks, and drills magnify a patient's apprehension and can induce great fear. Fear itself increases pain, makes patients more tense and uncomfortable, and will generally make any experience more unpleasant.

The effective use of hypnotic suggestion can alleviate a patient's fears and make any dental experience less unpleasant. The relaxation that accompanies hypnosis can go a long way toward increasing patient cooperation and the ability to sit open-mouthed for long periods while dental work is being performed. Proper suggestions can also markedly reduce salivation and bleeding during treatment.

When patients are put into even a light hypnotic state their pain threshold is automatically raised—they feel less pain—by the increased relaxation. Pain can be further reduced by specific suggestions to that effect. There have been many reports of tooth extractions, oral surgery, and other normally painful treatments in which no other anesthesia except hypnosis was used.

The phenomenon of hypnotically-induced oral anesthesia is illustrated by an experience reported by one of my former students. She was participating in an eight-week course in self-hypnosis in which we met once a week for three hours. The incident she reported occurred in about the fifth week of the course.

She had an unusually strong fear of dentists. So strong was her fear that she would drive several blocks out of her way just to avoid driving past her regular dentist's office. One winter morning, as she was shoveling snow from her driveway, she accidentally hit herself in the mouth with the shovel handle and broke off a tooth at the gum line. This obviously required immediate treatment, so she went straight to her dentist.

Sitting in the treatment room, surrounded by all of the arcane, terrifying paraphernalia of the dental profession, she almost backed out then and there. As the dentist approached her mouth with his hypodermic needle to inject novocaine into her gums, she grabbed his arm to stop him. This was the part she hated most, the needle in the gums.

"Let's try it without the novocaine," she said, unable to take her eyes off the needle. "Just give me a few minutes to mentally prepare myself and I won't need any anesthetic."

The dentist was taken aback and strongly resisted the idea at first, but she was persuasive, pointing out to him that it was her mouth and her money, and he finally relented. She closed her eyes and went rapidly through the self-hypnosis procedure she had now been practicing for several weeks. After a few minutes she told the dentist she was ready to proceed.

I'll spare you the gory details of all the things the dentist had to do. You can imagine that it was not a quick, easy procedure to remove the remainder of the broken tooth. The important point here is that this woman sat calmly and painlessly through the entire procedure with absolutely no anesthetic other than her self-hypnosis. And she reported a surprisingly speedy healing of her gums subsequent to the operation.

There is a large body of anecdotal evidence, such as the incident just related, which supports the idea that bodily healing processes are much faster and more efficient when suggestions to that effect are administered. In addition to better healing, hypnotic suggestion can be used to foster better follow-up procedures on the part of the patient. Various types of dental work, such as periodontal surgery, require much greater detail to things like massaging the gums, different methods and frequency of brushing the teeth, dental flossing, and so on. It is a frustratingly common experience for dentists to successfully carry through with a dental procedure only to have a lax patient lose ground because he or she does not perform certain required procedures at home.

The intelligent use of hypnotic suggestion can make a dramatic difference in such situations. Properly suggested, patients find it easier and more desirable to faithfully perform home duties. This makes it far more likely that they will show up regularly for dental treatments, instead of backsliding and putting off returning to the dentist's office until irreversible damage has been done.

Hypnosis in Business and Industry

The applications of hypnosis in business and industry are not as easy to come across as are those in the healing sciences. There are fewer professional journals in which one finds reports of hypnotic applications, and it is probable that the business world—being somewhat more conservative and "bottom-line" oriented—has not yet fully discovered the tremendous potential of hypnosis. Another problem is the distrust of business in general that has risen in recent years. Unions, for example, would be likely to view with suspicion any management-initiated program that included hypnosis.

Despite such impediments, the potentials of hypnosis are beginning· to be tested in commercial enterprises. The results thus far have been quite promising and, in light of our current need to improve national productivity, hypnosis will probably find its way into more and more business applications in coming years.

To consider some of the applications being made, and to consider some of the theoretical possibilities of other applications, let's arbitrarily separate business and industry by saying that industry is people working primarily with machinery, and business is people working primarily with information and/or other people.

In industrial situations it is common for employees to work mainly with machinery all day long. This raises two major, interrelated problems: safety and boredom. Hypnosis can be beneficial in both of these problem areas.

Hypnotic suggestion can be used to make workers more alert, over longer periods of time, to danger signals. Potentially dangerous situations and actions will be more or less automatically avoided. An assembly line worker, for example, will respond much more quickly and spontaneously to a danger-signaling light or sound if hypnotic suggestion has been used to enhance such perceptions and responses. Quick, accurate response to danger signals can often make the difference between a minor problem and a major catastrophe.

Even if we put humanistic considerations aside, boredom is a serious problem in industry because it leads to higher absenteeism and employee turnover, and to lower productivity. Hypnotic suggestion can diminish or even remove boredom from the job and give the employee a greater sense of involvement and fulfillment in his or her work. This reduces illness and goldbricking. It also increases safety because an involved worker is more likely to be alert than one who is bored and daydreaming.

Boredom at work leads to hatred of the work. Many industrial workers actually make themselves sick because they hate their work so much. By using hypnotic suggestions to improve their attitudes toward their work, workers have been able to dramatically improve their health, their happiness about their work and about their lives in general, their adjustment to working conditions, and their overall productivity.

In business settings, where people must work together, interpersonal relations are a key factor. Each employee, manager, executive, or owner must get along with every other member of the firm if everyone is to be happy and efficient. There are few things that can make life as miserable as a continuing, bitter conflict with someone at work. Such a situation can be especially stressful if the conflict is with the boss!

The most important variable in personal conflicts is usually attitude, which can be greatly affected by the proper application of hypnotic suggestion. It is relatively easy to condition oneself with suggestion to ignore, for example, the acrimonious taunting of a co-worker. Jibes, taunts, and snide remarks can then be laughed off—that is to say, genuinely laughed off without resulting in that inner seething that we have all experienced at some time in our lives. When such taunting behavior is laughed at or ignored, it eventually stops.

Relations with customers or clients can similarly be affected by the correct use of suggestion. Anyone who has worked with the public knows how frustrating and downright maddening it can be at times. But positive hypnotic suggestion can raise one's tolerance levels. This in turn makes work, and life in general, more enjoyable and productive.

Persuasiveness can also be increased through direct suggestion. Incidentally, it should be noted that the usefulness of persuasion is not limited to salespeople. We all need and use persuasion, whether it is to get a new idea accepted by others (and you know how difficult that can be), in getting a co-worker or customer to accept a particular situation, or even in getting a job.

Hypnosis and Self-Improvement

The ways in which hypnosis, particularly self-hypnosis, can be applied for self-improvement are virtually limitless. Anything that depends on your own efforts can be improved through the use of hypnotic suggestion. Here are some of the more popular areas in which self-hypnosis has been found to be extremely helpful:

Weight control. Overweight has rapidly become one of the most popular areas of hypnotic application. Most people who have a weight problem have tried all kinds of diets, pills, and gimmicks to achieve girth control. Those who have discovered the effectiveness of hypnosis, often after failing with every other method they could think of, have been amazed by the comparative ease with which hypnosis has worked for them. It is the only sensible way I know of to lose weight and keep it off without feeling deprived and miserable. If you have a weight problem, you will find a complete method for self-hypnotic weight control in Chapter 6.

Quitting smoking. Second only to weight control in popularity, becoming a nonsmoker is relatively easy and painless with the correct application of hypnosis. Chapter 7 is devoted to the smoker who wants to quit.

Fears. Fear has a natural place in our lives. It is quite natural to be afraid of a vicious dog or the Internal Revenue Service. But unusual and irrational fears can develop, such as the fear of flying, height, animals, close spaces, girls, and so on. Such irrational fears almost always dissolve when self-hypnosis is used, providing that they are not the product of severe psychological disturbance.

Self-confidence. Weak or nonexistent feelings of self-confidence are either situational or general. Situational lack of confidence occurs in specific situations and is related only to particular activities or abilities. A general lack of self-confidence manifests itself at all levels and in almost all activities. Both situational and general self-confidence can be improved with self-hypnosis.

Personality. The sum of individual characteristics we call personality can be improved with self-hypnosis. We do this by formulating and applying suggestions that are specific to the characteristic that needs strengthening or eliminating. Some of the characteristics that can be improved are positiveness and cheerfulness, consistency in dealing with others, responsiveness to the needs of others, shyness, and communication skills.

Concentration and memory. Regularly practicing self-hypnosis tends to produce a spontaneous improvement in concentration, and direct suggestions can be applied for even greater improvement. Improvement in concentration can be focused on specific situations or subjects, or it can be directed toward general improvement. As concentration improves, so will memory. Direct suggestions can be used for even greater enhancement. You will read more about improvement in concentration and memory in Chapter 5.

Sports. It is not at all uncommon for people to use hypnosis to improve their performance in sports. The most popular applications are

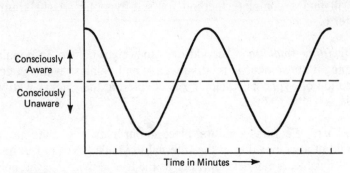

FIGURE 2-1 Typical pattern of drifting in and out of awareness during hypnosis.

in participant sports such as golf and tennis. And the use of hypnosis by professional athletes is widespread. Stamina, coordination, form, follow-through, and attitude are some of the factors that respond to direct hypnotic suggestion.

The applications of hypnosis listed here do not exhaust the possibilities. However, what has been said should give you a general feeling for the ways in which self-hypnosis can be used.

Now it is time to consider a definition of hypnosis—what it is, and what it is not.

HYPNOSIS DEFINED AND DESCRIBED

It will suffice for our purposes here to define hypnosis as a *pleasant state of altered awareness in which suggestibility is raised.* Please take careful note of how this definition is worded, especially the part about awareness. Awareness is *altered,* not removed. There are times, to be sure, when a person is so deeply hypnotized that he or she appears to lose all conscious awareness. But such hypnotic depth is the exception to the rule. On the other hand, it is fairly common for a hypnotized person to float in and out of conscious awareness in a cyclical rhythm. This is graphically illustrated in Figure 2–1, in which the wavy line represents the momentary lapse in conscious awareness that may occur every couple of minutes or so.

Sometimes this "in and out" experience is caused by a drifting into and out of ordinary sleep. For the beginner, it is often difficult to tell the difference between sleep and hypnosis. You will learn later, however, that there is a great deal of difference between sleep and hypnosis. The two are easily confused until you develop the required degree of inner sensitivity. If you experience this in-and-out phenomenon when you begin practicing self-hypnosis, don't worry about it unless you find that you are spending too much time in the unaware stage. If you do find yourself being more unaware than aware during your practice, you are probably falling asleep. Remedies for this will be presented later.

Every person who experiences hypnosis will have a different description of the experience. No two people will feel exactly the same thing, although there are some frequently occurring experiences, or telltale signs, that one can watch for.

One of the most commonly reported experiences is that of weightlessness. As the hypnotic state deepens, the body feels lighter and lighter. Sometimes this feeling becomes so pronounced that the hypnotized person feels as if he is floating on air. This is typically reported to be a pleasant experience.

Almost as common is the feeling of heaviness. First the limbs, then the entire body feels as if it were made of lead, feeling so heavy that the slightest movement would require a great deal of effort. Interestingly enough, many people report simultaneous feelings of both heaviness and weightlessness. However, some very good hypnotic subjects feel neither. They just feel very relaxed.

It is usually difficult for beginners to recognize the signs of hypnosis. Hypnosis begins very subtly and develops gradually, so the onset of hypnotic symptoms can be easily missed. This lack of recognition sometimes causes a blocking of further progress into a good hypnotic state. It is not unusual for the beginner to think that nothing is happening, and this instills a negative expectation which becomes a self-fulfilling prophecy that nothing *will* happen. The best advice here is to practice on faith. Don't try to *make* anything happen, just follow the prescribed routine with full confidence that hypnosis will eventually be developed.

On the other hand, the first experiences of hypnotic symptoms can also disrupt further hypnotic development. A typical example is when the hypnotic subject notices, for the first time, that her legs are feeling lighter and lighter. It is almost impossible for her to keep her attention from being drawn to this phenomenon, so it becomes a distraction which interrupts the whole process. With continued practice the symptoms of hypnosis occur more frequently—become more commonplace—and lose their disruptive quality.

Second-session syndrome is another experience common to hypnosis beginners. Everyone has experienced second-session syndrome in one

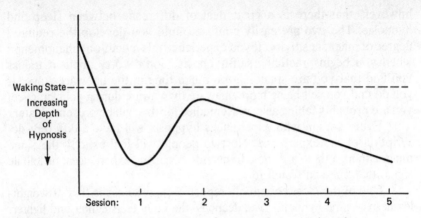

FIGURE 2-2 Typical pattern of hypnotic performance when second-session syndrome occurs.

way or another, often in sports-related activities. Often referred to as "beginners' luck," it typically goes something like this: You do very well, especially for a beginner, at something the first time you try it. But for some reason you don't do nearly as well on the second occasion, and it may take you a long time to get back to the level of your first performance.

Second-session syndrome can manifest itself the same way in hypnosis. A person achieves good depth with a number of novel feelings during the first induction attempt. But he doesn't get nearly as deep in successive inductions. This can be a disheartening experience for the person who does not understand what is happening—who does not know about second-session syndrome (which, by the way, is not limited to just the second session). If it happens to you, be assured that you will eventually achieve and exceed your initial depth, but it may take several sessions to do so. This is illustrated in Figure 2–2, in which the original depth of hypnosis is not achieved again until the fourth and fifth sessions.

Another commonly reported experience in hypnosis is a tingling sensation. It may be a localized tingling, such as in the hands, or there may be a tingling sensation all over the body. It is not an unpleasant sensation and need not cause alarm if it occurs. Nor need you be concerned that you are not hypnotized if you do not experience any tingling sensations.

These are certainly not the only sensations or experiences you might have in hypnosis. Every person has his or her own, individualistic experience. In your own development of hypnosis you may experience all of these phenomena and more, or your experiences might be entirely different. Whatever you experience, you can be assured that it will be pleasant. There are no "bad trips" in hypnosis. If you have an experience that is distinctly unpleasant, it is not hypnosis.

There are two minor exceptions to the pleasantness of a hypnotic experience. One is the mild headache that a few people experience after hypnosis when they are beginners. This phenomenon was covered at some length in the previous section on relaxation. These headaches, if they happen at all, should not recur after the first few practice sessions.

The other exception is a mild state of nausea. It is never serious, and like the headaches, is not likely to recur after the first few practice sessions. Headaches and nausea are both rare, so you are not likely to experience either of them in relation to your practice of self-hypnosis.

It is worth repeating at this point that hypnosis does not necessarily entail unconsciousness, nor is it necessary for you to experience any wildly euphoric, subjective states of mind. Hypnotic suggestion—which will be your main tool for change—will be effective even if you do not recognize any symptoms of hypnosis. Just practice the methods described in this book. The less you are consciously concerned about objective, recognizable symptoms of hypnosis, the more quickly you will achieve your goals.

Goal Achievement

The achievement of any goal requires either change or development (which is a form of change). Change requires energy. A major source of the energy required for inner change is your own mind. Many people are surprised when first confronted with the concept that their mind—and thought, the product of mental activity—is a source of energy. In the Western world, especially in America, we are taught from childhood that action—physical, mechanical action—is the only agent for getting anything done. Thought has been reduced to a position of relative weakness. This has become one of the primary intellectual propositions of our time, and a corollary is that thoughts have little if any reality and are therefore not very powerful.

Nothing could be further from the truth. As you will remember from what was said in the previous chapter about psychosomatic medicine, thinking can contribute largely to the onset of disease conditions. And thinking (particularly through hypnotic suggestion) can be instrumental in clearing up disease states. This puts thought in a central position relative to health and, by extension, to our entire lives. Just because thoughts cannot be weighed, measured, or burned as an alternative energy source does not mean that they are without substantive import.

One's own thinking is all-important in achieving any of the things that self-hypnosis is commonly used for: weight control, quitting smoking, increasing self-confidence, reducing tension, and so on. It is the redirection of thought processes into productive, energy-generating directions that yields positive change. Such effects of self-hypnosis are well documented, but the question still remains: What exactly is hypnosis?

At this time, a completely satisfactory answer is not available. However, I can offer a possible explanation and working theory of the cause and effect of hypnosis. To do so it is necessary to get a little technical. It is not necessary for you to thoroughly understand the theoretical basis for hypnosis that I am about to launch into. It is included here just in case you are interested. If you are not, feel free to skip to the next section (Common Questions About Hypnosis).

The pituitary and hypothalamus are believed to be the control centers of the involuntary nervous and glandular systems. In addition, there also exist many neurocirculatory hormones secreted by the cerebral cortex itself. These hormones directly affect the hypothalamus as well as the pituitary. This suggests that the cerebral cortex itself is the true control center of the hormonal and nervous systems. Thus a breakdown in the central nervous system will have a direct influence over these systems and result in marked metabolic disturbances throughout the body.

As far as we know at this time, all thought originates in the cerebral cortex. When the protoplasm of a cell in the cerebral cortex—or in any living cell, for that matter—is stimulated, an electric current is generated which flows along the length of the cell or tissue excited. And the very act of thinking is itself sufficient to generate this cellular electric current. Thought alone can therefore, in and of itself, be the stimulus to induce an electric current to flow down any nerve to the affected tissue. This demonstrates that thought is a source of energy.

Given that thought is a source of energy, the entire panoply of physiologic functions becomes subject to influence from "thinking," including the so-called involuntary systems. Thought-generated neuroelectric discharges in the areas of the thalamus, hypothalamus, limbic system, and reticular system, for example, will have dramatic effects on the emotions. If the stimulus is focused on the proper area of the hypothalamus, appetite can be increased or reduced. (Similar effects have been produced by stimulating areas of the limbic system in animal studies.)

In studies involving electrical stimulation of the brain (ESB), experiments on human subjects have demonstrated the ability to artificially stimulate a wide range of human emotions and sensations. Negative states such as anxiety, restlessness, panic, and intense pain can be induced through ESB, as can more agreeable feelings ranging from satisfaction to euphoria.

It is known that some of the "pleasure centers" of the brain have the ability to sharply reduce, or even suspend, any existing sensation of pain. Because of their inaccessible location in the human brain, these pleasure centers have not been experimentally manipulated through ESB research. However, such areas are not inaccessible to endogenous stimuli.

ESB research has also concerned itself with the artificial stimulation of memory. First discoverd by neurosurgeon Wilder Penfield, patients whose cortex had been stimulated reported vividly recalling long-forgotten episodes out of their distant pasts. Moreover, they would continue recalling more and more about the episodes so long as the electrode providing the stimulation remained in the same place. Hypnotic subjects have reported this same phenomenon of mysterious recall while in hypnotic states.

Much more evidence of both a direct and indirect nature could be presented here, but the point has hopefully been made: Thought is an energy form, or the source of energy, which can affect biological functioning. So what is it about hypnosis that makes such thought a possibility, more so anyway than in a waking state? Princeton psychologist Julian Jaynes has provided the basis for at least a partial answer in his book with the unlikely title of *The Origin of Consciousness in the Breakdown of the Bicameral Mind*.

Jaynes' concept of the bicameral mind is similar to our division of the mind into "upper and lower houses"—the conscious and the subconscious. He takes the position that consciousness is not fully developed in humans until sometime around the age of seven, that in our development during early years we learn to suppress the subconscious with the gradually developing conscious mind. He further takes the position that this is both a phylogenetic and an ontogenetic model of development.

The conscious part of the bicameral mind has all of the learned limitations and "I-can'ts" which are socially forced upon us. During hypnosis this filtering part of the mind is "turned off," as it were, giving the subconscious room to operate without the ordinary critiquing and filtering that comes from the conscious. In terms of energy, the by-passing of consciousness permits a reestablishing of properly channeled energy that is consonant with the desired outcome.

Now to return full circle with this model, the by-passing of consciousness—hypnotic induction—is achieved through the repetition of the desired thought (namely "sleep"). A hypnotic state is not possible if (a) the subject has no concept of hypnosis, or (b) certain "suppressing" suggestions are not made during the initial induction process. These suppressing suggestions will inevitably include concepts of "downness," "drifting," or "floating." But the key concept is *down* which, if nothing else, introduces to the subject at least a metaphor for sleep. It is this thought which, sooner or later, achieves sufficient energy to influence the appropriate brain functions and results in a hypnotic condition.

This hypnotic condition is not "sleep" in the ordinary sense of the word, but sleep is the closest, most accurate metaphor for describing it. Parts of the cerebral cortex which correspond to perceptual or cognitive screening are suppressed or "put to sleep." The larger the area thus suppressed, the deeper the hypnotic trance.

COMMON QUESTIONS ABOUT HYPNOSIS

The following questions and answers will serve two functions. First, they will answer the most commonly asked questions concerning hypnosis. Second, they will provide more information that will be helpful to you in developing self-hypnosis.

Is hypnosis different from sleep?

What we think of as ordinary, nocturnal sleep is not the same thing as hypnosis. It is true that the word "hypnosis" comes from the Greek word *hypnos* which means "sleep." James Braid, the eminent nineteenth-century British physician who coined the word, thought that hypnosis was a special form of sleep. However, there are many observable, measurable differences between the two states.

In ordinary sleep, blood pressure drops and heart rate slows down. In the hypnotic state, both heart rate and blood pressure can be made by direct suggestion to either speed up or slow down.

Another difference between sleep and hypnosis is found in metabolism, which is the process by which energy is provided for vital processes in the body. Metabolism rate is lowered in sleep, but not in hypnosis (unless specific suggestions are made to change it). Also lowered in sleep is urinary secretion, but not in hypnosis (again, unless specifically suggested).

Neurological effects are also quite different in the two states. During most stages of sleep, skeletal muscle is relaxed and there is a loss of tone and therefore a loss of the deep reflexes, such as knee and ankle jerks. But under hypnosis, these natural responses are the same as in the waking state.

One of the major differences between sleep and hypnosis is conscious awareness. One is not consciously aware of anything during sleep. But during hypnosis, there is always at least a thread of conscious awareness. In fact, it is not uncommon for hypnotized subjects to report a significant increase in alertness and awareness.

Can everyone be hypnotized?

Hypnosis is a skill that develops with proper practice. Anyone who is within the limits of what we think of as normal—the reference here is mainly to intelligence and sanity—can develop hypnotic states. It is true that only about one person in five can quickly and easily achieve a deep state of hypnosis, but this is simply an indication that some people are better at it than others.

Whatever your natural skill level, if you have the determination, time, and desire to practice a lot, you can probably become a real whiz at hypnosis even if it doesn't come easily for you in the beginning. However, most people find they can achieve their goals without having to develop very deep, "fantastic" depths of hypnosis.

Is hypnosis an artificial state?

Hypnosis is actually a natural state that everyone has experienced many times. One passes through a state of hypnosis on the way to sleep at night—the drowsy, semiawake state that precedes sleep is referred to as a *hypnagogic* state. A similar state of hypnosis is again present just before waking from sleep; this semiconscious state is referred to as *hypnopompic*. Most of us go through these states so quickly that they are not recognizable or noteworthy, but everyone has had at least one experience when the hypnagogic or hypnopompic state was prolonged. If you can remember having such an experience, you know it is a very pleasant, dreamlike state in which you feel great and very relaxed.

Does a person lose control under hypnosis?

All of the research—and all of my experience—leads to the conclusion that people cannot be made to do anything in hypnosis that they would not do in a waking state. The catch here is that you can never be sure what a person might be willing to do until you test the person. It is possible to trick a person when he is hypnotized, but only to the extent that he could be tricked without hypnosis. To my knowledge, there is not one verified case of a hypnotic subject being made to do anything

47

that violated his or her moral or ethical values. In the case of self-hypnosis this question is not likely to come up at all.

Is hypnosis dangerous?

Hetero-hypnosis (where one person is being hypnotized by another) can, under certain circumstances, be dangerous. Such circumstances are rare, but the fact that the possibility of danger does exist militates against ever putting yourself in the hands of anyone except a qualified professional. By "professional" I mean someone who is qualified in psychology or psychiatry. This eliminates most stage hypnotists and party entertainers because they have seldom been trained to deal with the human mind. A good rule of thumb is to never volunteer for a stage hypnotist, nor for the extravert at a party who claims to be a hypnotist.

Self-hypnosis is never dangerous. You have all of the safeguards working for you in self-hypnosis that you have in your normal waking state. You have nothing to fear from working with hypnosis by yourself.

Is there ever a problem waking up from hypnosis?

There is never a problem in getting out of the hypnotic state. You will spend all of your time getting into it, not out of it. Sometimes a hypnotized person is enjoying the state so much he doesn't want to wake up, but that is a matter of desire, not ability. Tell him to take off his clothes and he'll wake up in a flash (unless, of course, he's a little kinky).

Is a weak-minded person a better hypnotic subject?

The term "weak-minded" lacks an exact definition, but as I understand it, it refers to a person who has poor concentration, perhaps low intelligence, and probably no resistance to suggestions made by others. With any one of these criteria—or all three—the answer to the question is an emphatic *no!*

Poor concentration actually hinders the development of a good hypnotic state, while good concentration is a definite asset. If you have trouble concentrating, you will find that your hypnotizability increases only as your concentration improves. (Don't be disheartened. The exercises for developing hypnosis also develop concentration. And in the section dealing with suggestion application, you will learn how to apply suggestions to further develop your concentration.)

As far as intelligence is concerned, the person with normal or higher intelligence makes a better hypnotic subject than does a person with subnormal intelligence.

Gullibility—the inability to resist the suggestions of others—is the third factor mentioned above, and there is a lot of confusion about the difference between gullibility and suggestibility. It can be said that gullibility is suggestibility out of control. It is interesting to note that many people who consider themselves to be gullible become less so after they begin practicing self-hypnosis. Learning how to increase or turn on suggestibility at will also teaches one how to turn it off. And the ability to develop good states of hypnosis is by no means an indication that one is gullible.

HYPNOTIC INDUCTION METHODS

Hypnosis is a skill that is developed and improved with practice, and it is important to practice correctly and regularly. For the beginner, twice a day is ideal, and three or four times a week is probably a minimum practice schedule. When starting, you can expect to spend about twenty to thirty minutes on each practice session. As your skill develops, this time will become shorter. It is possible to achieve a level of skill in which one can go into a hypnotic state, apply the desired suggestions, and terminate the exercise all in a matter of a few minutes or even seconds. But this ability is developed only after a period of many months, perhaps years, of diligent practice.

It is unfortunate that some people give up on hypnosis shortly after starting with it. They are initially excited by the possibilities of achievement through hypnosis, but they give up too soon because they don't experience any magical, other-worldly states right off the bat.

The novice at hypnosis is ill-prepared to gauge his own progress. The beginning, developing symptoms of hypnosis are subtle and gradual, and it requires a good awareness of self and self-functioning to be able to recognize these symptoms. It is as if our life experiences cause us to form calluses that make us less sensitive to our inner experiences. With time and practice, these calluses go away and make us more sensitive and responsive to our inner environment. But until this begins to happen, it is often necessary to practice hypnosis and apply suggestions on faith.

If you don't experience anything recognizably different when you first start, give yourself six weeks to practice before giving up. I guarantee that you will not be able to practice for six weeks without noticing some positive differences.

The best time of day to practice is that time of day in which you feel at your best. Later, when you have become more skilled with hypnosis, you can use it to perk up the more sluggish part of your day. But until then, you need everything going for you, so practice at a time of day when you feel sharp and alert. Practicing self-hypnosis is difficult if you are tired or sleepy; it is not supposed to be practice at going to sleep.

Avoid practicing within an hour of eating, and don't try to make yourself more susceptible with drugs. Getting drunk or high to practice won't help. In fact, it will get in the way. If you take prescription drugs, continue to follow your doctor's advice. While drugs will not particularly help you in the development of hypnosis, most prescription drugs will not hinder you, either. A notable exception is any drug in the amphetamine category. Any of these stimulants will make hypnosis difficult if not impossible. If you are taking amphetamines, especially for weight control, ask your physician to reconsider the advisability of your taking them. The long-term effectiveness of amphetamines for weight control has been found highly questionable. Many medical researchers and practitioners have even advocated the abolishment of such drugs for weight control.

Some people find that practicing hypnosis gives them energy and stamina, leaving them alert and ready to "get with it." Others experience a pleasantly lethargic, relaxed condition following hypnosis. The way hypnosis affects you is an important consideration in determining when you will practice. If it energizes you, don't practice just before trying to go to sleep at night. If it leaves you feeling nicely limp and mellow, don't practice just before going to work or doing anything that requires you to be fully alert.

Preparing To Practice Hypnosis

There are some common-sense preparations you should make before actually starting your hypnosis session. For one thing, try to eliminate the possibility of any interruptions while you are practicing. It is advisable to get your family's cooperation, or the cooperation of anyone with whom you live, so that they understand what you are doing and won't disturb you for trivial things while you are trying to practice.

The position in which you practice is not critical, although most people prefer to practice while lying down or sitting back in a reclining chair. When you become more skilled, you can practice hypnosis in virtually any position, but start out as comfortably as possible.

Loosen any tight clothing and remove any distracting jewelry. If you wear contact lenses, remove them while you practice unless they are the kind that don't bother you when your eyes are closed. Your legs should not be crossed, and your hands and arms should rest comfortably at your side. It is also helpful if there is no one else in the room with you.

50

The key factors for good practice are comfort and the absence of distractions. A television or radio can be very distracting and won't help you a bit. Hypnosis requires concentration, a kind of concentration which we don't normally learn. Most people associate concentration with such things as pursed lips, squinted eyes, and clenched teeth. The kind of concentration you want to develop now is just the opposite—it is a loose kind of focused attention that is much easier on you, once you get the hang of it. This more desirable kind of concentration will develop naturally as you continue to practice hypnosis, so don't try to force it.

If you try forcing it, your efforts will get in the way of the development of a good hypnotic state. The secret is to achieve a compromise between trying to make something happen and doing nothing. You can do this—develop good concentration and self-hypnosis—by practicing in the prescribed manner and keeping uppermost in your mind the thought that you are not trying to make anything happen. You will be learning to *let self-hypnosis happen.*

The Four Major Parts of Hypnotic Induction

The self-hypnotic induction process can be divided into four distinct phases: relaxation, countdown or deepening, scene visualization, and termination.

The process of relaxation has already been discussed at length in Chapter 1. Relaxation is both a preparation for, and a beginning of, hypnosis. You must be relaxed to achieve a positive hypnotic state, and you actually begin to develop hypnosis as you become more and more relaxed. So your self-hypnotic induction begins with the deep relaxation process described in Chapter 1. You will simply be adding the next three phases to the deep relaxation procedure to turn it into a hypnotic induction.

The countdown or deepening procedure, which immediately follows the relaxation procedure, involves counting backward and imagining yourself drifting down toward a pleasant, sleeplike state of hypnosis. Think of your goal as being a state that is similar to sleep, but one in which you continue to be aware.

It should be mentioned at this point that at no time during the induction exercise will you need to speak out loud. You may if you want to, but it is not necessary. When counting down, for example, it is sufficient to think the numbers to yourself. If you are using an induction recording, this will all be done for you, but more about the use of recorded inductions later.

When you first start practicing self-hypnosis, begin your countdown at a relatively high number. The higher the number you start with, the longer you will have in which to achieve hypnosis. As a beginner, it is a good idea to start with a number such as one hundred. As you become more skilled you will be able to more quickly develop hypnosis, so later you will be able to start your countdown with lower numbers. The example of an induction talk (or induction "think") presented here will begin the countdown at twenty. Feel free to vary this starting number in accordance with your own needs.

While counting down, it is helpful to imagine yourself on an elevator or an escalator, riding down as you count down. You might imagine that each number represents a different floor level and see the numbers lighting up on a panel as you move downward. Your goal is the basement (zero) and to be in a state of hypnosis when you get there.

If you don't like elevators or escalators, you can just imagine yourself floating down. Or, if downward motion does not appeal to you, use horizontal movement. Some people like to imagine a white mist or cloud moving toward them as they count down, imagining that they are gradually being enveloped by the pleasant whiteness. With the aid of your imagination you can make the cloud become more dense as your hypnotic state deepens.

The use of your imagination during this phase, and during the scene visualization phase that follows, is extremely important. It is unfortunate that our culture has been so disparaging of imagination in adults. While it is true that unbridled imagination can be a problem, this does not justify the disrepute into which imagination has fallen. The constructive, positive use of the childlike (not child*ish*) qualities of imagination can be your most potent tool for change and achievement. Use imagination to your fullest ability, both in the development of hypnosis and in the application of suggestion (which will be covered in a later chapter).

If your ability to make pictures in your head has atrophied and you find it difficult or impossible to see things with your mind's eye, here is an easy exercise that will help you. Pick a small, simple object, such as the tip of a pencil. Hold the object in front of you and gaze at it for a few moments, noting all the details you can. In the case of a pencil point some of the things you might notice are its colors and general shape, whether the point is rounded or sharp, the grain of the wood where the pencil has been sharpened, and so on.

After a minute or two of observing the object, close your eyes and try to re-create it in your mind's eye. With a few practice sessions you will discover that you are rapidly recovering the ability to visualize things in your mind, and you can move gradually to more complicated objects.

A small percentage of people are "literal minded." They have never used mental images as part of their imagination. If you are such a person and you don't want to go to the trouble of developing your visual imagination, this need not deter you. You can imagine the sensations of riding down in an elevator without "seeing" it happen. Another tactic might include "hearing" the numbers being called out as you move downward during the countdown procedure. Or you might be able to visually imagine lightness and darkness, making the intensity of lightness increase as a white mist overtakes you (or have it darken as you go deeper—whatever seems pleasant and relaxing to you). Whatever your abilities, the more you can utilize your imagination, the more effective you will be in your use of self-hypnosis and suggestion.

Now, to continue with the countdown procedure. As you proceed to count down, imagine yourself becoming more and more drowsy. You know how it feels to be so drowsy that you can hardly stay awake. Imagine that you are feeling drowsier and drowsier as you continue your countdown. You will find that such feelings and experiences come more easily as you increase your skill. Feelings of lethargic drowsiness are natural when one is deeply relaxed.

When you have reached zero in your countdown, visualize yourself in some peaceful scene. Do *not* "see yourself" as if you were standing back, looking at a picture of yourself. Instead, see yourself in the sense that you would experience it if you were actually there.

Your scene visualization can be a place in the mountains on a pleasant spring day, a beach or south sea island, a pleasantly furnished room, or any other place that is peaceful and serene to you. The important characteristics of a scene visualization are tranquillity and peace; it should be a place that is relaxing for you, and in which you are alone with no distractions. It is your own personal place in which no cares or worries are allowed.

The scene you imagine does not have to be conventional. One woman I know of liked to imagine herself sitting in a rocking chair in a cornfield in Iowa. An ex-Navy man enjoyed lying on a mattress on a raft floating on the ocean. Your scene can be anything that makes you feel peaceful, serene, and relaxed.

What follows are a few examples of scene visualizations, presented in detail to give you a feel for properly structured scene visualizations. You may use any of them as presented, if they feel right for you, or you can make any modifications that would improve a particular scene for you. Or you may want to construct one that is entirely different. Just keep the basics in mind: Be alone in the scene, keep it peaceful, and imagine as much detail as possible. One more thing: Don't use a remembered scene from past experience if there is anything negative related to it. For example, if you remember a beautiful spot on the beach where you once had a picnic, but where you also got a terrible sunburn, don't use that scene.

Mountain scene. You are walking along a mountain path. It is a beautiful, warm spring day. You can feel the warmth of the sun shining through the pine trees and smell the scent of pine in the air. You are walking uphill on the path and your legs are getting more and more tired. You think to yourself how nice it would be to lie down and rest.

Eventually you come to your own private place, which is a level clearing in the trees, overlooking a beautiful mountain valley. Your clearing is lush with green grass and shrubs, and there is an abundance of mountain flowers. There is a small, rippling stream flowing through your clearing. Just at the edge of it is a hammock in which you lie down and rest. The gently swaying hammock is very pleasant. You feel serenly peaceful and drowsy as you lie in the hammock, listening to the sound of the stream, the birds singing in the trees. You can smell the scent of pine as you gently sway back and forth in the hammock.

Beach scene. You are walking barefoot on the beach and you can feel the warm, dry sand between your toes as you walk. You are alone on this stretch of beach which is your own private place. You can feel the warmth of the sun on your skin and smell the fresh sea air. Walking in the sand is pleasant, but your legs, ankles, and feet are tiring. Eventually you lie down in the warm sand (or you can have a hammock or cot in the trees a few yards back from the edge of the beach). As you lie there soaking up the warmth and feeling drowsy, you are aware of the sound of the ocean and an occasional seagull.

Cloud scene. You are lying on the slope of a hill in the country. It is a beautiful spring day. The grass is green, and you can feel the warmth of the sun and smell the clean country air. There are beautiful, billowy white clouds floating lazily overhead. As you watch the clouds, seeing the many shapes, one of the smaller clouds separates itself from the others and gently settles on the ground next to you. The cloud gently scoops you up and you begin to float upward, moving safely and gently.

You have no cares or worries—you are completely at peace—as you are gently moved through the sky by the breeze.

It is during your scene visualization that you will apply suggestions. This topic will be covered completely in Chapter 4.

The fourth and final phase of an induction procedure is the termination. A termination process is necessary to mark the end of the hypnotic state, when you tell yourself to awaken and return to your normal, waking state. You could, of course, just get up and walk away when you are finished with your self-hypnosis session. But it is much better to have a familiar procedure to follow before doing so.

The easiest and most effective form of termination procedure is to count slowly to three, giving yourself termination suggestions between the numbers. This process will become clear to you as you read the full induction talk given below.

HYPNOTIC INDUCTION SCRIPT

With the following script, you can either think your way through a hypnotic induction, or you can record it and listen to your recording for hypnotic induction. If you think your way through it you will have to become very familiar with the whole script because you obviously cannot read yourself into a hypnotic state. You don't have to memorize it word for word, but you will want to master some of the phrasing and know the sequence of major points. And change the "you's" in the script to "I's."

You could also have someone else read the script to you, but this seldom proves satisfactory. Hetero-hypnosis (where one person hypnotizes another) requires quite a bit of practice to get the timing, phrasing, and intonation right, even with a script. This same problem arises when beginners record their own voices reading the script. The best procedure is for you to become thoroughly familiar with the script and think your way through it. Or purchase one of the professionally done induction talks available on cassette tape.

There are a number of commercially produced cassette tape recordings of hypnotic induction talks available on the market. Naturally I think mine are the best. (A catalog of my tapes is available from Biocentrix Corporation, P.O. Box 10003, Denver, CO 80210.)

Some sort of background sound is helpful when you are first learning to use self-hypnosis because it blocks out distracting sounds. The static that you get when a radio is tuned between stations (unless you have a newer model with a static suppressor), or the sound of a television tuned to a "blank" or unused channel, are very similar to what we call "white noise." And, of course, there are white noise generators. If you happen to have one, use it. Otherwise, make do with the radio or TV static, but don't turn it up too high. You will find that you quickly learn to ignore the static sound, forgetting that it is even there.

The induction script that follows begins at a point immediately after your deep relaxation exercise. In other words, go through the deep relaxation procedure you learned in Chapter 1, then continue with the induction procedure. Further deepening of the relaxation will be achieved with the blanket method with which the script opens. After you have used the tensing-releasing method of deep relaxation for five or six weeks, the induction as presented in the script will be all you have to do because it starts with the blanket method of deep relaxation.

> We'll start with an imaginary blanket. Every part of your body that is covered by the blanket will completely relax. Just imagine that your muscles are unable to be tense if they are covered by the blanket. You should be in a comfortable position. Imagine the blanket moving over your toes, arches, and ankles. The blanket is now covering your feet. Keep your concentration on the blanket. Other thoughts and sounds are unimportant and do not distract you. As you imagine it, the blanket is becoming more and more real to you. You may even notice a sensation of warmth every place that the blanket covers you. With the blanket covering your toes, arches, and ankles, you can imagine all of those muscles becoming very relaxed. All tension is flowing out.
>
> Notice how nice it feels to let the tension flow out as you concentrate on the relaxation and imagine the blanket. Now the blanket is moving up slowly, moving up to your knees. All of the muscles and tendons in your knees and in your legs, all the way down to your toes, are becoming relaxed. They're becoming limp and floppy.
>
> Now the blanket is continuing to move up slowly, gradually, moving up to your waist. All of the muscles in your lower abdomen and hips are relaxing. The muscles in your legs are becoming limp and loose, all the way down to your toes.
>
> Imagine that your body is like a rubber band; all tight and tense when it is wound up, but limp and loose when it is unwound. You are unwinding, becoming limp and loose.
>
> Just listen to my voice and ignore everything else. You are becoming more and more relaxed, and beginning to feel sleepy. If they are not already closed, your eyelids are getting heavier and heavier. Soon you'll be so relaxed, you'll be unable to keep your eyes open.
>
> Now the blanket is moving up over your stomach, over your chest, up to

your shoulders. There are a great many muscles in your shoulders, chest, and stomach. Imagine all of the muscles in those areas becoming limp and loose. They're covered by the blanket, so they are relaxing. All tension is going away.

Now the relaxation is spreading outward, from the shoulders into your arms. Your arms are becoming more and more relaxed as the tension flows down and out of your body. Your hands and fingers are becoming limp and completely relaxed. If your eyes are not already closed, they soon will be. Your eyelids become so heavy, it feels as if they are made of lead. You can imagine them made of lead—very heavy, so hard to keep open. As you deepen your relaxation, they'll continue to get heavier and heavier. They eventually get so heavy you can't hold them open any longer.

Now the muscles and tendons in your neck are relaxing. This is an important area, so pay particular attention to the back of your neck. All of the muscles are getting so relaxed that your neck is limp and rubbery. All of the tendons and muscles are becoming more and more limp. From the back of your head, down to the back of your shoulders, all tension is flowing out of your neck.

Now the relaxation is spreading into your mouth and jaw muscles. You may notice a temporary increase in saliva as you relax your mouth muscles. Don't let it bother you—it's temporary and will go away shortly. Go ahead and swallow if you need to. The muscles in your jaw and mouth are becoming more and more relaxed. The relaxation is spreading into your cheeks and forehead. All of your facial muscles are becoming limp and loose. As the muscles continue to relax, your eyelids are becoming very heavy. If they have not already closed, don't fight it any more.

Let your eyes close, and slip deeper into relaxation. Don't try to make anything happen, just let it happen. Now that your eyes are closed, your eyelids feel so heavy that it would be practically impossible to open your eyes again without tensing up. Just imagine yourself very limp and floppy. With every breath, you're drifting deeper and deeper into relaxation.

Now I'm going to count backwards from twenty. As I count down, let yourself drift down pleasantly. Imagine yourself riding down on an elevator or an escalator, or just floating down through clouds like a feather. As I continue to count downward, imagine yourself drifting down with each count. You are drifting into a sleeplike state. By the time I reach zero, you'll be in a very pleasant, sleeplike state. It'll be like sleep in some ways, but different in others. You'll hear my voice and you'll understand my instructions.

You can rouse yourself any time you want to, or need to, but unless you need to awaken for something, you'll drift deeper into relaxation and follow my instructions.

Starting down now: twenty . . . nineteen . . . eighteen . . . seventeen . . . sixteen . . . fifteen . . . fourteen . . . thirteen . . . twelve . . . eleven . . . ten . . . half-way down, floating deeper and getting sleepier and sleepier with each count . . . nine . . . eight . . . seven . . . six . . . five . . . feeling so sleepy . . . four . . . three . . . sleepier and sleepier

. . . two . . . one . . . zero. Sleep and relax. Sleep and relax. Drift deeper and deeper into relaxation and sleep with each word that I speak and with each breath you take.

Now you're going to a very pleasant and a very special place. You're walking along a path in the woods. It's a beautiful spring day in the mountains. You're alone and feeling very peaceful, walking along the path. You can see the sun shining through the trees. You can smell the clean, mountain air.

You're walking slightly uphill, and your legs are beginning to get tired. It's very pleasant walking through the trees in the forest, but your legs and feet are beginning to get very tired. You're going to your own special place, and you're looking forward to getting there so you can lie down and rest.

Your legs and feet are becoming very tired. They feel so heavy. It would be so nice to lie down and rest. Now you are coming to your own special, private place. It is a small clearing by a pleasant stream. There is a hammock stretched between two trees, and you lie down in the hammock.

It feels so good to lie down and rest. The hammock is gently swaying— just enough to be pleasant. You can hear the sounds of the stream, of the birds in the trees. You can smell the scent of pine in the fresh, clean, mountain air. You feel so serene and calm. No cares or worries, just a pleasant awareness of yourself in your own private place.

As you lie in the hammock, gently swaying back and forth . . . back and forth . . . you feel very positive about life. Life has a way of always working out, and you feel very good about that. You know that every day you are becoming more and more relaxed, secure in the conviction that things will work out the way you want them to.

You are developing stronger and stronger feelings of well-being . . . feelings of well-being that stay with you throughout your day. You are sleeping better and better at night, because more and more you look forward to each new day. The inner forces of your mind are tuning in to health and happiness. You are being led to the accomplishment of your goals by the power of your mind. Even without consciously thinking about it, you are moving closer and closer to the accomplishment of your goals . . . closer and closer . . . closer and closer.

You know that all things are possible, and that you can be anything you want to be. The power of your inner mind can direct you to the accomplishment of your goals. You are being led to those accomplishments by the power of your inner mind. You know that all things are possible, and that you can be anything that you want to be . . . anything that you want to be . . .

In a moment when you hear me say "direct yourself," I am going to be silent for a few minutes so you can think positively about all the good things you want to be and do. As you think about these things, you are directing your inner mind to help you achieve them. Vividly picture yourself being the way you want most to be . . . doing the things you want most to do . . . make your visualization as vivid and detailed as you possibly can. When you again hear my voice, after this self-directing period, it will not disturb your relaxation. Ready now . . . direct yourself.

[This self-directing period is the time for suggestion application. It should typically last about five minutes, but longer periods are perfectly acceptable.]

Now listen to my voice . . . listen to my voice and remain relaxed. All of the instructions that I have given you, and all of the directions that you have given yourself, will be effective because you want them to be. Positive changes are taking place in your life, and you are directing those changes.

Each time you practice deep relaxation and self-hypnosis you are getting better and better at it . . . better and better each time you practice. You will never have a problem slipping into hypnosis accidentally. You can relax whenever you want to, but only when you want to, and when you intend to. When you awaken, you will feel relaxed and happy with no unpleasant side effects.

Now, as I count to three, you will slowly, gradually, pleasantly awaken. You will return to your normal, waking state, except for the positive directions and instructions that will remain effective. Now, starting up . . . one . . . becoming more alert . . . two, getting ready to wake up . . . three, open your eyes, wake up, and return to your waking state.

Depth of Hypnotic Trance

Measurement of the depth of a hypnotic trance presents several problems ("trance," as used here, simply means a hypnotic state). There is really no standard of measurement, just as there is no uniform way of measuring something like love or desire or any other internal feeling state. We might say that one person wants something more or less than another person, but it would be difficult to describe the actual difference between wanting something a lot more and wanting something just a little more.

In the same sense, we can say that one hypnotic trance is deeper than another, but we run into trouble when we try to give some objective measurement to the difference between the two trances. Many attempts have been made to do this by devising scales of hypnotic depth in which the more easily achieved phenomena indicate a lighter state of hypnosis, and increasingly deeper states are indicated by the ability of the hypnotized person to evince more and more difficult phenomena. (Three well-known attempts at such scaling are the Davis-Husband Scale of Hypnotic Susceptibility, the LeCron-Bordeaux Scale of Hypnotic Susceptibility, and the Burgess Tests of Depth of Trance.)

Figure 2–3 presents a scale of trance depth that I have found helpful in teaching self-hypnosis to others. It was originally developed with the aid of college students in a self-hypnosis course I was teaching. Especially constructed for self-hypnosis, it is not particularly satisfactory for use

FIGURE 2-3 Scale of hypnotic depth with particular application to self-hypnosis.

HYPNOIDAL	1.	Flutter of eyelids. Feelings of heaviness in arms and legs. Local sensations of warmth.
LIGHT TRANCE	2.	Eye closure, feeling that it would be too difficult to open eyes. Automatic movements possible.
	3.	Consciousness almost normal; some floating in and out of consciousness.
	4.	Slower and deeper breathing; slower pulse.
MEDIUM TRANCE	5.	Strong lassitude (unwilling to move, speak, think or act).
	6.	Partial feeling of detachment.
	7.	Recognition of hypnotic trance; difficult to describe but definitely felt.
	8.	Glove anesthesia possible.
	9.	Rigidity of limbs possible with direct suggestion.
DEEP TRANCE	10.	Illusions of touch possible.
	11.	Illusions of taste possible.
	12.	Illusions of smell possible.
	13.	Fantasies and day-dreams become vivid.
	14.	Partial post-hypnotic amnesia may occur.
	15.	Ability to open eyes without affecting hypnotic trance state.
	16.	Fixed stare when eyes are open; pupilary dilation.
	17.	Positive auditory and visual hallucinations possible.
	18.	Limited age-regression possible.
	19.	Negative auditory and visual hallucinations possible.
PLENARY TRANCE	20.	Stuporous condition in which all voluntary activity is inhibited. Rare in self-hypnosis.

in hetero-hypnotic research or practice. The divisions between the various trance depths are somewhat arbitrary and are intended to serve only as a general guideline.

Bear in mind that no scale will be completely accurate for any one person. The symptoms of various hypnotic depths can sometimes be radically different from one person to the next. For example, I have placed eye closure—that point at which it is just too much effort to keep the eyes open—at the beginning of the light trance state. Almost all scales devised so far place eye closure in this approximate position, yet I have seen several cases where very deep hypnotic states were developed without any eye closure at all. So if you find that your experience does not conform to the scale presented in Figure 2–3, don't let it alarm you.

Some of the terms in the scale need further definition, so here are some notes to clear up any confusion about them.

Automatic movements are body movements that are the result of suggestion, and for which no conscious effort is required. Interestingly, such movements are usually unfelt; the hypnotic subject has to see them to know they are happening. If, while in the hypnotic state, you were to repeatedly imagine your right hand floating effortlessly into the air, it would begin to rise without any conscious effort on your part. This would be automatic movement. You can do it, but it usually takes five to ten minutes of suggestion to achieve it (and it can sometimes take longer).

Glove anesthesia refers to the removal of all pain sensations in the area of your hand that would be covered by a glove. This anesthesia (or, more correctly, *analgesia*) can then be transferred to any part of the body by merely touching it with the anesthetized hand.

Post-hypnotic amnesia is the inability (partial or total) to remember what occurred during the hypnotic trance. Sometimes this occurs spontaneously, but it is usually the product of suggestion. It is this phenomenon of post-hypnotic amnesia, by the way, that often convinces people that they were "out" during the hypnotic session.

A *positive hallucination* is the condition in which something is believed present when it is not really there. A *negative* hallucination is the inability to perceive something that really is there. So a positive auditory hallucination, for example, would entail hearing a bell (if that were the suggested stimulus) when there was in fact no such sound. A negative auditory hallucination would involve not hearing a bell (if so suggested) when there really is a bell ringing.

Depth of trance is almost always a matter of interest and concern to the beginner. It is true that increased trance depth increases suggestibility, and therefore the rapidity with which suggestions are effective. But it is also true that suggestion is effective without any hypnosis at all! You will learn that *waking suggestions*—suggestions applied while in a waking state—are also effective when properly applied. If this were not true, there would be a lot less advertising.

Regular practice and the correct application of suggestion should be of more concern to you than the depth of trance you achieve. You will be able to develop greater depth as you continue to practice, but you do not have to reach any particular level before suggestion is effective. So keep your attention focused on regular practice and proper technique, avoiding too much concern about the depth of your hypnotic trance.

As you continue to practice, you will find that some days are better than others. If you have one of those days when you are not doing as well with your self-hypnosis as you have been, it does not mean that anything is broken. Nor does it mean that you have lost your touch. Such ups and downs are natural with any skill, including self-hypnosis.

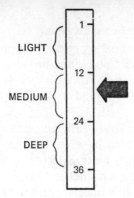

FIGURE 2-4 Yardstick and pointer technique for measuring the depth of self-hypnotic trance.

Self-Measurement of Hypnotic Depth

There are several ways you can measure the depth of your hypnotic states. The methods presented here will be for self-comparison, rather than for comparing your own with the depths of other people. These methods are somewhat subjective and will take some practice for you to become comfortable with them. But once you are comfortable with them, you will find them quite reliable. They mostly require, once again, the use of imagination, and all are done in the hypnotic state.

One of the most popular methods of self-measurement is the yardstick and pointer technique. As you know, a yardstick is thirty-six inches long; this will be your depth scale. When you are at the point in your hypnosis practice that you want to measure, picture in your mind a vertical yardstick and a floating pointer (see Figure 2–4).

The floating pointer is to indicate the depth of hypnosis you are in at that moment. It is helpful to "see" the pointer being very springy at first, bouncing up and down before it finally comes to rest at the appropriate number on the stick. In Figure 2-4, the pointer has stopped at about eighteen, indicating a "medium" depth of hypnosis. Regularly practice this method of measurement and you will find that it quickly becomes reliable. As mentioned earlier, don't be dismayed when you find that achievable depth varies from day to day. Your self-hypnosis will still be effective, even in the very lightest states.

There are several methodological variations that utilize the basic concept represented in the yardstick method. One variation is to see a gauge similar in concept to the gas gauge in your automobile (see Figure 2–5). The idea and application are the same as with the yardstick; only the format is different.

It is worth repeating that the actual depth of hypnosis is not as important as regular and correct practice. One of the major objectives

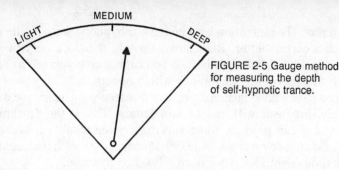

FIGURE 2-5 Gauge method for measuring the depth of self-hypnotic trance.

in using hypnosis is the increase in suggestibility that it develops. For optimum results in your program of suggestion application, it is desirable to develop a recognizable state of hypnosis. You are doing this when you know, during hypnosis, that something is different. This "something" may be any of the symptoms mentioned earlier, or it might be a feeling or experience that is uniquely your own.

Don't try to force any special symptoms of hypnosis on yourself, and try not to let yourself be influenced by Hollywood's versions of hypnosis that you may have seen on television or in movies. Above all, don't try to force anything to happen. Practice, be patient, and let things happen naturally.

Alternative Deepening Techniques

Here are a couple of alternative methods for deepening the self-hypnotic state. You can experiment with these techniques to see if you like them better than the conventional counting-down method.

Try counting down from five, repeating each number three times, with a pause of about three or four seconds between each number. During the pause, visualize the number appearing on a screen in your mind—something like a digital counter—then let the number fade away before repeating it (or before moving down to the next number). Imagine that this digital print-out in your mind is a measure of your deepening hypnotic state.

When you reach the third and last zero, hold the zero in your mind and visualize it enlarging into a movie screen. See your scene visualization on the screen, putting in all the detail you can muster. When the scene is clearly formed on the screen, move yourself into and continue with your scene visualization in the normal way.

Although not as popular with most people, some do prefer to use letters of the alphabet in place of numbers. Instead of counting down, you start through the alphabet beginning with "A" and continuing one letter at a time. The intention is to be in your hypnotic state by the time you reach a certain letter. Remember, though, there are only twenty-six letters in the English alphabet, so you cannot give yourself as much time with this procedure as you can with numbers.

If you have a good imagination, here is a deepening technique which completely dispenses with numbers or letters. This is the "mapping" method and it can produce some very interesting results. It takes the place of counting down and should be commenced, as with the counting-down method, right after your deep relaxation exercise.

Imagine a large, three-story house with a basement. You begin your deepening procedure by walking into the house through the front door. Walk up the three flights of stairs, thinking as you go how comfortable the house is and how relaxed you feel when you are in it. Enter one of the rooms when you reach the top of the stairs. There is a straight-backed chair in the room, and you sit down in it. As you sit there, feel the relaxation beginning to seep into your mind. Spend a moment or two there, then rise and return to the stairway.

Start walking down the stairs, heading for the second floor. Take each step deliberately, feeling more and more pleasantly lethargic as you move down the stairs. When you reach the second floor you enter one of the rooms where there is a softer and more comfortable chair waiting for you. Sit down in that chair and notice that you feel even more relaxed, comfortable, and drowsy than you did in the chair on the top floor.

By this time you are feeling very lazy and drowsy, and it is with reluctance that you leave this comfortable chair and room. But you know that you are going to an even more comfortable place on the ground floor. Again, take each step down the stairs deliberately and slowly, going deeper and deeper with each step.

As you enter a room on the ground floor, you see a large, comfortable reclining chair awaiting you. Seating yourself in it, you lean back and feel so comfortably relaxed you could almost melt into the upholstery of the chair. Sit there for a moment or two, almost overwhelmed by feelings of comfort, relaxation, and just plain feeling good. But now you must push yourself out of this chair because you know there is an even better place awaiting you in the basement. You find it very difficult to get up because you are so relaxed in this chair and room that you feel as if you could stay here forever. But you do get up, leave the room, and start down the stairs toward the basement. You move even more slowly down this last flight of stairs because by now you are almost floating, and nothing is very important except the delicious enjoyment of your own self and sense of awareness.

Your basement room is at the base of the stairs. There is a doorway into this room with a massive door that can be bolted from the inside. Just outside the door is a strong chest that you open before entering the room. In your pocket are three (at least three) fat envelopes. Each of these envelopes is labeled, and you read the labels as you put the envelopes in the chest. The first envelope is labeled WORRIES, and it contains all of your worries and cares. The second envelope is labeled ANXIETIES, and it contains all of your anxieties, fears, and anything else that could make you nervous. The third envelope is labeled TENSION. It contains all cares, problems, and concerns not included in the first two envelopes.

The purpose of these envelopes, as you have no doubt already guessed, is to provide a symbolic way of emptying your mind of all distractions, especially those that might be negative in nature. There may be times when you want to add envelopes with more specific labels to deal with current problems. For example, an envelope labeled BILLS might be a good one if you are beset by money problems.

Deposit your envelopes in the chest, visualizing every detail of closing and padlocking the chest. You want those problems securely locked away where they will not intrude themselves into your mind while you are practicing self-hypnosis. You have plenty of time for worrying without doing it at this time.

Now you are ready to enter your basement room, which is like no other room in the world. Soft, relaxing light radiates from the walls and ceiling. The light is multicolored, changing and moving in the most beautiful patterns you have ever seen. Hauntingly beautiful music is playing in the background, music that sounds like the celestial spheres moving in natural harmony through the universe.

In the center of the room is a special couch, contoured to fit only you. You lie down on this couch and feel more comfortable than you have ever felt in your life. Lying on this couch in this room makes you feel as if your mind has entered another dimension, one in which you can be anything and everything.

If you will practice this scene visualization several times, you will eventually be able to go directly to the basement without traversing the whole house. This is particularly convenient for short breaks during the day. You can also experiment with reversing the procedure, starting at the lowest floor and culminating at a special place on the top floor of the house.

Accelerating Hypnotic Induction

As you continue to practice you will become faster at developing a self-hypnotic state, and the trance state will become deeper. It is not uncommon, after several months of practice, to be able to use a recall method of induction (closely related to the recall method in deep relaxation). With this method it takes only a few seconds to develop self-hypnosis.

The recall induction method is basically simple: You recall, or remember, what your hypnotic state feels like, and re-create it. While the procedure itself is simple, getting to the skill level required to do it takes time and practice. Depending on how often and correctly you practice, it will probably take at least several months of practice to achieve this ability. And it can take much longer. (On the other hand, there are some people who can do it almost immediately, but that is rare.)

It would seem logical to move directly from hypnosis to suggestion. In other words, to follow the present chapter on hypnotic induction methods with a chapter on suggestion formulation and application. After all, it is suggestion applied during hypnosis which makes hypnosis so valuable. It is through suggestion that the programming, or directional, aspects of goal achievement are made possible.

However, there exists a problem with such a sequence. In order to be effective, suggestions must be properly formulated. And you cannot be assured of correct and proper formulation of suggestions without the use of autoquestioning. This is true for many of the same reasons that you cannot tell another person how to get somewhere until you know where he is starting from, where he wants to go, and how he will be traveling.

So the next chapter is on autoquestioning, which I think you will find exciting, interesting, and worthwhile. Then, in the following chapter, we will consider suggestion formulation and application.

3

Autoquestioning

You probably want to make changes in your life. They may be large-scale changes, or they may be more limited modifications. Whether you are interested in limited or massive changes, you must learn to obtain information from your subconscious if you are going to effect desired changes in yourself that will be permanent. The kind of information you can get from the subconscious part of your mind—through autoquestioning—is helpful or necessary for several reasons.

THE PRIMARY GOALS
OF AUTOQUESTIONING

There are three primary reasons for getting information from the subconscious part of the mind. Each of these reasons is a possible outcome toward which you are striving. The first of these is *insight*.

Insights are more difficult to describe than to recognize. The autoquestioning process gradually pulls up information from the subconscious about the problem area being investigated. When enough information has been brought to the conscious level, an insight may occur which gives you a new awareness of the meaning and subconscious origin of your behavior and symptoms related to the problem. When the insight reaches full conscious awareness, it becomes the familiar "light-going-on" or "ah-ha!" phenomenon. When this happens you may remember the particular event that originally started the problem. It is frequently something that you have not remembered or thought about since the time it happened.

The foregoing remarks apply to problems caused by a specific event or series of events. It is also possible to reach a *relational* insight. This kind of insight is not a memory of a specific event. It is the dawning of awareness of a condition, attitude, relationship, or inner truth about something from your past. Sometimes these kinds of insights are very general in nature; it is not the memory of a specific instance that comes to you, but an awareness of a general fact or relationship.

It is not always possible to reach an insight through questioning. Even if you do not, you will put the information from your questioning to good use when formulating suggestions.

A second goal of autoquestioning is actually an offshoot of reaching an insight into the source of the problem. The process of autoquestioning is often abreactive and leads to *catharsis*. Catharsis is the release, liberation, or reduction of emotional tension. It can happen when repressed, traumatic, symptom-producing experiences are brought to the conscious level. When catharsis occurs, we say that the problem has been removed by the conscious awareness of its cause.

The third goal of autoquestioning is relevant in those situations where conscious awareness of the source of a problem is not sufficient to remove or change it. It is then that you formulate and apply suggestions that will do the job. Any information, even a small amount of information, about the subconscious causes of a problem is very helpful in formulating suggestions that are tailored to your own needs.

The alternative to tailored suggestions is simply Positive Thinking. I have capitalized the "P" and "T" in "Positive Thinking" because I want to distinguish it from the lower case "positive thinking."

Positive thinking, or "thinking positively" to make the distinction even clearer, is a Good Thing that can be very helpful in promoting the achievement of goals. But Positive Thinking has become a quasi-religious cult for many people. It is too often crutched by its adherents as an alternative to the diligent pursuit of logical, well-thought-out plans.

Aside from the fact that Positive Thinking is often just a substitute for thinking, its major reason for failure is that it can set up tremendous resistance in the subconscious. Telling ourselves that we are going to do something that subconsciously terrifies us will result in subconscious rejection. We may not consciously know that the subconscious terror exists, and that we are subconsciously putting up resistance that makes the situation worse instead of better. (Sometimes we subconsciously overreact, making things even worse than they were, in order to assure that we will not reach the feared objective.)

It is a fundamental concept of self-improvement that you can't fight city hall. "City hall" is the subconscious mind. If you are going to get anywhere with your efforts, you must enlist the aid and cooperation of "city hall." To do that you've got to have at least some idea of your subconscious needs and fears. And that's where autoquestioning comes in.

SUBCONSCIOUS BLOCKS TO ACHIEVEMENT

There are times when information alone is sufficient to remove a block to achievement, but the usual case requires information to be sent back to the subconscious that is designed to either eliminate a block or change the subconscious viewpoint. Such transformations of the subconscious viewpoint must be accomplished in order to bring the power of the subconscious into line with consciously desired goals.

You have probably already experienced failure in something at which you tried very hard to succeed. Perhaps others had easily succeeded in the same area and you wondered why they could do it but you could not. The answer is in your subconscious, not in some obscure quality like the "strength" of your mind or the luck of the Irish. There was subconscious disagreement with your conscious goals. The possible reasons for subconscious disagreement with conscious goals are many and varied, and they seldom seem reasonable in the light of common sense. Fortunately, the subconscious can be changed to bring it into line with conscious goals.

An example of a subconscious block to success can be seen in the student who finds herself unable to do well in a particular subject for no apparent reason. Statements such as "I have a mental block about mathematics" or "I just don't do well in chemistry" and so on, are laments frequently heard around high schools and colleges. But my experience in teaching self-hypnosis and autoquestioning to college students has demonstrated that the elimination of such blocks to learning is often very simple. There is usually some attitude, viewpoint, or belief held by the subconscious that prevents the student from concentrating on the blocked subject, and which causes her to quickly forget anything she does manage to learn.

To eliminate such blocks to learning, the subconscious must be questioned until the cause of the problem is discovered. In some cases, conscious knowledge of the cause is enough to eliminate it as a source of trouble. But if it is not, the proper application of suggestions will eliminate the subconscious block. Then the student can achieve passing grades in the previously troublesome subject. Not only that, but students sometimes excell in the recently unblocked subject, apparently making up for lost time.

SOURCES OF DYSFUNCTION

Subconscious ideas, beliefs, or viewpoints that block success in any area (weight control, quitting smoking, financial improvement, social skills, sports, and so on) are called *sources of dysfunction.* A "dysfunction" is a function that is disordered or impaired. Overeating when one wants to lose weight, losing when one wants to win, or an inability to concentrate or study are all dysfunctions if they are caused by a relevant negative quality in the subconscious. It is *conscious* desires or intentions that determine whether or not something is a dysfunction. If you chew your fingernails but would like to quit, then nail-chewing is a dysfunction for you. On the other hand (pun intended), if you enjoy chewing your nails because you find them tasty and nutritious and have no desire to quit, then nail-chewing is not a dysfunction. For our purposes here, you are the one who determines whether something is or is not a dysfunction.

Dysfunctions are the products of fixed ideas in the subconscious. Just why and when certain ideas get imbedded in the subconscious, while others do not, is not really known. We do know that the probability of an idea being fixed in the subconscious is increased when a person is in a more emotional state than usual. But the fixing of such ideas can also occur in relatively unemotional states of mind—sometimes in very subtle ways.

Fixed ideas, beliefs, and viewpoints that become the sources of dysfunction are not the ordinary content of memories stored in the subconscious. It is therefore convenient to borrow a term from the field of ethology and call sources of dysfunction *imprints* to distinguish them from ordinary memory content. Imprints, then, are *fixed ideas, beliefs, and viewpoints that have special importance for the subconscious, and that are marked for special influence.*

Not all imprints are negative, or sources of dysfunction. Everyone also has subconsciously fixed ideas—imprints—that are positive. These positive imprints are the bases of functions, as opposed to *dys*functions. Positive imprints and their functions are of little concern to us here.

Once an idea or belief becomes imprinted in the subconscious, one is motivated to behave in accordance with the imprint, and these imprints are highly resistant to change. It is only through the correct application of communication with the subconscious that such ideas and beliefs can be brought into line with conscious desires.

A case in point is a student I knew who suffered from acrophobia (fear of height). He was unable to travel by air or even stand close to upper-story windows where he might become aware of how high he was in the building. This was a particularly acute source of trouble for him because his office was on the third floor of a two-building complex, and his work necessitated going from one building to the other several times a day. There was a third-floor walkway connecting the two buildings, but he couldn't use it. He would go all the way down to the ground floor and cross the street rather than use the walkway each time he went from one building to the other.

Although he had no conscious memory of the event that precipitated his acrophobia, he was able to uncover it using autoquestioning. He was then able to formulate and apply self-hypnotic suggestions that eventually freed him from his acrophobic condition. Here is his summary of what he learned through autoquestioning:

> When I was four years old my parents and an uncle took me to the county fair. There were carnival rides at the fair and my uncle took me for a ride on the ferris wheel. At some point in the ride the ferris wheel was stopped abruptly when we were at the highest point. The chair in which we were seated rocked slightly, allowing me a glimpse of the ground far below. In the same moment I started to slide forward on the seat. My uncle had a firm grasp on me and there was probably no danger whatever. But the panic and fear I felt in that brief instant, as I was looking down at the ground, formed the imprint that left me terrified of heights for over thirty years.

> I still do not consciously remember the incident, but my parents have verified that we did go to the county fair when I was four, and my mother's brother went with us.

> Since uncovering this imprint I have been applying suggestions to overcome it and have made dramatic progress in just a few months. I now use the breezeway between our buildings every day, and have moved my desk closer to my third-floor office window to enjoy the view. However, I am not yet ready to get on a ferris wheel.

Even though his experience lasted but a brief instant, and there was no real danger, the connection between fear and height was imprinted in his subconscious. From that point on his subconscious would react with fear whenever he was very far above the ground, just as if he were still four years old.

The precipitating events or experiences that result in imprints are often buried beyond conscious recall and cannot be consciously remembered. But it is sometimes surprising how willing one's subconscious mind is to answer questions relative to some buried experience. At times it is almost as if the mind were eager to divest itself of a fixed idea or value that it knows to be dysfunctional, but that it has been unable to spontaneously eliminate. It is more common, however, for the subconscious to tenaciously hang onto its imprints, necessitating elaborate questioning procedures to first uncover them, and then the correct use of suggestions to change them.

An often asked question is, "Why doesn't the subconscious eliminate dysfunctional ideas on its own, since it is aware of everything the conscious mind knows?" The answer to this question lies in the difference between ordinary memories and imprints. All consciously accessible knowledge is stored in memory. Any part of knowledge will be treated as nothing more than memories unless it gets "tagged" or labeled as being of particular importance to one or more of the three major functions of the subconscious: preservation, protection, or procreation. From a subconscious standpoint, all other knowledge is much like a can of gasoline in the trunk of an automobile—it is of no value in making the engine run until it is put into the gas tank.

An understanding of the inability of the subconscious to use certain forms of logic is helpful in explaining many subconscious phenomena that otherwise appear contradictory or paradoxical. The single most important factor in subconscious reasoning is its inability to use inductive logic, evidently functioning mainly with the use of deductive reasoning. This characteristic makes it possible for the subconscious to host two or more fixed ideas—imprints—that are opposites in reality.

The presence of opposing imprints can create uncomfortable and distressing situations. A person with an imprint against success may also have one or more imprints against failure. The result is a constant teeter-tottering back and forth between being motivated to avoid success and being motivated to avoid failure. This kind of conflict can exist in virtually any area of human endeavor, and most people do experience conflicting imprints of one sort or another.

Although the limited logic of the subconscious is responsible for many of our problems, it is this same logical limitation of the subconscious that makes it possible for suggestion to be effective, even when what we are suggesting seems to contradict reality. The subconscious does not know the difference between fantasy and external reality because of its peculiar logic. Therefore we can, through suggestion, reconstruct our realities to more closely conform to our conscious wishes.

One of the greatest difficulties in autoquestioning is that of knowing what questions to ask. The process of appropriate questioning is fundamental to all education, and it is certainly no less so in learning about oneself. Most students of self-communication are surprised by the ease with which problems can be eliminated after the proper questions have been formulated and asked.

Difficulties in questioning can be considerably lessened by structuring the most common kinds—and causes—of problems into categories. By putting labels on sources of dysfunction, we reduce the number of questions required to zero in on a trouble source. Categories and labels also provide starting points for questioning.

So far, a number of references have been made to "fixed ideas," "imprints," "viewpoints," and "beliefs" of the subconscious mind, and so on. These terms all fall under the general heading of *sources of dysfunction,* defined earlier as something firmly planted in the subconscious that makes us respond or behave in a manner not in agreement with conscious desires or goals. It should be clear by now that the removal, or alteration, of these sources of dysfunction is the key to achieving permanent self-improvement or personal development.

The key concept in self-motivated change is communication, a two-way communication between the conscious and subconscious parts of the mind. It is seldom possible to carry on a conversation with the subconscious in the same way you can talk to another person. (Anyone who can do this is probably stranger than most of us care to be.) So we have to use autoquestioning to get information from the subconscious.

Attempts at autoquestioning without a strategy are likely to end in confusion and frustration. To avoid this kind of disappointment, start with the assumption that *there is no such thing as random behavior.* I am using the term "behavior" in its broadest sense: Thinking, acting, moving, bodily functioning such as heartbeat and breathing, are all forms of behavior. Every action, whether it is a private thought or the movement of an arm, has a cause. It follows that every subconscious belief also has a cause.

In autoquestioning, we are attempting to learn the real cause of dysfunctional behavior and the original source of the dysfunction. These causes frequently stem from early childhood experiences, but not always. The causative experience could have been one specific, perhaps traumatic, event. Or the cause of a dysfunction could be a compound of several similar events or experiences which have added up over time. And, whether caused by one event or several, whether occurring early in life or later, the subconscious ideas formed by such significant experiences are highly resistant to decay. We ordinarily think of things growing weaker with age, but this is not usually the case with subconscious ideas and beliefs. They can retain their potency throughout one's lifetime if not either spontaneously or purposely changed.

Subconscious Imprinting

You are already familiar with the terms "imprint" (the fixed idea in the subconscious) and "imprinting" (the process of creating an imprint). But the importance of the concept of imprinting is sufficient to justify some repetition and further clarification here.

Imprinting is a form of learning that usually occurs early in a person's life and remains relatively unmodifiable from then on. It occurs when the subconscious mind accepts an idea as being of particular importance relative to any of the three major subconscious functions of preservation, protection, and procreation.

Although most imprinting takes place during childhood, it can occur at any time of life. All of the necessary conditions that cause imprinting are not known, but it is known that the subconscious is more susceptible to imprinting when emotions are aroused.

Repetition is another factor that contributes to the formation of imprints. If an idea is repeated often enough, the subconscious will eventually imprint that idea. It is not known whether it is the buildup caused by repetition of the idea that eventually spills over and causes the imprint, or if repeating the idea sooner or later catches the subconscious in the right condition for imprinting.

Any kind of information received by the subconscious can be the source of an imprint. Imprints are often the products of remarks spoken by others and overheard by chance. Parental conversations that take place when the parents think their child is asleep have created countless imprints in children. But remarks need not be made by parents to have the same effect. Imprints can be caused by the comments of teachers, relatives, neighbors, passing strangers, or something heard on radio or television.

Visual information can also form imprints. Seeing an automobile accident, and the injuries or deaths resulting from that accident, might cause the imprinting of the idea that automobiles are dangerous (!) and frightening. Such an imprint would make a person feel uncomfortable in an automobile.

Information received through the sense of touch is equally potent in forming imprints, although in actual practice most people have fewer imprints caused by tactile experiences than by those of the other senses. An example of an imprint caused by something felt is the case of a young boy who was wading in a pond when he felt something slither past his leg. This frightened him and created a fear of water that prevented him from learning to swim until he eliminated the imprint many years later.

Because of the literal-mindedness of the subconscious mind, imprints often create physically uncomfortable symptoms. These often result from clichés or figures of speech that have been imprinted. If a statement such as, "Joe is a pain in the neck" becomes imprinted, the presence of Joe might actually precipitate a pain or ache in the region of the neck (a headache would be the same thing). Many people have reported chest pains that were the product of imprinting caused by some expression that included the term "heartache." Such imprints are the products of *organ language*.

We will divide sources of dysfunction into two broad categories: *information* imprints and *identification* imprints. A subcategory is *guilt* imprints which are a special form of either information or identification imprints. Guilt imprints are dealt with separately because they are so widespread, and because they have their own unique characteristics.

Information Imprints

An information imprint is the product of any information becoming fixed in the subconscious. As in the case of any imprint, it is something that the subconscious mind holds to be important to the individual's preservation, protection, or procreation. The input of the original information can have been through any of the perceptual senses. It was either seen, heard, smelled, touched, or tasted, or any combination of these senses.

The input that results in information imprints can be further divided into *verbal* and *nonverbal* sources. A verbal source is information conveyed by language, either written or spoken. Nonverbal sources are information that is not in language form. Symbols, signs, images, pictures, fantasies, as well as smells, textures, and unspoken sounds are examples of possible nonverbal sources of information imprints.

Imprint-producing events, whether verbal or nonverbal, can range from extremely subtle events that would not bother most people, to obviously traumatic events. Seemingly innocuous remarks made by parents can be subtle sources of imprints. For example, little Johnnie might ask his mother why they don't have a big car (or some other, similar question).

His mother might answer with something like, "I'd rather be healthy than wealthy." Literally translated (and the subconscious takes things literally), her answer suggests that one must be unhealthy to be wealthy. On another occasion, Johnnie may ask his father why his playmate across town has a horse of his own and he does not, and receive an answer like, "Having everything you want won't bring happiness." Again, the literal translation of Dad's remark might be, "Having 'things' will make you unhappy." Naturally, Johnnie wants to be happy and healthy, so he will be subconsciously motivated to be unwealthy and not have "things" for the rest of his life. That is, unless he discovers and deals with his negative imprints.

It is not the nature of the information itself that causes imprinting, but the individual's *response* to that information. The response may be strictly subconscious and therefore unnoticed by the person at the time. It is only after studying and working with imprints that one begins to develop a conscious awareness of them and when they are occurring. This increased awareness and ability to detect the imprinting process is especially beneficial because it allows conscious intervention when undesirable imprinting is occurring.

Many practictioners of autoquestioning have reported the uncovering of information imprints that occurred before birth. Human perceptual senses begin their development before birth and there is evidence to suggest that bumps, loud noises, maternal emotions (which produce chemical changes in the prenatal environment), and various other factors can be sources of imprinting. I mention this here in case, in your own autoquestioning, you uncover evidence of prenatal imprints. Don't think you have gone off the deep end if you make such a discovery; others have, too. This is a vast area with a great deal of promise, but much more research is needed before we can really say much about it.

Identification Imprints

Identification is the internalization of the beliefs, ideas, or values of an individual, group, or role. Internalization is a term borrowed from earlier psychoanalytic writings (as is the term *identification*). It refers to learning, or the state of having learned, in which the learner is not aware that he or she was learning anything.

The initial processes of identification take place during early childhood and extend over several of the individual's most formative years. What is the subconscious motivation to identify with groups, individuals, and roles? It has already been pointed out that the subconscious mind is primarily concerned with the preservation, protection, and procreation of the individual. Although we do not talk about "instincts" when discussing human beings, we do have inherent *predispositions* toward certain things. Two predispositions that play important roles in identification are *goal seeking* and *group membership*.

An individual is subconsciously (and often consciously) motivated to seek goals that will support the major subconscious functions. Preservation, for example, might be promoted by being strong, able to exert power over others rather than being controlled by others (and therefore at their mercy). Thus, the achievement of certain types of power becomes a goal for many people, and may lead to identification with powerful people.

Group membership is an equally powerful motivator. Whether built in at birth (genetically endowed) or developed early, we all subconsciously recognize that group membership is essential to preservation, protection, and procreation. The groups in which we strive for membership vary with each person and can range from such exalted groups as the brother/sisterhood of humankind to the family or a small group of friends. Nations, states, communities, churches, schools and universities, athletes, Masons, Girl Scouts, and political parties are just a few examples of groups with which we may want to identify.

Because most identification takes place during childhood, the initial objects of identification are usually members of one's immediate family. Parents are the most obvious choices, but we can also identify with brothers and sisters, grandparents, aunts and uncles, teachers, neighbors, TV personalities, movie stars, or anyone else we have an opportunity to observe.

In this process of identification the subconscious adopts aspects of the target personality as its own, and all subsequent behavior is modified to fit that pattern. The assimilation of the other personality and value system is never total, even though in some cases it may look as if it is.

The development of identification is always a subconscious process of which the conscious mind is unaware, and its force in shaping subsequent behavior remains unknown to the conscious. It is often possible, however, to infer an identification by comparing behavior. If the behavior or values of one person are similar to those of another, then it is possible that one of them identifies with the other (especially if one is younger than the other and had contact with him or her during childhood). We frequently see this in cases where a person's behavior or values remind us of his or her parents.

Because behavior or values are internalized, the identifier is unaware of the conditions that motivate him. When someone is asked why he does something a particular way, or why he believes a certain way, and he responds with an answer such as, "Because that's just the way I am" or "Don't ask silly questions; everyone knows that," it is probably safe to assume that the behavior or belief in question is the product of subconscious identification.

Not all identifications are bad, of course. It is only when identification interferes with conscious goals that it is a source of dysfunction. Eliminating a source of dysfunction, when identification is involved, does not mean eliminating the entire identification. Identification is so universal and important to our development that it would be impossible to eliminate all identifications, or even all of a single identification. When identification is associated with a dysfunction, we want to eliminate or change only that part of the identification that is troublesome.

The dynamics of group and role identification are the same as for individual identification, except that it is a group or role that provides the behaviors or values that are internalized. When one identifies with a group, she internalizes some of the values and behavior norms of that group and considers herself a member of it.

Americans, bankers, mechanics, psychiatrists—all have certain characteristics common to each group. A person who identifies with any such group will exhibit some of that group's characteristics. Most adults choose their vocations on the basis of pre-existing identifications. It is much easier to fit into and feel comfortable with any group with which we identify.

Everyone identifies with one or more roles. It is probably safe to say that everyone identifies with a multitude of roles, and that different roles are expressed by different behavior under different circumstances. For example, a man will behave one way at home and another way at work. A woman may be a completely different person at a party than she is at home with her family. Like the other kinds of identification, most roles are assimilated without conscious effort or awareness.

When one is familiar with the concept of role, group, and individual identification, the process of questioning the subconscious for sources of dysfunction is considerably shortened. It is seldom necessary or even possible to uncover an entire identification pattern. Because identifications cover such a broad range of behavior, it is necessary to narrow down the specific aspects of an identification to just those that apply to the immediate problem.

One cannot rely on the advantages of insight when questioning the subconscious about identifications. There seldom occurs a flash of insight that allows one to "feel" or "know" the identification. Because it is difficult to consciously experience identification, the process of questioning about, and dealing with, identification is very much like dealing with another person.

Some people have opposing identification factors that can alternately push them in opposite directions. When identification factors—imprints that are part of the total identification matrix—are in opposition, they are almost always of such a nature that they do not motivate behavior at the same time. This is fortunate because the simultaneous activation of opposing identification factors creates intolerable stress for a person.

Guilt Imprints

Everyone suffers from guilt feelings to some extent. Guilt is usually defined as the emotional feeling associated with the realization that one has violated an important social, moral, or ethical value. One usually thinks of guilt as having its origin in some act committed by the person who feels the guilt, but guilt feelings can also be produced by thoughts and imagined transgressions.

Everyone has experienced the conscious feelings of guilt—the cross word we later regret, or the anguish for an act we should not have committed. But it is the guilts we don't consciously know about that do the most harm. Subconscious guilt can change behavior and performance in such subtle ways that one can be directed away from successfully achieving a goal without consciously knowing what has happened. The subconscious sometimes does this to punish the individual for guilt feelings.

Making sure that a person is punished for guilt feelings (real or imagined) is one of the ancillary (but nontheless impactful) functions of the subconscious mind. The expiation of guilt that relieves the pressure of guilt feelings, and reduces the need for punishment, is not directly possible in the case of subconscious guilt. Because they are not consciously known, subconscious guilts have no direct outlet, so they must find release in symbolic expiation. Self-punishment in its myriad forms is the mode of atonement of the subconscious.

Sometimes the atonement "takes," sometimes it does not. There are certain kinds of transgressions for which one episode of self-punishment will be subconsciously sufficient. An example of this is the "don't brag" imprint that many people have. A person with this imprint dare not make statements such as, "I never catch colds" or "I haven't had a traffic ticket in years." Such boasting will result in the catching of a cold or the receipt of a traffic ticket. (Some people can get around this by "knocking on wood," a symbolic act of contrition which may eliminate any sub-consciously-felt need for further retribution.) If boastful statements are made and a cold is caught or a ticket received, that will usually be the end of the matter; the sinner has paid the price and nothing more will happen until he or she boasts about something again.

But there are other kinds of guilt for which no amount of punishment will be adequate retribution. Such guilts most often stem from conditions over which the person has little or no control. Many people have strong subconscious guilts about being a woman, being black (or for being a member of any ethnic group, including white), being successful or un-successful, for being alive (this often happens to survivors of accidents or catastrophes), or even for being strong or weak. For these kinds of subconscious guilt feelings—remember, the person is unlikely to have any conscious awareness of the guilt—no amount of punishment is suffi-cient. So self-activated punishment just goes on and on.

Self-punishment can take many forms. One may be unable to break the smoking habit because smoking is a release for subconscious guilt feelings. Overeating is another common form of self-punishment. The discomforts and embarrassments of being fat—not to mention the dangers to health—provide a meaningful and relatively constant state of punishment from the subconscious viewpoint. Guilt may also motivate the subconscious to frustrate all attempts to achieve financial success. In fact, virtually any failure may be caused by the subconsciously-felt need for punishment.

Many, perhaps most, subconscious guilt feelings originate in child-hood. A child's understanding of the laws of cause and effect is poor and often distorted. A child can believe that he was the cause of something that, in fact, he had nothing to do with. The egocentrism of childhood may cause a child to blame himself for nearly everything that happens in his world. The death or illness of a member of the family, the divorce of parents, or any misfortune that affects the child may be interpreted by him as being his fault.

Any form of rejection by the parents may create guilt feelings in a child because she believes it is her own inadequacies that have caused the parents' rejection. Experiences such as rejection can develop feelings of inadequacy that are further complicated by guilt. All of this can occur at the subconscious level, or part of it can be consciously experienced.

Maturation of the individual does not change guilt feelings later in life. What was significant and formative for the child may later seem silly and insignificant to the adult, but guilt feelings in the subconscious will retain their impact, regardless of the conscious maturation of the adult.

Religious teachings often contribute to the development of subconscious guilt feelings. If a child is taught that it is sinful to want what is not his, he may feel guilty for wanting things he does not have. Many Western religions teach that an illicit thought is as sinful as committing the act, so a child who even fleetingly entertains thoughts of swiping his playmates' toys may feel as guilty as if he had actually committed the theft.

This is not meant to imply that children should not be brought up in the teachings of the church, temple, or synagogue. There is no perfect environment in which children will develop absolutely no guilt. The point here is that childhood religious teachings and experiences are worthy areas of inquiry with autoquestioning.

The society in which we are raised and live can contribute to the formation of guilt feelings. The child who comes from the "wrong side of town" is a particularly good candidate for serious guilt problems related to inadequacy. The child subconsciously reasons that it is her fault that she does not have equal social status, so she feels guilty for being inadequate. Sentiments of resentment and hostility toward those who enjoy better circumstances in life may develop guilt feelings. And the child from a better part of town might have equally strong guilt feelings for opposite reasons. He may have a sense of superiority that develops guilt feelings because it is not entirely acceptable to feel superior in a democracy.

If a person is treated as if she should be guilty, she probably will develop guilt feelings. This often happens with the children of convicted criminals. Other children treat the convict's child as if it were she who had been sent to prison. Because of this treatment, the child begins to assume the guilt for her father's transgressions against society. A child who does not have a father is often treated as if it were his fault that he is fatherless. Even if the child does not develop guilt feelings as a direct result of such treatment, he will be likely to develop strong resentment toward the absent father. He may eventually hate his father for abandoning him. Parents who are called off to war, who leave the family because of divorce, or who die, are often resented by their children for having abandoned them. These emotions of hatred or resentment can lead to strong guilt feelings at the subconscious level.

Other people's guilt feelings can also be inherited through identification. If a child identifies with a person who has strong guilt feelings, those feelings may very likely be incorporated in the identification. They remain a powerful force in shaping behavior, even though the identifier was innocent of the experience that originally caused the guilt. This is true whether the object of identification is an individual, a role, or a group. One can feel guilty about the plight of minority groups without ever having contributed directly to their misfortunes. Members of minority groups can, in the same way, inherit guilt feelings about being a member of their minority group.

The methods of uncovering and dealing with guilt feelings are much the same as those used for other sources of dysfunction. If it is understood that any situation or condition is capable of inducing guilt feelings, and that guilt feelings may be known only to the subconscious and therefore not consciously related to a problem, then it becomes possible to question the subconscious with an open mind.

Autoquestioning can be a tricky business because the subconscious is sometimes devious and evasive. The cleverest questions may result in frustration, especially when trying to get to the source of guilt feelings, but perseverance is usually rewarded. If you reach a dead end in questioning, and no other questions come to mind, walk away from it and give yourself a rest. Come back to the subject an hour or a day later, and fresh questions will usually come to mind. But if all efforts fail to produce information beyond the establishment of guilt as the source of trouble, go directly to the application of suggestion. In such a case, the suggestion can only be generally directed at removal of the guilt.

What follows is the essence of a questioning sequence that uncovered a guilt-caused block to success. This questioning was conducted with the Chevreul pendulum, which you will learn about shortly, Each "Q" is a conscious question, and "A" is the pendulum response, or subconscious answer to the question. Most of the unproductive questions have been edited out of this example to give it clarity and continuity.

Q: Is there something in my subconscious that sometimes keeps me from being successful?
A: Yes.
Q: Does guilt have anything to do with my subconscious resistance to success?
A: Yes.
Q: Is the need for these guilt feelings caused by one or more imprints?
A: Yes.
Q: Do these imprints have anything to do with religion?
A: No.
Q: Do they have anything to do with my parents?
A: Yes.
Q: Both parents?
A: No.
Q: Just my father?

A: No.

Q: Just with my mother?

A: Yes.

Q: Were these imprints caused by something my mother said to me?

A: Yes.

Q: Was it something that she said to me in many different ways over many different times?

A: Yes.

Q: Did these things she said have to do with material wealth?

A: No.

Q: Did these things she said refer to success in general?

A: Yes.

Q: I remember she used to tell me not to brag. Is that what caused the imprints?

A: Yes.

Q: Do I think I am bragging when I think about being successful?

A: No.

Q: Would being successful be a form of bragging?

A: Yes.

Q: Does this cause "anticipatory" guilt feelings that make me do things to block success?

A: Yes.

AUTOQUESTIONING TECHNIQUES

The basis for the autoquestioning techniques we will be using is *ideomotor action*. Briefly stated, ideomotor action occurs when *thoughts or ideas are automatically translated into specific patterns of muscular activity*. For the most part this muscular movement, executed under the influence of a dominant idea, is automatic and not volitional. In other words, an idea can cause muscular movement without our conscious intention or control of that movement.

The validity of ideomotion has been both experimentally and clinically proven. A practical example of the use of ideomotion is the polygraph, or lie detector. The polygraph works by measuring four different aspects of bodily functioning that change when a person lies. These bodily changes are outside the conscious control of the person being tested, and polygraph operators say that indications of lying can show up even when the subject does not consciously know that he or she is lying. In a sense, we also think with our bodies, and bodily movements can be used as a connecting link between the conscious and subconscious parts of the mind.

The polygraph works the way it does because conscious intervention cannot override subconscious control of bodily functions. We can utilize this dynamic to get answers from the subconscious. Fortunately, we do not have to have anything so complicated and elaborate as a polygraph. There is a much simpler and less expensive method of measuring ideo-motion when we are questioning only ourselves, and it is one that works for everyone: The Chevreul pendulum.

The Chevreul Pendulum

The Chevreul pendulum is named after Anton Chevreul, the man who first discovered its uses in the eighteenth century. To construct a pendulum, tie a bob to the end of a length of thread or string. Any light object, such as a button, ring, or washer, will serve as a bob. The thread or string to which it is tied should be about twelve inches in length, and the total length of thread should be lighter than the object to which it is tied.

When the pendulum is made, seat yourself comfortably at a desk or table with your elbow resting on the surface. If you are right-handed, use your right hand to hold the pendulum. If left-handed, use your left hand. Hold the loose end of the pendulum between the thumb and fore-finger, and adjust the length of thread hanging from your hand so that the bob (button, ring, washer, etc.) is suspended about an inch from the surface of the table (see Figure 3–1). Place a piece of paper beneath the pendulum, have a pencil or pen handy, and you are ready to begin practicing.

On the paper, draw a straight line extending away from you, as if you were drawing an arrow pointing at someone seated directly across from you. This is the vertical axis. Hold the pendulum over the center of the line and imagine it beginning to swing up and down along the vertical axis. Don't make any conscious effort to move the pendulum; that is, don't purposely move your arm just to make the pendulum swing. Just hold it over the line and *imagine* it swinging back and forth along the axis. Once the pendulum begins to swing, don't make any conscious effort to interfere with its movement.

It is necessary to start in this simple fashion and develop this one direction of swing before going to the next step. For some people, the pendulum will begin to swing immediately. For others it may take a little longer. You will probably be able to get an identifiable swing along the axis within a minute or two. If you do not, it sometimes helps to put the pendulum down and walk away from it for a few minutes. Then return to the pendulum and try again.

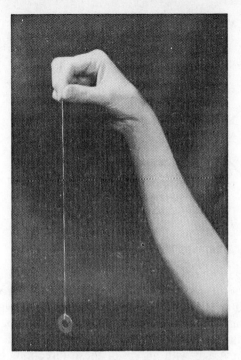
FIGURE 3-1 Using the Chevreul pendulum.

If this tactic fails to get the pendulum moving, have someone else give you suggestions that the pendulum will swing along the axis. As you sit and look at the pendulum hanging over the line, the other person should keep repeating statements to the effect that the pendulum will begin to swing along the axis. If the pendulum still refuses to move (or, more correctly, if your subconscious still refuses to make your arm swing the pendulum), put it aside for a few hours and try again later. I have seen very few cases where it took repeated efforts over a period of two or three days to get the pendulum into action. Such cases are rare, but if you do have this kind of difficulty, don't give up—I have encountered only one person in several years who could not get the pendulum to move.

Don't be concerned about how far the pendulum swings. If it swings just enough for the direction to be definitely recognizable, that is all you need. When you have achieved a definite swing along the vertical axis, draw on your paper another line perpendicular to and intersecting the midpoint of the vertical axis. This is the horizontal axis. You should

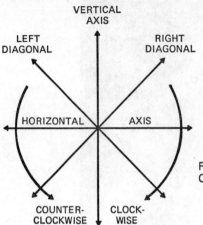

VERTICAL
AXIS

LEFT
DIAGONAL

RIGHT
DIAGONAL

HORIZONTAL   AXIS

FIGURE 3-2 Signal directions of the
Chevreul pendulum.

COUNTER-   CLOCK-
CLOCKWISE   WISE

now have a large cross or "+" drawn on your paper. Follow the same procedure to get the pendulum to swing along the horizontal axis.

When you can get both horizontal and vertical swing by thinking about them, you have four more directions to develop. These are the left and right diagonals, clockwise circle, and counter-clockwise circle. The complete diagram with all six of these directions is illustrated in Figure 3–2. When you can get the pendulum to swing in all six directions (one at a time, of course), you are ready to start asking questions of your subconscious.

Before you begin asking questions, directions for specific answers must be established. The five most commonly and successfully used answers are *yes, no, maybe, don't want to answer,* and *rephrase the question.*

The procedure for establishing directions of pendulum swing for specific answers is as follows: Gaze at the pendulum as it is suspended above your diagram (from Figure 3–2) and think "yes." Think to yourself that you want a direction of swing that will indicate the answer "yes" to any questions you ask if "yes" is the correct answer. Just gaze at the pendulum thinking "yes" until it begins to move. If the pendulum swings along the vertical axis in response to this procedure, this is your direction for "yes."

Now follow the same procedure for establishing the "no" direction. If the pendulum moves along the horizontal axis, for example, then that direction will indicate a "no" answer when given in response to a question. Incidentally, vertical swing for "yes" and horizontal swing for "no" are common directions of response, probably because these are the directions we shake our heads to indicate approval (yes) or disapproval (no).

Once you have the "yes" and "no" responses, do the same thing to obtain the "maybe," "don't want to answer," and "rephrase the question" directions of swing ("don't want to answer" is usually abbreviated DWA). The "yes" and "no" signals will have taken up two of the six possible directions of swing, so there are four remaining directions from which the subconscious can choose. When signals for all five answers are established, it is a good idea to mark all five signals on your paper so you don't get confused when you begin to ask questions. Leave the sixth direction unassigned. If the pendulum swings in that direction in response to a question, that means none of the five answers is appropriate.

Always re-establish your answer directions before each questioning session. You may find that you always get the same signals for your answers, or some or all of them can be different from time to time.

The reason for having more answers than just "yes" or "no" is the obvious fact that not all questions can be answered with a "yes" or "no." There are many times when a question is ambiguously stated, and there are also questions to which the subconscious does not know the answer. The only questions that can be validly answered by the subconscious are those for which the subconscious can know the answer. This excludes questions about the future. If you try to use this method for, say, gambling, you will probably find the tuition very high for the lesson you will learn. I have never known anyone who could get reliable information about the future with the pendulum questioning technique.

Questions about other people are in the same category. Don't use the pendulum to ask if your girlfriend really loves you, or if your husband is playing around on you. The answers obtained by the pendulum come from your own subconscious mind only, so the only questions you should ask are those that pertain to yourself and your own past.

When you get "maybe" or "DWA" for an answer, there are several possible reasons. The question may have been phrased in such a way that "yes" or "no" would be incorrect. Paraphrasing, especially if it simplifies the original question, will often change the response to a more definite answer. If no amount of paraphrasing will change an indefinite response like "DWA," there may be subconscious resistance to answering the question in any form. Sometimes there is a subconscious belief that the answer would be too painful, and that the self is not consciously prepared to cope with the answer.

Fortunately, most experiences are not buried so deeply that we cannot get answers about them. The procedures presented later will show how to approach a problem from different directions, eventually uncovering an area that was initially resisted by the subconscious. If the proper application of all techniques fails to break down the resistance to answering certain questions, the need for professional guidance may be indicated. If you do encounter an area of deep resistance, and you suspect that it is causing problems you cannot cope with on your own, seek professional help.

It is always a good idea to keep a record of your questions and answers because it is difficult to remember them later. And your questions will be much more succinct and better thought-out if you write them first. Normally, it is not possible to write down in advance all of the questions you will be asking, so be prepared to keep a record of your questions and answers as you engage in autoquestioning.

At the end of each session, write a brief summary of what you learned. This makes a more concise reference, and writing it initiates certain subconscious dynamics that make subsequent questioning sessions more fruitful.

There is a tendency to suspect the validity of answers when first beginning to work with autoquestioning. Thoughts such as, "Are the answers really coming from my subconscious?" or "Am I affecting the pendulum with wishful thinking?" are not uncommon. Of course, common sense is in order in accepting answers, and the pendulum itself can be used to check on the validity of the answers you are getting. Use the pendulum to answer questions like "Are the answers I am getting coming from my subconscious?" You should get a "yes" to this unless you know that you consciously manipulated the pendulum. Awareness is, after all, part of the definition of consciousness. If you consciously know you did it, you consciously did it.

Here are a couple more checking-up questions: "Did I get that answer because of wishful thinking?" and "Did I get that answer because my subconscious thinks it is the answer I wanted?" After checking on yourself a few times, your subconscious will become convinced that only correct answers are appropriate and acceptable, and you will develop more confidence in your autoquestioning responses.

There is an initial learning period when answers are not entirely to be trusted. But with sincere conscious motives the subconscious soon gets the idea and will not lie. With a little training, usually two or three hours of using the pendulum, you can get correct answers to questions even while you are consciously thinking the wrong answer. Test this by asking yourself if your name is Harry (provided that it is not; any name that is not your own will do) and thinking "yes." You will get a correct answer ("no") even though you were thinking "yes." If you do happen to get a "yes," have a little talk with yourself to the effect that you want only correct answers. Then try it again. Repeat this procedure until you get it right.

The first time you sit down to engage in autoquestioning with the Chevreul pendulum, use the following questions to give yourself a proper start:

"Is there a part of my mind of which I am not normally, consciously aware?" (Your answer should be "yes" to this question. If it is not, have another little talk with yourself to reinforce the notion that this is a serious activity. It is not a game, and you want only correct answers to your questions. Repeat this procedure until you get a "yes" answer.)

"Can I refer to that part of my mind as my subconscious?" (You should also get a "yes" to this question. If you do not, follow the procedure outlined above.)

"When I use this or any other questioning technique, will I get honest, truthful answers from my subconscious?" (Same response and procedure as above.)

These questions lay the groundwork for future questioning. You need not repeat them again once you have received satisfactory answers. These questions formally establish the autoquestioning concept within your own mind, and the answers you receive form a commitment by the subconscious part of your mind. Later in this chapter you will learn how to continue with your questioning—how to obtain information related to whatever problem you are working on—when we cover strategies for questioning.

Children should not be taught the use of the pendulum, nor should they see anyone else using it. Suggestibility is at its strongest in childhood, and a wrong answer from the pendulum could create needless problems.

Ideomotor Spelling

Questioning strategies which simplify the problem of knowing what questions to ask will be presented shortly. But even the best of questioning strategies will not keep you from sometimes coming up against a brick wall in your questioning. When you do—when you reach one of those points when you cannot think of another question to ask—it is very helpful to get a spelled-out clue from your subconscious. The procedure for doing this is basically simple, although it usually requires a fair amount of time.

Start by determining the existence of a subconscious clue with the following questioning strategy:

"Is there a word or phrase of which I am subconsciously thinking that will help me?" (The answer should be "yes.")

"Is it one word?" (Assume for the sake of this example that the answer to this question was "no," meaning the clue is a phrase of more than one word.)

"Are there five or fewer words in this phrase?" (Assume an answer of "yes." If the answer had been "no," the next question would have continued the bracketing, five words at a time: "Are there between six and ten words in the phrase?", and so on.)

"Are there four words in the phrase?" (Move down one word at a time to determine exactly how many words are in the phrase. Assume an answer here of "no.")

"Are there three words in the phrase?" (Assume the phrase you were subconsciously thinking about had three words, so you would get a "yes" to this question.)

You now know that you are subconsciously thinking about a clue composed of three words. The next step is to determine the number of letters in each word:

"Does the first word of this three-word phrase have five or fewer letters?" (Assume a "yes" answer.)

"Does it have five letters?" (Assume a "no" answer.)

"Does it have four letters?" (Assume a "yes" answer.)

So you now know that the first word of the three-word phrase has four letters. Continue with this procedure to determine the number of letters in each of the remaining words. To keep track of this, put the correct number of blank spaces on a piece of paper and number them accordingly. To continue with the present example, suppose you learned there were two letters in the second word and nine letters in the third word. Your paper would then have a blank space for each letter of the three-word phrase as indicated in Figure 3–3.

$\overline{1}\ \overline{2}\ \overline{3}\ \overline{4}$ $\overline{1}\ \overline{2}$ $\overline{1}\ \overline{2}\ \overline{3}\ \overline{4}\ \overline{5}\ \overline{6}\ \overline{7}\ \overline{8}\ \overline{9}$

1   2   3

FIGURE 3-3 Three words to be spelled with autoquestioning using ideomotor spelling charts.

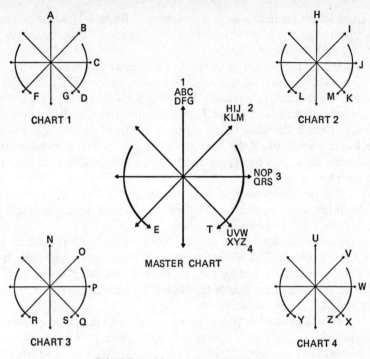

FIGURE 3-4 Ideomotor spelling charts.

You are now ready to find out what the phrase is by getting one letter at a time with autoquestioning. Referring to the ideomotor spelling charts in Figure 3-4, you will notice that there is a Master Chart and four smaller charts numbered 1 through 4.

The Master Chart has all twenty-six letters of the alphabet on it. The vertical axis represents the letters *A, B, C, D, F,* and *G.* The "1" on the vertical axis refers to Chart 1 which has each of these six letters represented by a separate direction the pendulum can swing. The right diagonal, horizontal, and left diagonal directions on the Master Chart also represent groups of six different letters of the alphabet. The letters *E* and *T* are not on any of the smaller charts because they each have their own circular direction on the Master Chart.

To start the questioning, hold your pendulum over the center of the Master Chart and ask yourself which of the directions contains the first letter of the first word. You may do this questioning silently, simply thinking the questions. If the pendulum swings along the vertical axis, you know that the first letter of the first word is an *A, B, C, D, F,* or

G. These letters are individually represented on Chart 1. Hold the pendulum over Chart 1 and repeat the question; the direction the pendulum swings will tell you the specific letter.

If the first direction of swing on the Master Chart had been a right diagonal, your second question would have been over Chart 2. With this method you can determine each letter with a maximum of two questions. If the letter happens to be an *E* or a *T,* only one question is required because these letters are by themselves on the clockwise and counter-clockwise directions of the Master Chart. These two particular letters have been chosen to be represented on the Master Chart because they are the most frequently occurring letters of the English alphabet.

Fill in the blanks on your paper as you proceed with this questioning. In the three-word example used here, you would need a maximum of thirty questions to spell out the phrase.

You should not resort to the ideomotor spelling procedure until you have exhausted all efforts to think of questions using the simple-answer procedure. It seems that subconsciously we place little if any value on anything that is free or too easy. If we have to work for something, that makes it more valuable.

You will create problems for yourself if you jump too quickly into the spelling method. If, as soon as you have read this, you whip out your pendulum and ask, "Okay, what's wrong with me and what'll fix me?" you will probably end up with a bunch of gobbledygook.

Codes and jumbles are not uncommon products of ideomotor spelling. If you use the spelling charts and get nonsense words, return to the simple answer process and ask yourself if the letters you have obtained are in code. Also ask if the letters are jumbled. If they are, you will have to go back through again to get the correct letters. It is even possible that you will have to do this more than once.

An example of the intricate processes of the subconscious mind, and the methods of penetrating its defenses, is the following case of a man who wanted to be a writer. He was in his late twenties at the time and had for many years felt a strong, conscious desire to write. But, except for school assignments, he had never actually sat down and written anything.

In his autoquestioning the letters STR WF SZF appeared several times, but he could not figure out what these mysterious letters meant. He had a very strong gut feeling that they were somehow important, but he did not know how or why. Then one day it dawned on him that these letters might be a coded message. (An observer probably would have thought of this much sooner; this is an example of how the subconscious mind can block conscious awareness of something that would be obvious to others.)

Using the simple-answer method (not ideomotor spelling), he began to question himself about the meaning of these letters. The following is an abbreviated transcript of his questions and answers:

Q: Do the letters STR WF SZF have any meaning?
A: Yes.
Q: Does that meaning pertain to my inability to write?
A: Yes.
Q: Do they have something to do with identification?
A: No.
Q: Do they signify an imprint.
A: Yes.
Q: Do they spell English words?
A: Yes.
Q: Are the letters in a cryptogram?
A: Yes.

A great deal of questioning was then required to decipher the cryptogram (the letters were also jumbled). Starting with the first letter *S*, he used a bracketing procedure to learn the real letter of the alphabet that *S* represented (this was a time-consuming method—the spelling charts had not yet been devised). Each of the eight letters had to be determined in the same manner. Questions that determined the first letter are given to show the procedure:

Q: Does S represent an A, B, C, D, or E?
A: No.
Q: Does it represent an F, G, H, I, or J?
A: Yes.
Q: Is it an F?
A: Yes.

In this laborious manner, and after going through the letters several times, he came up with FAG DODGE. And wham! As soon as he realized what the letters spelled, he had an almost overwhelming flash of insight, remembering an experience he had had in his youth.

When he was about fifteen years old, he had an older friend who was a freshman in college, and who wanted to be a writer. Whenever this friend was home from college they would spend time together, talking about philosophy, psychology, and literature. One day, after he had been visiting with his college friend, the fifteen-year-old's father asked him, "Why do you spend time with that fag?"

And that was it! That one question from his father was enough to create the imprint that scholarly activities, scientific endeavors, and certainly anything to do with writing, were done only by "fags." This was in a rural American community where a fag was a sissy and probably homosexual, the opposite of being the Real Man every male was supposed to be.

Further autoquestioning revealed that this one imprint was responsible for many of his failures in life, including flunking out of college his first year. (He was consciously striving for the kind of educated, literate status that the imprint prohibited, unaware that his subconscious mind was not about to let him be anything like that.)

This man applied suggestions to eliminate the troublesome imprint. He was able to finish college, eventually earned a doctorate, and now enjoys at least a modicum of success as a writer. This book is one example of his work.

THE FINGER RESPONSE METHOD

The finger response method of ideomotor questioning substitutes fingers for the pendulum. The major drawback of this method is that not everyone is willing to spend the time to make it work. Virtually anyone can quickly use the Chevreul pendulum, but it takes some people longer to learn to get answers with finger signals. The advantages of this method are that it eliminates the need for a pendulum or any other paraphernalia, and it can be used much less conspicuously than can the pendulum. It is very difficult to avoid attracting attention if the pendulum is used around other people, so one normally uses it only when alone and isolated. But the finger response method can be used in the middle of a crowd without anyone else knowing what you are doing.

The method for developing finger signals is essentially the same as that used with the pendulum, but finger movements are substituted for pendulum actions. To develop finger signals, get comfortable and place your hands in any relaxed position in which you can see your fingers (the hands must not be clasped together or gripping anything). As in the pendulum method, begin by establishing movements that will indicate the various answers ("yes," "no," "maybe," and so forth). Look right at your hands and think "yes," if that is the answer you are establishing first. Watch for even the slightest movement in any one of the fingers or thumbs. When a discernible movement is made without conscious aid, that signal will be the sign for "yes." Proceed to establish the rest of the answers with the remaining fingers.

More patience is required to develop the finger response method. As with the pendulum, or any other form of learning, the responses become quicker and stronger with practice, but the initial development may require you to wait several minutes or longer.

The magnitude of response in finger signals can vary from a very slight quiver of the finger to an inch or more of movement. Since the movement is ideomotor action and subconsciously motivated, it is ordinarily not felt. You must be able to *see* the finger movement, and do not doubt its validity if you don't feel it. As with the Chevreul pendulum, the magnitude of finger movement is not important as long as the signal is definite and observable.

The Ouija Board

The Ouija board ("Ouija" is a trademark of Parker Brothers Games, not a generic name) is a smooth board about twenty-by-thirty inches in size with the letters of the alphabet and numbers printed on its surface. A planchette, on which you place your hand, is used with the board, and you wait for it to move to the letters that will spell out a message.

Some people erroneously associate the Ouija board with the occult, thinking that the spelled-out messages come from spirits or ghosts or other nefarious entities. To my knowledge, this is not the case. The movement of the Ouija board planchette is motivated by ideomotor behavior, just as it is with the Chevreul pendulum or the finger response method. There is nothing occult about the Ouija board; any messages that are spelled out on it are messages from the operator's own subconscious mind.

Because it requires a higher order of neural integration to move one's entire arm and hand, the Ouija board may take longer to learn to use than the pendulum. Very slight movements can effectively control the direction in which a pendulum swings, but the Ouija board requires much larger and more complex movements. Some people find themselves moving the planchette as soon as they put their hand on it. Others have to practice for hours before they finally achieve truly ideomotor movements. It is likely that anyone can learn to use the Ouija board if he or she is willing to invest the time.

The basics of autoquestioning are the same with the Ouija board as with the pendulum or finger response method. The major difference is the degree to which one can consciously direct the questioning. Those who use the Ouija board find that they may or may not get answers to their consciously placed questions. Sometimes the subconscious veers off onto other subjects which it considers to be more important. Be prepared for this if you use the Ouija board.

Ideomotor Writing (Automatic Writing)

Automatic writing is writing without conscious control. It is a form of ideomotor action that is still more complicated than any of the other three methods of autoquestioning. Once a person is successfully able to "automate," the subconscious gives up its material much more readily than it does with the other methods, and it is generally easier to accept material written by one's own hand. Answers achieved through the other methods do not have the impact that subconsciously written material has. Some people can quickly and easily write automatically. However, for some people it takes hours to develop and may not be worth the time and effort.

Automatic writing provides two benefits when a person is working with herself for self-improvement. One is the possibility of discovering subconsciously fixed ideas by direct communication. The pendulum and finger response method of autoquestioning are limited to a specific set of answers, but automatic writing can draw from the full range of language as it is known to the person.

The second benefit results from clues for further questioning that are taken from the automatically written material. Automatic writing does not always give whole sentences and neatly constructed thoughts; the products of automating are often just single words or phrases, and sometimes only nonsense syllables. But these words and syllables can provide clues for further questioning that might not otherwise occur to you.

Mirror writing is an interesting phenomenon that sometimes occurs in automatic writing. This is writing that is reversed and must be held up to a mirror to be read. Mirror writing may occur alternately with normal, forward writing. One person reported by the late A.M. Mühl, a psychiatrist who was considered the leading authority on automatic writing, was able to write forward normally on one line, then dip down at the right Margin and write mirror-wise to the left on the next line, then dip down at the left margin and write forward, and so on, without ever removing the pencil from the page.

There is no set method of initiating automatic writing that is best for everyone. One usually has to experiment with various means until the best one is found. Faster results are obtained if the normal, physical resistances to natural writing are removed. This can be achieved by constructing a sling that allows the arm and hand to swing freely without having to rest on the writing surface. A sling suspended from a ceiling hook is best. It can be made of stout string, leather, or anything that will withstand the weight of an arm resting in it. A small towel can be folded and placed in the loop. Allow the forearm to rest on the towel, leaving the wrist and hand free. The sling should be adjusted so the wrist clears the paper by about an inch. With this arrangement, the slightest impulse has a chance to produce an unhindered movement.

Now, with the arm and hand hovering over a sheet of paper, and a pencil or pen in hand, begin to read something interesting. The reading material should be interesting enough to hold your attention—something that diverts your attention away from automatic writing. If marked automatic activity exists, writing will begin almost immediately, and connected statements may be produced. More frequently, early attempts result only in seemingly meaningless scrawls. Most people will write connected accounts only after several practice sessions. However, even nonsense syllables sometimes create insights that are valuable clues to further questioning.

If automatic writing is not achieved on the first attempt, keep trying. Automatic activity has been achieved after as many as a dozen unsuccessful trials. Once the path from the subconscious is fully established, it becomes increasingly easier to obtain good writing activity.

If you cannot automate with the hand with which you normally write, try the other hand. A right-handed person will often discover greater automatic activity when the pencil is held in the left hand, and vice versa.

You need not necessarily read while attempting automatic writing. Some people find it more productive to carry on a conversation, while others find counting to be effective. Once you achieve good automatic writing activity, you can dispense with the sling and write in the normal manner to which you are accustomed. (Some people never need the sling to automate.)

Automatic writing is usually an undirected activity in which the subconscious is left free to write whatever it wants to. Meaningful and useful material can be obtained in this way, but it is sometimes desirable to direct the subconscious to a particular subject. This can be done, once automatic activity has been well established, by thinking of the subject of interest while automating. One will sometimes encounter difficulty in getting anything relevant out of the subconscious in one session, only to find in a later session that the subconscious goes on and on interminably about the previous subject of interest. Such time lags are not uncommon and seem to indicate a need for the subconscious to have a little time to prepare itself to divulge meaningful material.

AUTOQUESTIONING STRATEGIES

Autoquestioning is a form of self-inquiry and, in a limited sense, self-analysis. To approach it with the same attitudes and assumptions that we bring to conventional, external inquiry is a mistake. For most people the subconscious mind is new and uncharted territory which, without proper preparation, can be confusing and frustrating.

The ability to come up with the right questions is a skill that can only be developed through practice. There may be times when you want to just walk away from it and forget the whole business. Don't! Stick with it, and you will find that it was not all that difficult when you look back on it later. And it will certainly have been easier and more rewarding than years (or a lifetime) of failure.

A little skepticism is natural when applying these techniques for the first time. I often hear comments such as "It just seems too easy . . . I don't know whether to trust it or not." Actually, I like to hear people make such statements because it is a good indication that they are probably doing something right.

Some people ask if it is dangerous to stir around in the deeper parts of their minds. They are afraid they might create more problems than they solve. This attitude would be correct and appropriate if I were proposing that you probe around in someone else's mind. But when it comes to self-inquiry, you can put such fears aside. You will not discover more than you can handle at the time, and you will certainly not create any new problems for yourself. What you discover about yourself might make you uncomfortable, however. Such discomfort is a little like discovering that you don't have as much money in the bank as you thought you had. You are better off knowing how much or how little is there so you can do something about it, even though you may not like the idea.

In all aspects of autoquestioning, you will be most effective if you develop a spirit of ruthless honesty about yourself. If you do not constantly strive for scrupulous veracity with yourself, you will find it very difficult to penetrate your own camouflage. We know subconsciously how best to fool ourselves. This is why we can sometimes see someone else's problems more clearly than our own. Mental camouflage very effectively hides problems from oneself, but not necessarily from others.

When you are engaging in autoquestioning, try to establish everything with questions. In other words, keep your assumptions to a minimum. For example, use questions to get subconscious acknowledgment that a particular situation is a problem. The differences in logic between the conscious and subconscious minds make it unsafe to assume that what you consciously consider to be a problem is viewed the same way by the subconscious.

The answers you give yourself in autoquestioning form commitments. This is both an advantage and a disadvantage. The disadvantage can arise if you ask dead-end questions. A dead-end question is the ultimate question: "Can I lose weight?" "Will I be able to quit smoking?" or "Will I ever be successful?" They are called dead-end questions because you will have literally reached a dead-end in your attempts to change if you get a negative answer and take it seriously. If you happened to get a "no" to such questions (which would be incorrect), you have simply added a commitment to failure. It would not guarantee your failure, but it would make more work for you, plus it would be unjustifiably disheartening. Avoid dead-end questions by always assuming the positive. You *can* lose weight; you *can* quit smoking; you *can* be successful; and so on. Expend your efforts working on the "how," not the "if."

The advantages of commitments formed by answers should be rather more obvious. If I ask you to do something and you ignore me, I don't really know whether you are going to do it or not. But if you say "Yes I'll do it," I can be more confident that you will. This same principle applies to dealing with the subconscious mind. If you ask yourself whether or not a particular suggestion will be effective and you get a "yes" answer, then that suggestion will be more effective than it would be without the subconscious commitment.

It has already been mentioned that uncovering the cause of a problem is sometimes sufficient to remove the problem. But a feeling of relief does not in itself prove that the solution found is the real one. Feelings of relief can result from the fact that by hitting upon a pseudo-solution, the crucial problem is temporarily circumvented. However, this does not mean that the subconscious part of the mind gives out purposely false information.

I have never known of a case in which subconscious responses were out-and-out lies. Evasions of the truth in autoquestioning are usually just that—evasions that are the result of not offering more information than is consciously asked for. (Methods for validating obtained information will be presented later.)

Even though your subconscious is not likely to lie to you, it can be pretty tricky. You may subconsciously take advantage of any loopholes that logically exist in your approach or program. Sometimes it is a little like dealing with a child. If you ask a child to clean up her room, and she says she will, where have you made your mistake if you let it go at that? If you are a parent you probably know immediately what is missing: *When?* In the same spirit, if you have asked yourself if a particular suggestion will be acceptable and effective, don't stop questioning just because you get a "yes" answer. Continue your questioning to ascertain some reasonable expectation of increments of change, how soon the change will be taking place, and so on.

Overcoming Subconscious Resistance

You should not think that autoquestioning is "a piece of cake." You are very likely to encounter resistance, especially at the more significant levels of self-inquiry. You have learned, in the process of living your life, a complicated set of responses for dealing with your environment.

Subconscious resistance to self-communication is an attempt to keep things as they are. Resistance does not come from a subconscious desire to remain dysfunctional as such. It is usually not the discomfort or suffering that we subconsciously want to keep or maintain, but those aspects of it which have proved to be of subconscious value, and which hold the promise of future security and gratification. In other words, you are going to experience resistance when you subconsciously feel threatened in something essential to the internal structures you have built.

Unless you have unusually severe problems, this resistance need not—will not—stop you in your quest for self-improvement and personal development. It will simply require a little more work on your part.

When you begin your autoquestioning, emotional reactions to your findings are likely to occur. You may find yourself feeling apprehensive, ashamed, guilty, or irritated about what you discover in yourself. These defensive emotional reactions may result in defensive inhibitions or evasive maneuvers, but they need not be serious if you are aware of their existence and their source. You should be particularly alert for the following symptoms of defensive resistance:

1. *Initial resistance to analyzing a problem.* This symptom is usually manifested

in feelings of vague discomfort when you think about anything related to the problem. These are feelings of threat that can keep you from starting to work on the problem if you give in to them. A gradual, step-by-step approach that will be described later is the best way to begin with any problem that triggers this symptom.

2. *A general block to questioning.* Most of the techniques of autoquestioning require you to come up with the right questions. Emotional resistance can impair your ability to think about a problem and formulate relevant questions. There may be no discomfort, just a blank mind; you just cannot think of any way to get a handle on the problem. Recognize it as a subconscious ploy and don't let it deter you. The autoquestioning strategies will show you how to overcome this blockage.

3. *Lack of comprehension.* Defensive resistance can block your understanding of what you are uncovering. This confusion, which can be very frustrating, usually clears up with persistence. Try to remember that virtually every form of subconscious resistance dissipates gradually as you progressively discover that you really can cope with the truth and reality. You discover that not only can you cope with the new information about yourself and your world, but that you actually feel better for it.

4. *Rejection of findings.* An immediate, negative response to anything you learn about yourself should always make you suspicious. Such emotional rejection may be a symptom of resistance. After all, what better way to keep yourself from acting on information than to convince yourself that it is not true? While this symptom may be caused by resistance, it can also be the result of faulty questioning. You will have to learn to do a balancing act between the recognition of resistance and healthy skepticism (never accept more than you can really believe).

The above four categories of resistance are very common. They will not be a problem if you learn to recognize their symptoms and refuse to give in to them.

If, during your questioning, you are getting a lot of "DWAs" and "maybe's," ask yourself if it would be better to leave the subject for now and come back to it later. Sometimes a postponement as brief as a few minutes can make a world of difference in subconscious willingness to answer questions about a particular subject.

Always use a gradual, delicate approach to questioning. Avoid head-on confrontations with yourself. It is the subconscious mind that is always victorious in any open battle with the conscious. So respect the subconscious part of your mind and be diplomatic; never excoriate yourself if information comes slowly. Autoquestioning is a skill that develops with practice and familiarity. If you get impatient and try to rush things, you will only increase subconscious resistance. When a DWA answer is given, back up and gradually approach the question again.

If repeated, gradual approaches fail to get any answer other than DWA, it is time to question the source of the resistance itself. Once the nature of the resistance to answering the particular question is understood (brought to consciousness), the subconscious may then answer the question.

The following set of questions and answers is an example of one technique for overcoming a DWA response. A "backing up" procedure is first tried after getting the DWA, but when that fails to change the answer, the cause for the resistance is then questioned. The final result is a change in the answer.

Q: If I give myself the suggestion that I will do better in math, will it be easier for me to understand math?
A: DWA.

Q: Is there something in my subconscious that has made math difficult for me in the past?
A: Yes.

Q: Does that "something" affect me when I study other subjects?
A: No.

Q: Will positive suggestions change my subconscious viewpoint toward math?
A: DWA.

Q: Is there resistance to answering questions about math?
A: Yes.

Q: Is it important for me to do poorly in math?
A: Yes.

Q: Was this subconscious belief caused by something that happened to me in the past?
A: Yes.

Q: Was it caused by something I heard?
A: Yes.

Q: Was it something said to me by one of my teachers in school?
A: No.

Q: Was it something said to me by one of my parents?
A: Yes.

Q: My father?
A: No.

Q: My mother?
A: Yes.

Q: I remember Mother telling me when I was eight that I "would never be any good at arithmetic." Was that what I heard that caused the belief that I should do poorly in math?
A: Yes.

Q: If I give myself the suggestion that my mother did not want me to do poorly in math, and that I can be good at math, will I then be able to do better in math?

A: Maybe.

Q: Will those two suggestions be acceptable?

A: Yes.

(Don't be misled by the apparent simplicity of this questioning process. While all of the autoquestioning examples in this book have been taken from actual cases, they have also been edited to remove all of the questions and answers that do not address the point being made in the example. The example you just read is composed of fifteen questions. The original transcript from which it is drawn consisted of over forty questions.)

Another symptom of resistance in ideomotor questioning is that of getting the same response to all questions. It is possible, of course, to word all questions in such a way that the same answer to all of them is correct. But this seldom happens in actual practice.

To assure yourself that you are not doing this, word your questions in a way that will give you a variety of answers. If the same answer keeps recurring, ask a simple question that has an obvious answer, such as "Is it raining outside?" or "Is this Wednesday?" If you are getting a "yes" to every question, ask a simple question to which the correct answer is "no." If you get a "yes" to the question, put the pendulum down and think to yourself how you want correct answers and will not settle for just any response (have another one of those talks with yourself). Then resume your questioning, asking simple questions that require a "no" answer until you get it. When the subconscious becomes convinced that hysterical responses are not satisfactory, they are not likely to reappear.

Because there is no end to the ingenuity of the subconscious mind in devising forms of resistance, there is just no way to cover all possible symptoms of resistance here. If you understand and remember that the questioning technique itself can be used to uncover resistance to autoquestioning, most problems can be recognized and eliminated before they become serious blocks to self-communication. With the principles presented in this chapter you have a basis for dealing with any resistance that might occur in your questioning.

A Schematic For Questioning

Be as elemental in your autoquestioning as possible, and remember that it is your *behavior of interest* (BOI) that is the key focal point. If you are interested in achieving weight control, then *eating* is your BOI, not

103

the state of being overweight itself. You will sometimes have to go far afield in your questioning, but keep the BOI uppermost in your mind at all times. This will be particularly applicable when we get into suggestion formulation and application in the next chapter.

When you first start an autoquestioning session, it is a good idea to ask yourself a few warming-up questions. These should be fairly easy questions to which you know the answers, such as "Is today Thursday" or "Am I wearing a red hat?" Ask one or two questions that require a "yes" answer and one or two "no" questions. Then proceed to questions that will establish the existence of your dysfunction.

Do not assume that you subconsciously agree with what you consciously consider to be a problem. If your answers indicate subconscious agreement—that is, that the dysfunction is indeed a problem—then it is probable that your subconscious mind believes that life without the problem would be worse than the problem itself. To illustrate, if you are overweight and you subconsciously agree that being overweight is undesirable, then the real source of the dysfunction is related to the BOI. The BOI in this case would be overeating, from which you are subconsciously getting something besides nutrition (for example, love, attention, reinforcement, and so on).

Once your questions have established the dysfunction, ask if it is okay to ask questions about the source of the dysfunction at that time. If it is not, determine when it will be. In ten minutes? An hour? Tomorrow? Sometimes this approach is necessary because the subconscious part of your mind wants to call the shots. You can't take it out and spank it, so you might as well go along with it as gracefully as possible.

When you have received subconscious approval to proceed, you are ready to get into the actual interrogation of the subconscious about the source of the dysfunction. The four interrogatives *what, when, who,* and *where* provide an excellent schematic for autoquestioning. Getting answers relative to these four interrogative categories will lead you logically to a good deal of information about any dysfunction.

"What" questions. You want to know what kind of imprint is at the root of the dysfunction: Is it an information imprint, an identification imprint, or a guilt imprint? The questions can be straightforward and simple, if you understand these three kinds of imprints. Here are a few sample questions:

"Did an information imprint start this dysfunction?"
"Is the source of my problem related to identification?"

"Is this problem caused by guilt?"

If the source is an information imprint, question further to determine whether it is verbal or nonverbal. If it is verbal, was itsomething said to you, or something you overheard, or something you read? If it is nonverbal, was it something you saw, heard, smelled, touched/felt, or tasted? Pursue the questioning to determine as much about it as you can. When you know the *what,* move on to the *when.*

"When" questions. Bracketing is the normal procedure for determining when an imprint was formed. Do this with age groupings of about five years each until the relevant age bracket is determined:

"Did [the "what" in question] occur before I was six years old?"
"Did it happen when I was between six and ten?"
"Between ten and fifteen?"

Continue this way until you get a "yes" to a particular age bracket. Then question one year at a time to determine the specific year of occurrence. Continue this way until you know the specific year (see the earlier discussion about prenatal imprints). It is sometimes possible to narrow down even further, particularly if the imprinting experience occurred on some special occasion such as the first day in kindergarten, a birthday, Christmas, and so on.

If you don't already know, you will want to determine whether this was a specific event that caused the imprint, or a series of events. If it was a series, then you can determine the first significant event that started you on the way to forming the imprint. This is not appropriate in all cases, so you may have to content yourself with knowing the general period in your life in which the imprint was formed.

After learning when the imprint was formed, double check with questions to determine that this was *the* event that caused the imprint. The subconscious will sometimes "cop a plea" (plead guilty to a lesser charge in order to avoid the consequences of a more serious one). Carefully formulate your questions to ascertain that you are not doing this. Ask if this is the original, *main* source of the dysfunction.

"Who" questions. By "who" is meant who was or were the person(s) involved in the formation of the imprint. First determine how many people were involved and who they were. If the source of the dysfunction was something said to you (or something that you overheard

being said), who said it? By this time you will already know what kind of imprint it is and at what age it happened. This information may give some clue about who was likely to have been involved. In general, parents are the first suspects for questioning, followed by close relatives, teachers, friends, and neighbors. Not all imprints are caused by events involving specific people, of course, and it is possible that the people involved in an imprint-forming event were not known by you. Check on these possibilities if you are not getting anywhere with your "who" questioning.

"Where" questions. Once you know the *what, when,* and *who,*the *where* is usually relatively easy to determine. What you have already learned about the imprint-forming event will significantly narrow the number of guesses required to learn where it happened. Be as specific as possible in determining where it happened. If the event occurred at home, try to find out just where at home—in the house? the yard? the garage? If it did occur in the house, determine the specific room in which it occurred.

In learning the *what, when, who* and *where,* you will have collected a great deal of information on which to base the formulation of suggestions. And, you will recall, there are times when the conscious awareness of these factors is itself sufficient to remove the source of dysfunction.

AUTOBIOGRAPHY AS A BASIS
FOR AUTOQUESTIONING

The sources of dysfunction described in the previous pages provide handles for concepts that would otherwise be unwieldy and hard to employ. It is much easier to ask questions about constructs such as identification now that they have been defined. These labels for the general categories of sources of dysfunction therefore shorten the autoquestioning process. Defined sources of dysfunction also provide clues to good starting points, but there are times when it is difficult to know where to start. Indeed, some people have to begin without having any clear-cut ideas about what it is they need to work on. Even when one does have a vague idea of the direction in which he or she wants to develop, the question of where to start can be vexing.

A way to get started in such cases is by writing an autobiography that can be used as a basis for initial questioning. The earliest memories are the starting point for the autobiography, and it should not end until the present is adequately covered. It should be written as fast as you can get the words on paper, with no concern for style, spelling, or punctuation. It should be as uninhibited as possible, with no concern for content during the writing. You are writing it strictly for yourself, so don't waste time editing it as if it were for publication.

Although there is no strict format that must be followed, the following general categories provide an overall scheme that is helpful in writing an autobiography:

Early childhood memories. Start with the earliest memories, even if they are hazy and indistinct. It is usually worthwhile to record the earliest memories that include parents. This stage of your autobiography should extend up to about the age of seven.

Parents in your childhood. This section should deal with what your parents were like in your childhood. Record any thoughts about your parents until you were about twelve. Include any thoughts about what your home life was like, and thoughts about any divorces, deaths, or illnesses in the family.

Childhood emotions. Record any fears, likes, or dislikes that you remember having as a child. This should include recurring dreams or any unusual fears you may have had. Also try to remember how you felt about other people in general at various stages of your childhood.

Childhood experiences. Put down any and all childhood experiences that come to mind. Unusual experiences usually form strong memories and should be included. These can be either positive or negative, pleasant or unpleasant. There are also memories that are strong and easily recalled, but that do not seem to be important. Write them down whether they seem important or not. Sometimes the most significant material comes from seemingly unimportant memories. Do not try to evaluate the material while you are writing—just write down whatever comes to mind.

Religion. Cover the earliest remembered experiences concerning your (then) religion. This should include how you felt about those experiences then, and how you feel about them today. Include the general religious orientation of your family as a child and of your present family. Write down any thoughts you have about God and religion in general.

Teen-age experiences. The experiencing of "firsts" accelerates during the teen-age period: the first date, the first kiss, the first cigarette, and so on. Include any of these experiences that stand out in your memory, as well as any irrational fears or serious problems that occurred during this period.

Marriage. If you are married, record whatever comes to mind about your marriage. Include thoughts about husband or wife, children, and the institution in general.

Vocation. Give your mind free rein in writing about your job. If you do not work out of the home but your spouse does, write your thoughts about his or her job.

This form is just a guideline, so do not hesitate to deviate from it if it feels natural to do so. The key concept in writing an autobiography for use in autoquestioning is spontaneity.

When the autobiography is completed, go back through it and underline all words, thoughts, or phrases that might have some meaning for the subconscious. There is no way to know, while picking out these parts, if they are in fact meaningful. Just underline a key word in every major thought or phrase. In the following example, the italicized words or phrases are those chosen for autoquestioning, and the superscript refers to the question that follows for that particular word or phrase.

> . . . then when I was five my mother took me to *kindergarten*[1] and I played in the *sandbox*[2] a lot and remember the *back of the building*[3], it was made of brick with trees and grass. I *didn't have any friends*[4] there and I can't remember the *teacher*[5] at all and I know I went to kindergarten a long time but can only remember playing in the sandbox. We lived in [*city*] then and the *streetcar*[6] came by our house and the *people who lived next to us*[7] were not very friendly . . .

Question 1:
Did something happen in kindergarten that presently causes me to behave in any way that I do not consciously like?
Question 2:
Was there something about the sandbox in kindergarten that was instrumental in creating a subconscious state that opposes my present goals?
Question 3:
Is the back of the building significant?
Question 4:
Is the fact that I did not have any friends in kindergarten significant?
Question 5:
Was there anything about the teacher that was subconsciously significant?

Question 6:
Do streetcars have anything to do with present problems?
Question 7:
Were the people who lived next to us subconsciously significant?

This technique of questioning elements taken from an autobiography can be very productive. There is always enough material in even the shortest autobiography to keep you working for a long time uncovering things that you might otherwise never know about. It will certainly provide direction for the person who does not know where to begin.

WHEN TO BE CAUTIOUS

One of the great things about these techniques is that their proper use creates no dangers for the person using them for self-improvement and personal development. But anything can be abused, and my purpose here is to warn you about what constitutes abuse. Another purpose is to indicate limitations that have not been stated elsewhere in this book.

The procedures presented in this book will not take the place of psychotherapy, any more than you can take the place of a qualified psychotherapist (even trained psychotherapists do not treat themselves). The techniques of self-hypnosis and autoquestioning should not be employed while one is in therapy unless the therapist approves their use. It is not that these techniques will make the patient worse. But they can confuse the therapeutic program or distract the patient from the goals of the therapist.

You should not attempt to deal with physical ailments until they have been thoroughly investigated by a physician. It is always dangerous to ignore any physical symptom whose source is not known. Frequent headaches, for example, may be caused by simple nervous tension, and the source of the nervous tension may be dealt with using these methods. But such headaches can also be the symptom of something much more serious, and only your doctor is qualified to determine whether it is serious or not. So don't try to treat any physical symptoms on your own until you have clearance from your doctor.

No matter how much explanation is given, there always seem to be some people who do not understand the nature of ideomotor action. The Chevreul pendulum, for example, is not made to move by some mysterious force. The swing of the pendulum is the product of movement in the arm and hand, which in turn is motivated by the subconscious mind working through normal, neuromuscular channels of internal function.

Autoquestioning cannot answer questions about other people's minds. Trying to learn how others feel about you is not a valid use of any form of autoquestioning. Attempts at questioning the future are in the same category. This includes questions such as "Will I move to Seattle next year?" or "What lottery number should I choose?"

There are only two conditions in which questioning of the future is acceptable. One has to do with questioning the effectiveness of a suggestion. Questioning whether a suggestion will be effective could be construed as questioning the future, but this is a permissible use of autoquestioning. Determining a time frame for the effectiveness of a suggestion might also be considered questioning the future, but the answers to this questioning, as well as to questions about the effectiveness of a suggestion, are based on present states of mind. By the way, you should never try to pin down the subconscious to a specific date in questioning how soon a suggestion will have done its work. Stick to general periods of time rather than trying for specific dates.

The other condition in which future-oriented questions are appropriate are when such questions are used to determine the *present* subconscious attitude about a future event or condition. The question "*Should* I move to Seattle next year?" would be appropriate in trying to determine the subconscious attitude about such a move. Such questions can be very helpful in determining possible subconscious resistance to future decisions. If the subconscious response was "no" to moving to Seattle, suggestions could be used to change the subconscious viewpoint and prevent resistance to such a move. But never use such questions simply to make decisions.

There is a fatigue factor that must be considered when using autoquestioning techniques. A proliferation of "don't want to answer" or "maybe" responses often means that a point of fatigue has been reached. Since the subconscious mind does not seem to ever get physically tired, what we are here calling "fatigue" is probably wariness, not weariness.

A fatigue point may be reached rather quickly in the first few questioning sessions, but practice extends the length of time that questioning can be conducted before the fatigue sets in. Most people are able to obtain answers for an hour or longer with a little practice. (One or two hours of autoquestioning may sound like a long time, but it is surprising how quickly an hour will pass when you are learning interesting things about yourself.) When you do suspect you have reached a fatigue point, quit for a while. The amount of rest needed before continuing with autoquestioning varies with individuals and situations. It may be as brief as a few minutes, or as long as several days.

In the beginning, it is normal to experience some skepticism about answers obtained in autoquestioning. Common sense must be used in accepting answers when you are first starting because it often takes the subconscious a while to get the idea that only accurate and serious responses are acceptable. Integrity in answering usually develops rapidly if the subconscious is led to understand that accurate answers are more important than the normal subconscious concerns for conscious sensitivity. For this reason it is important that autoquestioning techniques not be used capriciously or for playing games.

There is often a feeling that a question is being answered even before it is asked. This is not really surprising when we consider the nature of the phenomena involved. The subconscious knows the question, or at least its general nature, before it is completely articulated in the conscious. This subconscious awareness may be only a nanosecond ahead of the conscious mind, but that is enough time for the subconscious to thrust at least a hint of the answer into the conscious realm. This usually happens only with questions that are relatively simple and unimportant, or with questions to which the conscious knows the answer. With these kinds of questions one may have the feeling that wishful thinking is prompting the answers, but wishful thinking will not force incorrect answers if the proper subconscious attitude toward autoquestioning is fostered early in the learning process.

With these autoquestioning methods and techniques you can get information directly from the subconscious part of your mind. Sometimes this bringing of information to consciousness is sufficient to eliminate a dysfunction. When it does not do this, the information can be used to formulate suggestions. How to formulate and apply suggestion is our next topic.

4

Suggestion

Suggestions can change your life for the better if they are properly formulated and used. In fact, suggestions have already been a tremendous influence on your attitudes and behavior. One of the more obvious ways in which we are all influenced by suggestion is through advertising. Every day we are bombarded by countless suggestions imbedded in advertisements. Advertising agencies long ago discovered the potency of suggestion and the laws of suggestion. The brand of cigarettes you smoke, the kind of car you drive, the kind of soap you buy, and the brand of beer you drink are all influenced by the suggestions made through advertising.

It is practically impossible to go about our daily business without coming into contact with thousands of commercial suggestions. Newspapers, magazines, television, radio, billboards, mail, and many others are all sources of suggestions that are difficult to ignore. Sometimes the suggestions are subtle, sometimes they are not. The advertisement that depicts a masculine-looking cowboy smoking a particular brand of cigarettes is making several visual suggestions, one of which is that you, too, can be masculine if you smoke this brand. I think you know which brand this is—I won't promote them further by mentioning the name here, but they frequently invite you to come to "[brand name] country." As an interesting aside, this brand is more popular with women than with men. Figure that one out.

Television commercials for household cleaning products boldly suggest that you are unclean, unsanitary, and socially undesirable if you permit the existence of even the smallest amount of hidden dirt anywhere in your house. These and other suggestions conveyed through advertising have literally changed the way we live and think. It was just a century ago that toothpaste and deodorant did not exist, people made most of their own clothes or had them made to order, hardly anyone ever traveled more than about ten miles from their place of birth, and the phrase "germ free" was still many years in the future.

Very little advertising is intended to make you want to jump up and immediately run out to buy the product being advertised. Such a direct approach is not as effective as a slower, more subtle approach. The strategy of advertisers is to get their products accepted at the subconscious level. Through repetition of their advertisements they form a familiar identity in the minds of their viewers and readers. Once that identity is formed in the mind of a consumer, he or she will select that brand of product on the next shopping trip without really knowing the true reasons for the selection.

Now, I know that you are probably thinking, "Advertising doesn't affect me." Over the past several years I have asked literally thousands of people, in both formal and informal situations, how much influence they think advertising has on them. And I have never had even one person admit that his or her purchasing habits were influenced by advertising. Well, it's working on someone. A new advertising campaign for a product in a given geographical area will often produce an astronomic increase in sales. My point is that we are all susceptible to suggestion and the less we are aware of the suggestion, the more effective it can be. When you know the principles of suggestion, advertisements become fascinating topics of study because they contain some of the most masterfully constructed and delivered suggestions you will ever encounter.

Knowledge of the principles of suggestion is certainly necessary to apply suggestions effectively. That knowledge can also be used to prevent undesirable suggestions from being effective. Because suggestions surround us all the time, it is beneficial to know how they work in order to be more selective in what we allow to affect us.

One usually thinks of a suggestion as being a direct, verbal statement such as, "Why don't you sit down?" That is a suggestion, but it is only one of many kinds of suggestions. If all suggestions were of this direct, verbal type, they would be much easier to recognize and to work with. However, *practically any form or kind of information can constitute a suggestion if it is received at the right time and place.*

A brief glance at your shoes by someone else may plant a suggestion that results in your getting your shoes shined. A facial expression of even the slightest disapproval from certain people can make you change your behavior. Seeing a car wreck might suggest to you to slow down.

Anything we see, hear, smell, feel, or even taste can form a suggestion, or trigger a response that has been developed by previous suggestions. The respect for authority is a good example of how a condition of mind can be built up over time, and which can be triggered later to affect behavior. Parents are almost always the first authority figures in a person's life. Through a number of childhood experiences, a child learns that it is usually painful and uncomfortable to displease parents. As the child learns to avoid parental displeasure, he will respond more and more quickly to increasingly subtler suggestions that "keep him in line." A slightly raised eyebrow may be a strong enough suggestion to make the child stop whatever he is doing. This respect is later generalized to all authority figures: teachers, policemen, politicians, community leaders, and so on.

Once the respect for authority is firmly established and generalized, even the subtlest suggestion can affect behavior. The mere sight of a police car may cause a driver to slow down, even if she was not exceeding the speed limit. A television commercial that depicts a policeman being impressed with a certain make of automobile may form a suggestion that is followed on the next automobile purchase. A shopper is likely to be responding to suggestions made through advertising when selecting a particular brand of household item. The objective of many advertisements is to associate authority figures with the brand being advertised.

"Why," you may be wondering, "does Henderson keep harping about advertising?" My purpose is not to educate you about advertising per se, but to point out that advertising in America today represents the state of the art for certain types of suggestion. This is not to imply that I am in total agreement with the philosophy, purposes, and methods of American advertising. Lamentable as some advertising may be, it is not going to go away and it cannot be completely ignored. So, since you and I are going to be subjected to all kinds of advertising, we might as well try to learn something from it that suits our own purposes. One of the books you might find very informative and interesting is Key's exposé of advertising entitled *Subliminal Seduction*. (You will find a complete reference for Key's book or any other work mentioned here in the Selected Bibliography.)

Advertising presents a microcosm of American culture, illustrated by the fact that the only real cultural centers in this country are its shopping centers. To know and understand advertising is to know and understand much about ourselves. If you don't like this thought, then you will have to become more aware of the suggestive qualities of advertising in order to resist them—suggestion is always more effective when the recipient is unaware of it.

Advertising can also make it difficult to break old habits. Many advertisements contribute directly to dysfunctions such as smoking, over*eating, and drinking. The avowed purpose of all advertising is to make the consumer want to use the advertised product, to make him or her feel good about* using the product, and to make him or her feel good *while* using it. Tobacco companies make smoking look as appealing as possible. Food companies, especially those with junk food products, do the same thing. Breweries and distilleries follow the same principles— you will never see advertising in which a skidrow alcoholic extolls the virtues of a particular alcoholic beverage. Every element in advertising is designed to make the use of a product pleasant, appealing, even necessary to such subconscious needs as social approval and control.

Anyone who has ever tried to stay on a diet knows how suggestive or even seductive food advertising is. Although I have never known of a case in which advertising was overtly trying to induce overeating, advertising provides an ongoing source of suggestion that significantly increases the difficulties of dieting. If the dieter knows and understands how to use suggestion, he or she will be better able to counteract the influences of external sources of suggestion such as advertising. This applies to any area of self-improvement or personal development. Suggestions from external sources must be neutralized if they are in opposition to conscious goals. *The ability to resist suggestions is as important as being able to use them.* Fortunately, the study of the dynamics of suggestion helps build such resistance.

Suggestions are being applied all the time, whether you want them to be or not. Examples from advertising have already been presented at some length. Another kind of suggestion that is especially important are those statements you make to others about yourself and your world. Much of the research in this area has been done under the heading of "self-fulfilling prophecy." This means that expecting something to happen increases the liklihood that it will happen. For example, if you have persisted for years in making negative statements about your luck, such as "just my luck" or "with my luck, such-and-such is bound to happen," you have been contributing to your own bad luck.

This is not black magic, just subconscious dynamics. We know that what generally passes for bad luck is often the result of self-initiated mistakes, errors, or missed opportunities because we were not alert or ready for them. On the other hand, good luck is often the product of being subconsciously motivated to be in the right place at the right time, or sometimes just being alert to opportunity when it knocks.

So one of the first principles of suggestion is to not make statements that you don't want to be true. And, conversely, do make statements that are in line with what you want from your world. You can prove this principle to yourself with a simple test. Try telling several people over the next few weeks that your luck is improving. You'll find that you really do start getting luckier.

Another way in which suggestions are always being applied has to do with expectation theory. Howard Rosenthal and his research associates at Harvard University have shown that if person A expects certain behavior from person B, person B is more likely to behave in accordance with those expectations. If I expect you to be able to make significant, positive changes in your life through the intelligent application of suggestion—and I do, by the way—then you are more likely to do so than you would be if I did not expect it.

Consider for a moment those days you have experienced when it seemed as if everybody was out to get you (we all have them). At those times it is easy to get the feeling that all anyone wants to do is dump on you. The truth is, when things are going that way it is probably because you are subconsciously projecting negative expectations which are suggestions to others. Certainly there are other possible explanations, but the next time you are having "one of those days," try consciously working on the suggestion that others will start responding to you with courtesy, warmth, and acceptance.

In working toward self-improvement and personal development it is essential that you learn to recognize and reject negative suggestions that come from external sources. No matter how strong and independent-minded we might like to think of ourselves as being, at various times and in different situations we are all prey to outside influences. Here is an example from my own experience which shows how troublesome even a passing remark can be.

I was fat most of my life, weighing just under 250 pounds when I was up to my slaughtering weight. At the time this "passing remark" incident occurred, I was finally learning how to use self-hypnosis and suggestion, and I was really beginning to shed my excess weight. One afternoon when I came home a next-door neighbor was out watering her lawn. She greeted me, looked at me a minute, then said, "Wow, you're really losing weight! Are you sick?"

And that did it! That woman's clumsy question clearly implied an association between losing weight and being sick. And that association was sucked right into my subconscious mind. The subconscious logic was obvious: Sick people commonly lose weight, therefore I had better stop losing weight to avoid being sick. For several weeks after this incident, I would hear the echo of her question as I took my morning shower. (It came to me in the shower because the water was associated with the fact that the woman had been watering her lawn when she asked me that cursed question.) All through my shower I would have to "think down" the negative suggestion that weight loss meant being unhealthy.

Even before the "echo in the shower," I knew that my neighbor's question was either forming a new imprint or reviving an old one because of my subconscious gatekeeper. Having a gatekeeper is a good way to spot potentially troublesome negative suggestions. It is developed with your imagination. Imagine a wise old man or woman who guards the door to your mind. He or she is trained to recognize negative suggestions and to let you know immediately if one is trying to gain entry into your subconscious mind. Once alerted, you can either reject the suggestion outright or formulate countersuggestions if the intruding suggestion does manage to gain a toehold.

You might think that it would be easier to just have the gatekeeper automatically reject negative suggestions, whether you were consciously aware of them or not. That will not work as well because it puts the decision-making process in the subconscious part of the mind. And, as you already know, the subconscious is limited in its logical capabilities.

There are a variety of ways in which you can deal with unwanted suggestions. Practically any model that feels right for you will be effective after you have practiced it for a while. I know a writer who was so accustomed to getting rejection slips from publishers that she decided to issue rejection slips to unwanted suggestions. Another person I know literally flushes negative suggestions down the toilet. He writes the unwanted suggestion on a piece of paper, crumples it up, and flushes it down.

Just as external suggestions require constant vigilance, so do internally generated suggestions. As you are no doubt aware, your own mind occasionally generates negative ideas with no conscious help. As you continue to work with suggestion, you will become more alert to these negative suggestions, and you can deal with them the same way you deal with external suggestions.

Your own speech forms a hybrid of internal-external suggestion. You have a thought, which results in an utterance, which then has the double influence of also being an external suggestion. Research has shown that we respond to the things we say in ways that are similar to the ways we respond to what others say. So monitoring and controlling our own statements becomes very important. This has already been mentioned in the discussion about self-fulfilling prophecies and how they apply to our good and bad luck.

It would seem an easy matter to stop saying negative things about ourselves, but experience has shown that it is not as easy as it sounds. The subconscious gatekeeper is beneficial, but it is also helpful to enlist the aid of other people. Tell your family members, friends, and fellow workers that you would like them to help you keep track of how often you say something negative about yourself. Ask them not to correct you or tell you what you said, but to just indicate when you have said something negative about yourself. They can do this by holding up their first and second fingers in a V-sign and wiggling them at you. We call this "finger-twiddling." You will be surprised by how often you make negative statements about yourself. You will also be surprised by how much fun your friends will have twiddling you.

It should be clear by now that we are all constantly surrounded by external suggestions, and that our own behavior and speech are also suggestions. This brings us back to a point made earlier: Virtually any kind of information can be a source of suggestion. So far, we have discussed what might be termed *spontaneous* suggestions. Now it is time to turn our attention to the kinds of internally generated, purposive, or *intentional* suggestions that you will be using to achieve your goals. The autoquestioning techniques explained earlier are ways of obtaining information *from* the subconscious mind. Intentional suggestion is a way of communicating information *to* the subconscious. When enough information has been obtained about a source of dysfunction, suggestions can be formulated and applied to change or eliminate it. The formulation and application of suggestions is not a haphazard process; there are certain principles and procedures that, if followed, make suggestions more successful.

THE LAWS OF SUGGESTION

There are two very important laws that greatly influence the effectiveness of suggestion. The first one is usually referred to as the *Law of Concentrated Attention*. This law states that *whenever spontaneous attention becomes concentrated on an idea, that idea tends to be realized*. It has been said that if something is repeated often enough, people begin to believe it. When this happens, the Law of Concentrated Attention is in effect. For purposes of self-improvement, it is the attention of the subconscious mind that we want. The more attention the subconscious gives an idea, and the less the conscious interferes, the more readily the ideas which we instill will become accepted and acted upon. Conscious interference is reduced to a minimum by the use of proper techniques of formulating and applying suggestions.

The second law is the *Law of Reversed Effect*. *If there is doubt in the mind, the harder one tries, the harder it is to succeed.* This law can become active any time there is doubt about the outcome of anything one is trying to do. The doubts that cause failure in such situations can be very subtle and sometimes consciously unknown.

For example, every typist has experienced times when it is impossible to type something without errors. The greater the attempts to eliminate the errors, the more errors occur. Doubts begin to build up in such circumstances, and the harder one tries, the harder it is to avoid making errors. Insomniacs experience this when they try to sleep. Because of past experience they "know" they are going to have trouble getting to sleep, and sure enough they do. The harder the insomniac tries to go to sleep, the more wide-awake he or she becomes. If the insomniac stops trying so hard to go to sleep, or somehow eliminates doubts about being able to go to sleep, sleep comes quickly and easily because the Law of Reversed Effect is no longer being triggered.

This law was mentioned earlier in the discussion about passive direction. It is important to maintain a certain amount of passivity when using suggestion in order to avoid the reversed effects of trying too hard. In some ways, using suggestion is much like planting grass. First the ground is prepared, then the seeds are planted. You cannot make the seeds grow—all you can do is water them occasionally and wait for the grass to appear. Once the seeds are planted, you must leave them alone. Disturbing them will only slow the process of growth and perhaps even kill the seeds.

To relate this analogy of growing grass to suggestion, questioning and determining the sources of dysfunction, and formulating suggestions, are the ground preparations. The application of the suggestion is the equivalent of planting the seed, and repetition of the suggestion is the watering of the seed. When the seed begins to grow, behavior and performance in the relevant areas are changed. Once the suggestion begins to take effect, the changes are usually gradual and natural, just like growth in a plant.

Self-improvement that results from the repeated use of suggestion is almost always permanent because the subconscious has been brought into alignment with conscious goals and desires. When subconscious sources of resistance are removed, a person is free to achieve his ends without constantly experiencing self-initiated blocks to success. As one becomes aware of some degree of success resulting from the application of suggestion, further success is fostered because belief has been strengthened. Ultimate success is the product of incremental compounding of smaller successes along the way. The more you succeed, the greater the success you are capable of achieving.

For this reason it is best to begin any personal development program with fairly easy goals or subgoals. Make the first subgoal relatively easy, then move to the next subgoal when you have achieved it. This approach makes it much easier to, say, lose fifty pounds. All you have to do is lose one pound. Fifty times.

The question of symptom substitution is often raised by people studying self-communication techniques. The popular conception is that any symptom which is removed will pop up in some other form. This is never the case when the source of the symptom is removed. Having an appendectomy does not cause an appendix to grow somewhere else.

The person who quits smoking but immediately begins to overeat and gain weight does so because she did not deal with her subconscious desire or need to smoke. Even when the underlying source of dysfunction cannot be directly dealt with, there is seldom a problem with substitute symptoms. Success experiences in the realm of self-communication always bolster one's self-reliance and confidence. This in turn improves the individual's powers of adjustment to levels that are sufficient to prevent any transfer of symptoms, or relapse, from occurring.

SUGGESTION FORMULATION

Several key factors must be kept in mind when formulating suggestions. What should be one of the most obvious of these factors is often overlooked: The suggestion must be relevant and applicable to the case at hand. If a person has taken the time and trouble to determine that financial failure is caused by imprints originally caused by his mother's remarks, he should do more than just formulate a general suggestion about success. His suggestions should be directed at removing or changing the imprints, instead of overwhelming or bypassing them. An overweight person whose suggestions simply state that he will not eat sweets is ignoring the causes of why he wants to eat sweets.

Even if the source is undetermined, suggestions should be directed to the desire and motivation behind the dysfunction, not just to the dysfuncton itself. There are some situations in which a more general suggestion will be effective if there is subconscious understanding that the source of the dysfunction is to be eliminated by the suggestion. But a commitment to this effect must first be obtained from the subconscious through autoquestioning.

The subconscious characteristic of taking things literally must be remembered when working with suggestion. Every word should be chosen with care in order to avoid the use of ambiguous or slang terms. One student who was plagued by examination jitters before and during every test gave herself the suggestion that she would be "cool and calm" when taking tests. Her suggestion was effective in that she did remain calm during her next test. However, she nearly froze in a room that was warm enough for everyone else. Her subconscious mind had responded to the literal meaning of "cool" in her suggestion.

It is usually best to use the personal pronoun "I" in formulating suggestions that refer to yourself. Many people make the mistake of saying "you" in their suggestion when they mean "I." instead of "*you* are becoming . . . , " saaay "*I* am becoming . . ." The same goes for "it"—use "I" or "me" for all personal references and avoid formulations such as "*It* is becoming . . ."

Suggestions are more effective when they are realistic and reasonably logical. Using step- or subgoals is a way of assuring that your suggestions meet this criterion. If the goal of your suggestion is better memory, do not suggest that you will awaken in the morning with a photographic memory. Work instead with realistic concepts of gradual improvement or change.

Now, please do not misunderstand my use here of the terms "realistic" and "logical." If you have understood the earlier discussions about how the subconscious reasons, then you know that certain modifications have to be made in what would ordinarily be considered realistic and logical. But I do not think suggestion is going to help anyone regrow a missing limb or tooth, add another foot in height, change eye color, or visit Mars. (I find it interesting that, as I sit here trying to think of obviously absurd examples, not many come to mind that I feel certain are impossible. Today's impossibility has a way of becoming tomorrow's commonplace.)

I have been surprised on a couple of occassions to learn that people were using suggestions that spirits were going to come to their aid. Don't bother doing this. If indeed there are spirits, they have not shown any interest in responding to the suggestions of mortals.

The strength and efficacy of suggestions are always enhanced by positive formulation. Try to choose positive words and phrases whenever possible. Emphasize what you *are* going to do, not what you are *not* going to do. For example, "I am becoming more self-confident" is a much better formulation than "I am getting rid of my lack of confidence." There are times when the complete elimination of negative terms is difficult or even impossible. In those cases it will be necessary to go ahead and formulate the suggestion in negative terms. But before giving up and using negative expressions, try the method of antonyms, or opposite meanings. List your negative words down one side of a sheet of paper. Directly across from each word write its corresponding positive, or opposite, term. Here are some examples to show you what I mean, and to give you more of a feel for what is meant by "negative" and "positive" words:

Negative Word	Positive Opposite
adverse	favorable; beneficial
bad	good
destroy	build; form; create
difficult	easy
distraction	concentration
hinder	help
ignorant	informed; educated
recede	advance
reject	choose; accept
stingy	generous; charitable
stop or quit	start; begin
ugly	beautiful; handsome
worse	better

If the method of positive opposites fails to yield a positive formulation, you will probably just have to stick with the negative form. Negative suggestions are not ineffectual, but positive formulations are more desirable.

An important reason that positive formulations are desirable is the subconscious affinity for parsing sentences into their component parts. You experience this subconscious characteristic when a segment of a song or advertising jingle keeps running through your mind. When this happens, your subconscious mind has "parsed" the segment from the total song or jingle. Suggestions are sometimes parsed in the same way, resulting in the component phrases either floating around in the subconscious, unconnected, with each phrase having its own effect, or in a recombination of the segments into a different suggestion.

Fragmentation of a suggestion is not likely to cause problems if only positive terms have been used. Consider the following example of a suggestion (the slashes indicate a typical subconscious fragmentation):

*Every day, / in every way, / I am becoming
more and more / self-confident*

Any one of the fragments of this suggestion is still positive and conducive to the desired effect. No matter how the segments are rearranged it comes out safe and positive. But look at what can happen when a negatively phrased suggestion is parsed by the subconscious:

Every day / I am feeling / less and less / inferior.

All the subconscious has to do is parse out the "less and less" to produce a disastrous suggestion: "Every day I am feeling inferior." Just the opposite of the intended suggestion!

Whenever you are not sure of a suggestion, try chopping it up in this way. If the suggestion is not easily turned into an opposite or otherwise undesirable meaning, then it is safe. This subconscious parsing of suggestions does not happen all the time, nor does it happen with every suggestion, so it is not a constant problem. But beware the possibilities and try to use positive formulations whenever possible.

The parsing of suggestions, when it does occur, is apparently limited to *formal suggestions*. A formal suggestion is one that is fairly brief and has been composed with care. Once it has been formulated to convey exactly the right message, it is applied repeatedly without deviating from the original wording. All of the examples given so far have been formal suggestions.

Another form of suggestion that is used to strengthen the effect of the formal suggestion is the *elaborated suggestion*. Elaborated suggestions are applied by merely talking to oneself, so to speak. They express the formal suggestion at greater length and in greater detail. Because repetition is important for suggestions to be effective, it is helpful to state the suggestion in many different ways. It is sort of like giving yourself a sales pitch. As an example, take the formal suggestion used above: "Every day, in every way, I am becoming more and more self-confident." For this formal suggestion, the elaborated suggestion might go something

123

like this (remember, the elaborated suggestion is an ad lib, so it is likely to be different every time):

> Every day I am developing more positive feelings about myself, responding to new situations in a relaxed and self-confident way. My self-image is improving to the point where I know I can handle any situation that might come up without feeling fearful and apprehensive. My nerves are becoming stronger and steadier because every day I am feeling stronger and calmer. I am developing stronger and stronger feelings of personal safety and security, and I am learning to feel and act with greater confidence . . .

And so on. You may have discerned a few negative phrasings in this example of an elaborated suggestion. Negative forms are not much of a problem in elaborated suggestions, probably because the mind is kept busy enough not to have any desire to play around with the sentences. Even more important, no single phrase is repeated enough to trigger parsing. But it is still a good idea to keep everything as positive as is reasonably possible. Affirmations are always stronger than negations, regardless of the form of suggestion being used.

Timing is an important factor in the drafting of suggestions. A suggestion that is timed to take place sometime in the near future is much more effective for some people and for certain suggestions, whereas others will get a better response with a suggestion that is stated in the present tense. "I am self-confident" and "I am becoming self-confident are both present tense suggestions (the "I am becoming" does extend into the future, but the *am* implies present action, too). There is, however, a fundamental difference between the two forms just given. The first one—"I am self-confident"—states an *existing* condition. The second one—"I am becoming self-confident"—states a *developing* condition. Whether to use the *existing* or *developing* format for a given suggestion is best determined through autoquestioning. Simply formulate the suggestion both ways and ask yourself if one is better than the other.

"Tomorrow I will be more self-confident" is a suggestion in the future tense. "The next time I am in a meeting with my boss I will remain calm, relaxed, and alert" is another example of a future tense suggestion. Determining whether a future or present tense suggestion is best can also be done through autoquestioning.

You will have noticed that several of the formal suggestion examples have begun with "Every day, in every way . . ." It is a good idea to include this phrase in any suggestion that does not otherwise state a specific time for achievement of the intended goal. The subconscious is a great procrastinator, often preferring to put off until later the fulfillment of a suggestion. Keep this in mind, avoiding open-ended formulations that have no time goal in them.

It is often difficult, sometimes impossible, to accurately define one's ultimate goals in self-improvement or personal development. Goals are not much of a problem when the objective is something like losing weight or financial success. These are areas in which both intermediate and ultimate goals are easy to define in either pounds or dollars. But goals become harder to define in other areas. Confidence, relaxation and stress reduction, concentration, memory—these are examples of areas in which it is harder to attach numerical or quantitative values. This is why it is essential to include a "more and more" or "better and better" concept in the formulation of suggestions that do not include specifically stated goals. It does not make any sense to think in terms of a size nine memory or fourteen pounds of concentration, but it is easy to imagine these faculties getting better and better.

This provides us with a basic format for formal suggestions, a format into which we can plug a number of ideas:

Every day, in every way, I am becoming more and more _____.

The blank space can be filled in with words such as *relaxed, good-natured, disciplined, confident,* and so on. And suggestions for other qualities can be obtained with only slight modifications in wording:

Every day, in every way, my concentration is getting better and better.

Every day, in every way, I am becoming more and more disinterested in food. (Note that although the word "disinterested" is technically negative, no amount of parsing can turn this into a negative suggestion.)

Every day, in every way, I am becoming healthier and healthier.

These are all good examples of formal suggestions, but they are intended to serve as examples only. The actual appropriateness and subconscious acceptability of any suggestion for a particular person can only be determined through autoquestioning.

Testing for Acceptance of a Suggestion

Once a suggestion has been drafted in accordance with the guidelines presented above, the subconscious must again be questioned to determine whether or not the suggestion is acceptable. This can be done with any of the autoquestioning methods, but the pendulum or finger methods are usually best for this task. The only time this questioning need be carried to any great length is when the suggestion is not acceptable as formulated. If it is not, further questioning will be needed to determine what changes in the suggestion will make it acceptable.

The initial questions for determining tbe acceptability of a suggestion can be simple and direct. There are four questions that need to be answered:

1. Is the suggestion acceptable to the subconscious mind?
2. Will the suggestion produce the desired results?
3. Will results be achieved within a reasonable period of time?
4. What is the most effective way of applying the suggestion?

All of this refers to formal suggestions. It can be assumed that the application of elaborated suggestions will enhance the effect of formal suggestions, provided that the elaborated suggestions follow the general theme of the formal suggestions.

The first question concerning acceptability might include several questions for determining whether the suggestion should be in the present or future tense, and whether it should be a statement of fact or a "becoming" kind of suggestion.

When inquiring about the acceptability of a suggestion, it is a good idea to include a statement of the suggestion in the initial question. References to "this suggestion" or "it" are not as reliable as actually repeating the suggestion in the question.

After the acceptability of the suggestion is established, proceed to determine with further questions the results that can be obtained with the suggestion, some kind of time frame for results, and the beat methods of application (more about methods of application shortly). The suggestion itself need not be repeated in all subsequent questions because it was established in the first question. If any question is asked that does not relate directly to the stated suggestion, then the suggestion must be restated when the questioning comes back to it.

What follows is a sample transcript of a questioning procedure to establish the acceptability of our sample suggestion:

Q: Is the suggestion "Every day, in every way, I am becoming more and more self-confident" acceptable?
A: Yes.
Q: Will the proper application of this suggestion help me to become more self-confident?
A: Yes.
Q: Will I be able to actually feel the increased self-confidence?

A: Yes.

Q: Will my self-confidence begin to increase immediately?
A: Yes.

Q: Will my self-confidence increase at a rate that I will *consciously* think is reasonable?
A: Yes.

Q: Should I give myself this suggestion every day?
A: Yes.

Q: Should I give myself this suggestion more than once a day?
A: Yes.

Q: Should I give myself this suggestion fifty times a day?
A: No.

Q: Twenty-five times a day?
A: No.

Q: Ten times a day?
A: Yes.

Q: Should I give myself this suggestion more than ten, but less than twenty-five, times a day?
A: No.

Q: Ten times a day is adequate?
A: Yes.

Q: Should I spread the ten applications of the suggestion throughout the day?
A: No.

Q: Will the suggestion be more effective if I repeat it ten times in succession?
A: Yes.

Q: Should I repeat the suggestion ten times during my self-hypnosis practice?
A: Yes.

If the answer to the first question had been negative, then different questions would have been necessary to determine what to do about the suggestion. In actual practice it does not often happen that a properly formulated suggestion is rejected by the subconscious. But if this does happen, question every element in the suggestion until it becomes clear just how it should be changed to gain acceptance. Then change the suggestion accordingly and test again for acceptance. If you continue to fail with repeated attempts to get acceptance of a suggestion that has been changed several times, you may not have discovered the real source of the dysfunction. Go back to questioning about the dysfunction until the real source is uncovered.

Determining the best method of applying a suggestion can lead in many different directions. The case cited above is just an example. Don't be alarmed if you learn that your own best application of a suggestion is entirely different from the above case.

It is possible for the best mode of application to change during the process of change. If your results from the suggestion slow down or you hit a plateau in which no further progress is being made, return to the questioning to recheck the best mode of application. It may have changed and, if it has, make the necessary changes in your application of the suggestion. Your subconscious is not being capricious in calling for such changes—it is merely learning more about the processes involved.

People are sometimes surprised that the subconscious mind can give directions about how best to change itself. It would seem logical (*consciously* logical, that is) that if the subconscious knows both *how* to change and *what* will be required to change it, then it should be able to change on its own without help. The weakness of this argument is that it fails to allow for the logical limits of the subconscious mind. The subconscious is a whiz at deductive reasoning but a complete dunce when it comes to inductive reasoning. So it cannot generalize specific bits of knowledge or information to other, broader areas of application. In this respect the subconscious mind is like a surgeon without hands. The surgeon may know every detail required to perform an appendectomy, but when it comes time to "surge," someone else with hands must do the actual operating. For the subconscious, the "someone else" is the conscious part of the mind.

There is another reason for asking so many questions of the subconscious concerning the acceptance of a suggestion: *Answers given by the subconscious are commitments.* The subconscious has a childlike kind of integrity. Once it has agreed to do something, it makes every effort to carry through with that commitment. If the subconscious affirms that a suggestion will be effective, that suggestion will be more effective than it would have been had there been no commitment made. It usually turns out that the stronger the commitment, the better and faster the results of the suggestion.

SUGGESTION APPLICATION

Generally speaking, suggestions can be applied anytime, anywhere. In fact, you should try to fill your mind with them whenever you have the opportunity. The more you can make your suggestions the dominant theme in your waking thoughts, the more effective they will be, and the sooner they will produce results.

During self-hypnosis is the best time to apply suggestions, and that is the application that will be emphasized in most of the remainder of this chapter on suggestion. But you do not have to be in a hypnotic state to apply your suggestions. You can repeat them when you are driving, doing housework, mowing the yard, or plowing the north forty. Try to develop the habit of thinking about your suggestions any time you are not doing something that requires your full attention. In other words, apply your suggestions as often as you can.

There are two fundamental rules that must be followed in the application of suggestions. The first is the *Rule of Acceptance,* which states that the subconscious mind must be allowed to accept suggestions because it cannot be forced to do anything. It can be changed, but trying to force a change, or trying to challenge the subconscious to change, will often produce just the opposite of the desired results. This is the reason why we use suggestions instead of commands when dealing with the subconscious mind.

Suggestions must be applied in an almost leisurely manner. Any thought of those suggestions as being ultimatums, challenges, or demands must be avoided. The subconscious must be allowed to take its own time in accepting and implementing any suggestion. Every person's mind seems to have its own timetable in which it works, and trying to rush that timetable is like trying to make grass grow faster. Using proper techniques will facilitate the acceptance and effectiveness of a suggestion, just as improper techniques or faulty formulation can cause a suggestion to be rejected. But it is ultimately the subconscious mind that sets its own pace, not the conscious mind. It is not unnatural for a person to want changes to occur rapidly and dramatically, but it is unwise to try to force the subconscious to accelerate its own natural tempo.

Once a specific method of application of a suggestion has been determined, that method should be followed with as little conscious regard for results as possible. The more a person worries and frets about the results of a suggestion, the more the doubts of the conscious mind get in the way of the subconscious. Constantly checking on the effectiveness of a suggestion reinforces negative thoughts about the entire process. This may in turn form an opposing suggestion. Such opposing suggestions and doubts are more easily controlled if the positive suggestions are passively applied. This is done by establishing a routine that follows the method a person has prescribed for himself, and by following that routine without fanfare. You will be in good shape if you can make suggestion application as routine and effortless as brushing your teeth.

The second rule of suggestion application is the *Rule of Repetition,* which says that repetition of a suggestion is necessary for it to be effective. There are some exceptions to this rule, but they happen infrequently and only in unusual circumstances. The number of times a suggestion should be repeated, and (sometimes) how long it will take for it to be effective, can all be determined with the autoquestioning techniques with which you are now familiar.

Autoquestioning will usually establish that twenty or fewer daily repetitions of a suggestion are sufficient. The establishment of a specific number of repetitions applies only to formal suggestions applied during self-hypnosis and should not be confused with the earlier statements about repeating suggestions as often as you can.

An elaborated suggestion will consist of several paraphrased repetitions of the formal suggestion, so there is no need to establish a specific number of repetitions for it.

When to Apply Suggestions

Generally speaking, the most effective time to apply formal suggestions is just before beginning the hypnotic induction. After you have assumed your normal practicing position and become relaxed, repeat your formal suggestion (or suggestions, if there are more than one) to yourself. You don't have to say them out loud, just think them to yourself the specified number of times. You will know from autoquestioning how many times to repeat each suggestion. Then go on with your induction practice— you have put the suggestion into your mind by having repeated it several times, so you need not be consciously concerned about remembering it.

Your informal, or elaborated, suggestions will be applied during the scene visualization of your self-hypnosis induction practice. If you happen to have one of my taped induction talks, you know that there is a blank period of three or four minutes during the scene visualization. If you do not, allow yourself a few minutes during your scene visualization to apply your elaborated suggestions. As in the case of the formal suggestion, you need not speak out loud, just silently think the suggestions to yourself.

A good method for supplementing the regular applications of suggestion is that of connecting the suggestions to external cues. This is done by repeating the suggestion whenever the external cue is present. As an example, let us say that a person wanted to connect a formal suggestion with red lights. She would, for several weeks, make a conscious effort to repeat the suggestion to herself any time she saw a red light. If she were stopped at a traffic light, she would repeat the suggestion until the light turned green, looking at the red light as she did so. If she noticed a red neon light, she would repeat the suggestion at least once.

While driving at night, every once in a while she would look right at the tail light of the car in front of her and repeat the suggestion. After doing this for a few weeks, the presence of a red light becomes a stimulus that reinforces the suggestion, whether it is consciously repeated or not.

This kind of association can also be made with activities such as physical exercises. If you regularly do push-ups, a suggestion can be repeated with each push-up. While jogging is a good time to repeat suggestions. Any repeated exercise can be used in this manner. An exercise period will pass much faster if it is also a time of suggestion application.

A good non-hypnotic time to apply suggestions is just before going to sleep at night. A pre-sleep application is especially helpful because it gets your positive, goal-oriented thoughts and images into the sub-conscious so they will have a chance to work while you are asleep. Sometimes this leads to dreams that can really speed up the effectiveness of suggestions. "Alternate reality" dreams are the most efficacious for breaking bad habits or changing dysfunctions. Such dreams are frequently unpleasant, but their results are quite rewarding.

An example of how alternate reality dreams work is provided by the experience of a forty-seven year old man who was using self-hypnosis to quit smoking. He had been applying suggestions for several weeks without any observable change in his desire to smoke. Then one night he bad a dream in which he was looking at some X-rays. They were of his own lungs, and there was a spot on them which meant he had inoperable lung cancer. This dream was unpleasant, to say the least, but when he awakened he was completely rid of all desire to smoke, and he has not smoked since.

It is not known whether such alternate reality dreams are the result of the subconscious mind having finally gotten the message, or if the alternate reality portrayed in the dream is what actually induces the change. I favor the second explanation because fantasy, in this case the dream, is more real to the subconscious than is external reality. An internal experience is much more vivid and real to the subconscious than reality itself. I have known people who knew they were dying from emphysema but who could not quit smoking until they dreamed they were dying from the disease. External reality had no influence on sub-conscious motivations, but as soon as that reality was internally (sub-consciously) represented, it had a dramatic effect.

One question that is very hard to answer has to do with how long it takes to achieve something with suggestion. The amount of time required depends on a number of variables: your own personal dynamics, how regularly you practice and how you practice, and the nature of the goal you are striving toward. Some goals, such as getting a college degree or becoming a computer programmer, may take years to achieve.

In general, you should be able to see at least some results within a few weeks if you are following instructions and doing it right. If, within two or three weeks, you see absolutely no improvement or progress, re-examine your suggestions. You may find some negative element in them that escaped you earlier. If you do find something in a suggestion that you suspect might be blocking progress, change the suggestion. If you cannot find anything wrong, make some general changes in your suggestions and try the modified versions for a while.

On the other hand, if you are getting results from your suggestions but you are impatient with the speed of your progress, you will be better off to curb your impatience and leave the suggestions alone. It is very discouraging to try to improve on a working suggestion, only to have it stop working altogether. So change only those suggestions that show no signs of being effective within two or three weeks, and leave alone those suggestions that do.

Do not make the mistake of abandoning your suggestions immediately upon reaching your goal. Continue practicing and applying your suggestions for at least several weeks after you have achieved whatever it is you are working on. The observable symptoms or signs may disappear before an imprint is completely dealt with. Or, in the case of working to develop something such as better memory, the signs of development will usually manifest themselves before the new, positive imprint is thoroughly cemented in the subconscious. So always continue with your suggestions beyond the point of achievement to assure solidification of your gains.

It is very important that a positive attitude be developed toward both the subconscious mind and the suggestions with which you are working. The subconscious should not be thought of as an enemy lurking inside your skull. It is perhaps the most important part of your mind relative to your own individuality, and it has only your best interests at heart. The fact that the subconscious makes mistakes in judgment, and that it functions differently from the conscious part of the mind should not be allowed to cause negative emotions. Anger, hostility, and self-recrimination only get in the way of goal achievement. Being bitter toward the subconscious for the mistakes it has made is like hating an automobile tire for going flat. Your time will be much better spent in repairing the puncture and reinflating the tire, rather than in excoriating it.

You should also develop a positive attitude about the ultimate success of your suggestions. (Please do not confuse this with Positive Thinking!) Whenever a negative thought pops into mind, counter it with an opposite, positive thought. Every "I can't do it" can be overcome with a "Yes, I can." This may feel awkward at first, with a feeling of deceiving yourself, but with practice the negative thoughts diminish and dwindle away, leaving only the positive ideas.

Image Rehearsal

Image rehearsal is a form of suggestion application that is extremely effective for almost any kind of self-improvement. Simply stated, image rehearsal is practicing in your imagination. You just imagine yourself doing the thing at which you want to improve, and imagine that you are doing it without mistakes or errors.

The U.S. Olympic Cross Country Ski Team has found that five hours of real practice and one hour of image rehearsal are better than six hours of real practice. Their image rehearsal consists of imagining themselves skiing with the errorless form they want to develop.

You can use image rehearsal to improve at anything, whether it is an athletic activity or losing weight (this is elaborated further in the chapter on weight control). You can practice with image rehearsal during self-hypnosis, or at any other time that you can relax for a few minutes. Just as in real practice, one practice session is not usually enough to produce noticeable results. And image rehearsal will not supplant real practice. No matter how good you get with image rehearsal, you will still have to get in some practice by actually doing whatever it is you want to get better at.

The addition of positive visual imagery will make any suggestion more effective. If an image of the desired results is held in the mind, the subconscious is provided with a model for attainment, and suggestions relative to attaining that image are enhanced. The person who wants to lose weight will help herself by forming a definite mental image of what she wants to look like. This image should be thought of as often as possible, especially while applying suggestions. A woman might see herself in a bikini showing off her nice figure. A man might see himself looking slender and sharp in a new suit. The mental image should be as clearly and precisely formed as possible, and the person should see herself doing rewarding things that are congruous with her ideal image. The person who wants to improve his finances might form an image of himself counting large sums of money, or driving a new car, or anything that has meaning for him and is associated with his goal. The image should be as detailed as possible.

This is not just daydreaming—it is planning and building. Daydreaming is quite often negative in nature; one "dreams" of having or achieving things that he does not really believe are possible for him. So the more one daydreams in this negative way, the further he removes himself from the possibility of achieving the objects of his dreams.

Using positive mental imagery in conjunction with suggestions is planning, building, and anticipation. The visualizer *knows* he is going to achieve the image he has conjured up, and he is getting ready by thinking about it. No matter how far-fetched the image may consciously seem in the beginning, if it has been cleared through autoquestioning, and if it is held in the mind long enough, the subconscious will begin to shape the person's behavior to turn the image into a reality.

One final point relative to imaging and personal development: *You must be able to imagine what it is you want to achieve!* Whether you are literal- or image-minded, you must somehow be able to imagine yourself being the way you want to be. A good deal of evidence indicates that an inability to imagine something means an inability to achieve it.

If you have difficulty imagining yourself as you want to be, you are probably trying to bite off a bigger chunk than you can subconsciously chew. So break down your goals into smaller units that you can imagine. If you cannot really imagine yourself being slender, for example, imagine yourself weighing just a little less. Or imagine some smaller part of yourself, such as your hand, being slender. You will still be able to achieve your ultimate goal, but you will have to do it through a progressive series of subgoals. Just remember to *keep your goals within imaginable limits*.

Anticipatory Role Behavior

Anticipatory role behavior is both a form and an application of suggestion. Anyone who has been in the military knows that advancement in rank usually comes only after a soldier has partially demonstrated the ability to perform at the higher rank. A private who wants to be promoted to corporal must begin to exhibit some of the characteristics of a corporal in order to be considered for promotion. This same phenomenon can be observed in business and industry. A person is not likely to be promoted to a higher level until he has given some indication that he can perform the higher-level duties.

The dynamics of anticipatory role behavior are twofold. For one thing, the subconscious eventually becomes convinced that the behavior is legitimate and normal, and will motivate the person to further acts that conform to the new status. For another thing, anticipatory behavior prompts other people to respond to the person in a way that reinforces the validity of the new status. It is characteristic of human beings to react in ways they think they are expected to react. If one demeans himself and acts unworthy, others will treat him as unworthy, setting up a vicious cycle over the years that makes the person feel and behave increasingly more unworthy. There are, of course, subconscious sources of dysfunction that have started and maintained the situation, and they must be dealt with. But conscious adoption of anticipatory role behavior is a valuable addition to suggestions and will help in reversing the undesirable situation.

An adequate model of successful behavior is necessary to properly assume anticipatory role behavior. The model should be an eclectic composite of several observed behaviors. Such a model is formed by close observation and study of other people who are successful in the relevant areas. The model should be formed on the basis of observing lots of other people because no one is perfect. Elements of behavior should be abstracted from overall behavior patterns, with only positive, successful elements being selected.

In developing your anticipatory role behavior, do not pattern yourself after any one person. Wholesale adaptation to another person's personality will only lead to phoniness. You must identify and abstract elements of behavior for inclusion in your behavior model that develop and increase your own individuality. Just copying someone else will only destroy individuality. True individuality does not come from conscious attempts at being different, but rather from knowing your own mind and having the strength to do what you know is right for you. Anticipatory role behavior can help you mold previously improper behavior into a pattern that is consonant with your goals and ambitions. Starting to act the way you want to be is a form of suggestion that helps you reach your goals.

We make and receive suggestions all the time. Because we are all constantly subjected to our own and others' suggestions, it is imperative that we learn to deal with them.

Negative suggestions from external sources must be recognized and resisted. Otherwise, they will block progress in self-improvement and personal development. Negative internal suggestions must also be controlled. This includes the things we say and do.

Properly formulated and applied, suggestions become the impetus, the motivating force, behind self-directed change. As you become more knowledgeable about, and proficient with, suggestions, you will continually broaden the horizons of your own potential.

5

Selected topics and applications

KEEPING IT UP

Keeping up your self-communication practice can be a problem. Autoquestioning, self-hypnosis, and suggestion formulation and application are not social activities. They are solitary pursuits that are difficult to do with other people. Working alone is fine for a while, but sooner or later we need other ways of staying motivated.

Over the years, I have seen this pattern over and over again: A person gets interested in self-hypnosis and begins working toward self-improvement and personal development. Progress is made, improvements occur, and good habits are developed. But then the person gets distracted by other demands and stops working with his or her program of personal development. These people say they were doing great for a while, but for some reason stopped. When I see them they are wanting to get back to it and regain their skills.

To avoid this on-again, off-again pattern, self-communication must become a way of life. Actually, it *is* a way of life for all of us. Our only choice is whether or not we take command and control it.

To maintain momentum and enthusiasm, more is needed than just reading a book or two and deciding to make changes. Here are some solutions to the problem of "keeping it up":

Continued reading. Set aside an hour or so each week for reading new material on self-hypnosis, and for rereading things you have read before. You will come across new methods—the excitement of trying a new approach goes a long way toward maintaining enthusiasm. The rereading of material will remind you of things you have forgotten, and you will discover things you missed before.

Research in self-communication areas is going on all the time. This research is reported in magazine and journal articles. Check the *Readers Guide* in your public library from time to time under the subject of "hypnosis." I keep up with recent publications and conduct some of my own research. New methods, techniques, and procedures are reported each month in my Self-Hypnosis Newsletter (for information about the newsletter, write me at P.O. Box 10003, Denver, CO 80210).

Form a discussion group.   Find people around you who are also interested in self-communication (almost everyone is if they are properly introduced to it). Occasional discussions with just one or two people with like interests can make a big difference. The "discussion group" need not be formally constituted. It can be as simple as having lunch once a week with one or two friends to talk about self-communication.

Attend public programs.   Keep up with what is going on in your area so you can attend self-hypnosis courses, lectures, seminars, and workshops. If nothing like this is going on where you live, find local professionals who know something about the subject. Persuade them to give a talk or conduct a course.

FEAR OF SUCCESS

There has been a lot of discussion in recent years about the fear of failure. Failure is unpleasant and can lead to anxieties about failing. This is why many people will not put forth their best effort. If they leave something in reserve they have a cushion against failure—no one need take failure personally if he or she really wasn't all that involved in the first place.

However, the general prevalence of failure in the world indicates a greater fear of success than of failure. Assuming that human beings seek pleasure and avoid pain, we must conclude that, in relative terms, failure is preferable to success. And this is what many people have discovered through autoquestioning. They have found that they feared success far more than they feared failure. This fear is so great in some that they fail at practically everything they try. Or, if they do not actually "fail," they at least do not achieve anything that could be clearly defined as success. Their subconscious terror of success motivates them to "hold it down."

Success anxiety, or fear, can be caused and reinforced in a number of ways. One very common source of success anxiety is the complicated emotion, *envy*. Sooner or later, we all envy someone for something. If the envy is strong enough it can even form the basis for an irrational hatred of the envied person. Thus, envy is identified early in our lives as highly unpleasant. Some people go to great lengths to avoid being the object of envy and, at its worst, hatred. When this condition exists, the fear of success is really a fear of envy, or of being envied.

Anthropological studies have demonstrated that the fear of envy has occurred in all cultures throughout history. Every society has its protections against envy, or the envious eye (often referred to as "the evil eye"). In India, teeth, claws, strings of shells, obscene symbols, or practically anything that will flutter and dangle, are used to attract attention away from something that needs to be protected from envy, or the evil eye. Moslems used to disfigure their children, horses, and asses (the four-legged kind) to protect them from envy. Homer's heroes were taught self-disparagement as an approved pose. Soldiers of Imperial Rome would follow the chariot of a triumphant general, shouting derisive and sarcastic verses while the populace showered him with small stones and garbage (just as we shower a bride with rice). Modern residents of southern Europe do not permit their children to be praised or caressed; if an adult does praise a child, the praiser must slap the child lightly and spit to avoid the evil eye. Chinese children are often given ugly names such as "dog," "hog," or "flea" to avoid the evil eye.

In America we avoid the evil eye in many ways. Women often own jewelry which they seldom feel comfortable wearing, and new clothing makes some people feel self-conscious. It is considered very bad manners in rural areas to ask a farmer or rancher how many acres of land he owns, how many head of cattle he has, or any other question that refers to his material holdings. Parents are often perplexed by their children's demand that a new pair of jeans be washed several times before they will wear them. The fear of envy, or the need to avoid being envied, can strongly influence virtually any kind of behavior.

Guilt is another source of the fear of success, often originating in early childhood. Children are very inadequate in their cause-and-effect reasoning, often blaming themselves for events over which they really have no control. Children often blame themselves for some tragic event, such as a death, illness, or divorce. If the timing of the tragedy happens to coincide with the child's emerging assertiveness, she may associate

139

the two and feel that it was her assertiveness that caused the tragedy. From then on she will be subconsciously motivated to avoid being assertive, which assures that higher levels of success will never be achieved.

The birth of younger siblings sometimes develops success anxiety. The youngest or only child who rules the roost will have the unpleasant experience of being dethroned with the birth of a new sister or brother. If this happens at about the time of the child's emerging assertiveness, he may subconsciously view the whole situation as punishment for his assertiveness. Henceforth, he will shun success in order to avoid such unpleasant punishment.

There are many experiences that can cause a fear of success if they happen when a child is first expressing his individuality. The extent to which parents can tolerate strength and adequacy in their children is very important. Parents who have at least a modicum of emotional security and self-confidence are not only able to tolerate individuality in their children, they encourage it. But the parent who suffers from feelings of insecurity and inadequacy will inadvertently quash a child's attempts at expressing his own individuality and developing sense of adequacy.

When a child receives negative parental responses to her first crude attempts to be herself, she quickly learns that it is much more comfortable to "stay in her place" and "do as she is told." A child's early attempts at self-expression are likely to be awkward and, to an uninformed or insensitive adult, insignificant. The little girl who unreasonably insists on taking her doll to church with her may be asserting herself for the first time. An insecure parent will see this as a threat to his authority (the home may be the only place in which he has any authority at all). He will feel it his "duty as a good parent" to put his foot down and show that he is boss. After a few such unpleasant experiences, a child learns that aggressive and self-assertive behavior is painful and unrewarding.

We all need love and acceptance, especially from our parents. If parents are emotionally secure and competent in their own lives they will be pleased (*most* of the time) by their children's successes and signs of emerging individuality. They will reward and encourage their children's positive personality development whether they are consciously aware that they are doing so or not. But insecure parents only pay lip service to wanting their children to be successful. Little Johnny's parents may demand that he make good grades in school, but Johnny senses that they do not really want him to do that well, so he does not.

This is quite often the case with parents who themselves were poor students in school. Dad may have a subconscious, or even conscious, conviction that little boys who make very good grades in school are sissies. A child will perceive this and perform accordingly. In a similar vein, girls are often forced into a make-good-grades-but-don't-be-too-smart mind set: They are expected to make good grades in school, but they are also expected to not be too threateningly smart outside the academic arena. This makes it difficult to generalize school lessons ("book larnin' ") to life. With any luck, the recent sociological and cultural drives toward equality between the sexes will diminish the occurrences of this unfortunate phenomenon.

Parentally enforced abnegations of self-assertion in a child are eventually generalized to almost all areas of activity and thinking. Although the behaviors associated with failure are certainly observable, the internal, mental processes are strictly subconscious. Just as the subconscious mind causes a person's hand to jerk away from something hot, it will motivate a person to avoid any activity that might lead to unacceptable levels of success. The subconscious will continue to function in the same way until self-communication is employed to change it.

The phenomenon of identification is closely related to the processes just described. The parent or other person who is the target of identification may have a low tolerance for success. When the value systems of that person are internalized through the process of identification, the fear of success comes with them.

Imprints of any kind can contribute to the fear of success. Admonitions against bragging, as discussed earlier, are often sources of imprints that motivate a person to avoid unacceptable levels of success. An oft-repeated "Don't brag" may form an imprint that makes it unwise to speak of any achievements. The subconscious may consider any discussion of success to be boasting, and set forces in action that will negate whatever achievement was discussed. What the subconscious has interpreted as bragging causes guilt feelings that, in turn, call for punishment.

Guilt feelings about boasting are sometimes generalized to even the *achievement* of success because the person cannot help thinking about, or being aware of, a sense of achievement. This thinking itself then becomes a subconsciously-interpreted form of boasting. Anti-success behavior is then triggered to avoid, or pay for, the guilt for having boasted. This is a particularly nasty and frustrating syndrome that can eventually convince one that he or she is truly star-crossed.

Many people who fear success are able to tolerate higher levels of success if it is either transitory or the product of luck. Success that comes from a stroke of luck does not arouse subconscious guilt because the person was not personally responsible for the success. Some people have learned this and refuse to take credit for their successes, insisting that they have just been lucky. Close inspection of such people's successes usually reveals that it was not luck, but their own behavior, that led to their success. But they have learned to prevent guilt feelings, and the resulting destruction of their success, by absolving themselves of all credit for their success.

Anyone who has a desire to succeed, and who has experienced difficulty with succeeding in the past, must uncover any fears of success if any significant, lasting success is ever to be attained. Such states of the subconscious mind can be disclosed through autoquestioning. If a fear of success is uncovered, it can be eliminated or changed with the application of suggestion.

Problem Solving and Dreams

Self-improvement and personal development often involve problem solving. The first step in problem solving is to determine what the problem is. There is a big difference between knowing *that* a problem exists, and knowing *what* the problem is. Even if the problem seems obvious, it is helpful to write it down. Formulate the problem as exactly and precisely as you can. If it cannot be succinctly and clearly stated, more thought is needed. If a person has debts that exceed income, for example, that is certainly a problem. But debts are not the real problem. If the person had enough money, there would be no debts. So the real problem is how to make enough money to pay the debts.

Once the problem is understood, any subconscious blocks to a solution must be removed. Autoquestioning techniques will uncover any blocks that do exist, and suggestions may be necessary to remove them and bring the subconscious to a positive viewpoint. The subconscious will not attempt to solve any problems if it believes that the solutions are not in the best interests of the person. Sometimes the subconscious is wrong.

Once you understand a problem, and the subconscious blocks to its solution have been eliminated, you still need a solution. Solutions can be maddeningly elusive.

One way to enlist the subconscious in coming up with a solution is through sleep and dreaming. To do this, go to bed every night with the conviction that you are either going to dream the solution to your problem, or that it is going to occur to you when you wake up. You may not have your solution after the first night, or even after several nights, but remain positive that the solution will eventually appear. Be sure to keep pencil and paper near your bed so you can write down any thoughts that awaken you in the night, or that occur to you when you first wake up. If you do not get them down on paper quickly, they have a way of rapidly escaping. It is very frustrating to know, later in the day, that you had a really terrific idea, but you just can't remember what it was.

Dreams and nocturnal problem-solving processes can be prompted by subconscious commitments made through autoquestioning. With a full conscious awareness of the problem and all of the relevant information, obtain subconscious commitments with questions such as the following:

Q: Is my subconscious already beginning to work on a solution to my problem?

Q: When the solution is reached, will my subconscious present it to my conscious in a dream?

Q: Will I be able to consciously understand the solution? (This is very important because subconscious symbols tend to be highly abstract and esoteric.)

Q: Will the solution be cloaked in symbols that will need translating for me to consciously understand it? (A double-check on the above question. If the answer to this question is "yes," you may have to use autoquestioning later to determine the meaning of a symbolic dream.)

Q: Will I be able to remember the dream when I first awaken?

Q: Will I be able to remember it long enough to write it down?

Q: Will I have this dream tonight?

Q: Will I be able to have this dream within a week?

Problem-solving dreams can be cloaked in such abstract symbolism that even though the dreamer understands *what* they mean, he is at a loss to explain just *why* the symbols mean what they do. An experience of my own illustrates this point. I once had a dream in which a house, a train, and a cliff symbolized a particular statistical process for dealing with some research data. I don't know why these three elements had that meaning for me. I just knew when I woke up that that way of analyzing the data was the solution to my problem.

Problems that seem insoluble are often solved brilliantly by the subconscious. But the subconscious demands appreciation for its services: Every effort must first be made to solve the problem consciously. It is usually only after one has racked his brain for a solution that the subconscious comes to the rescue.

In addition to this direct problem solving approach, the study of one's own dreams can be fascinating and rewarding. With autoquestioning, you have the ideal technique for fathoming the mysterious meanings in your own dreams.

It goes without saying that you must have and remember dreams in order to be able to study and interpret them. The following is a five-step process for: (a) prompting dreams, if you seldom dream; (b) remembering dreams; and (c) working with dreams for better understanding of yourself and your subconscious processes.

STEP 1. *Suggestion*. Give yourself suggestions, usually just before going to sleep at night, that you want to have dreams and remember them the next morning.

STEP 2. *Avoid movement immediately after waking*. The memory traces of a dream are very weak, and there is something about movement that tends to erase them. So remain as still as you can upon waking in the morning.

STEP 3. *Review*. As you lie there after waking, review the dreams you remember having. This process of thinking about them strengthens the memory traces. It will only take a few minutes to do this, but it is very important.

STEP 4. *Write down key words*. When you have reviewed your dreams, get up and immediately write down some key words. Just a few words will be adequate to jog your memory later when you write a more detailed description of the dream.

STEP 5. *Write down the dream in detail*. Either immediately or at some more convenient time later in the day, write a complete description of the dreams with as much detail as you can remember. This should be done in a "dream book" in which you keep written descriptions of all your dreams. And even if you "can't draw a straight line," add diagrams and rough drawings of your dreams. Be sure to record your dreams before you sleep again.

After a few weeks of keeping dream records, go through your recorded dreams and look for recurring elements. A symbol that is repeated in two or more dreams is likely to be a representation of something that is troubling you, or that in some way is important. Isolate these repeated elements for autoquestioning.

When you first start autoquestioning to determine the meanings of dream symbols you will probably find it confusing and frustrating. It is largely a guessing game in the beginning but it gets easier as you develop a feel for the latent meanings of your own dream symbols. Take nothing at face value; everything in a dream is symbolic, and quite often the meanings of dream symbols are related to clichés. For example, a dream involving corn might have "corniness" as a referent. Or a dream involving fish might indicate that something is "fishy" in your life.

If you dream that you are careening down a mountain in a vehicle with bad brakes, you might question to see if something in your life is "out of control." It could be your life, your job, a personal relationship, and so on. Or the bad brakes in the dream might be symbolic of bad "breaks" in life that are costing you control in some vital area.

If you really get into working with your dreams and would like more information, pick up a copy of Ann Faraday's *The Dream Game* (see Bibliography). This interesting book is written for the lay reader.

Selected Applications

The ultimate goal of the techniques presented in this book is success. Success can be defined for this purpose as the *permanent achievement of a significant goal*. It is only when changes or developments are permanent that one can claim success.

The applications that follow are merely guidelines for improvement in areas of frequent interest. They are by no means exhaustive in scope or application. There are numerous areas of application not mentioned here, and every individual will find his or her own applications at least slightly different from the examples given. But the techniques and methods of approach are all fundamentally the same. Weight control and quitting smoking are covered in separate chapters because they are such popular areas of self-improvement. Even if you are not interested in either quitting smoking or weight control, you would do well to at least look over those two chapters because they contain a wealth of precedural detail that you can apply to other areas.

Increasing Personal Income

Very few people would not like to increase their material wealth. If for no other reason, one could use more wealth to help those who are less fortunate.

The first thing you will need to do is get rid of all preconceived notions about what you are worth. Just because you have been working for about the same amount for many years does not mean that that is all you are worth. If it truly is all you are worth, then your first project should be to develop more knowledge and skills to increase your value on the market.

Set your immediate goals by raising the standards of past achievement. A good rule of thumb is to add 10 percent plus the past year's inflation rate to your current annual income, or to your most common annual income. For example, at the time of this writing, last year's inflation rate came down to about 5 percent after being in the double-digit range for a few years. Add this 5 percent annual inflation rate to the base increase of 10 percent for a total goal of a 15 percent increase in the amount you would normally expect to earn in the next twelve months.

If $12,000 is the amount you would expect to earn in the next twelve months, add 15 percent for a figure of $13,800 (.15 x $12,000 = $1,800 which, added to $12,000 = $13,800). So your immediate goal is $13,800 in the next twelve *or fewer* months. When you reach your goal of $13,800, add another 15 percent, which gives a figure of $15,870. (This assumes a constant inflation rate of 5 percent; if the inflation rate varies, adjust your formula accordingly.)

Going from $12,000 to $13,800 as a first year goal may not sound very exciting, but look at it this way: If you work the next ten years for $12,000 per year, your total earnings will have been $120,000. But by simply adding 15 percent per year, your ten-year earnings will have been $280,191.27 with a tenth year income of $48,546.69! That's a lot more than you would have been earning if you had not done something about your subconsciously imposed limits. Besides, it way not take you a full twelve months to achieve each goal level, which means that you can achieve these figures in less time.

Now, with your immediate goal established, question the subconscious to learn what has kept you from being successful in the past. Following are some types of questions that will get you started:

Q: Do I have a fear of success? If the answer is "yes," then:

Q: Is it caused by childhood experiences?

Q: Is it caused by identification?

Q: Is it caused by other imprints?

Q: Do I have subconscious imprints that block success?

Q: Do I have subconscious identification that blocks success?

Q: Do I have guilt feelings related to success?

Q: Are there limits to how much I think I am worth? (If "yes," determine the amount.)

Q: Have I been afraid to try to succeed because of a fear of failure?

These questions are only starting points. They will give you a beginning, but your own questioning must be pursued with questions that are relevant to your own history and experiences. When you have obtained enough information to formulate suggestions, draft pertinent suggestions that are subconsciously acceptable.

Not all failure is the product of subconscious prompting. To be successful at anything requires learned skills relative to the endeavor. No one could reasonably expect to be successful as a banker, stock broker, or plumber without knowledge and experience. The process of learning any skill, trade, or profession must involve some failures along the way. In fact, it could be said that all learning is the product of many small failures. But when one reaches a point beyond which further skill cannot be developed, and continues to make the same number and kinds of mistakes, there is good reason to suspect the existence of subconscious blocks to further development.

It is important to understand the difference between internally and externally caused failure. Adverse market conditions, economic depression or recession, labor strikes, problems of supply or demand, and so on, are all *external* influences on financial failure or success. Unfortunately, it is always a temptation to blame failure on external forces, when in fact the subconscious may be the real culprit that is causing defeat. Subconscious forces sometimes combine with negative external forces, creating the appearance that a failure has been caused by external elements.

Autoquestioning can be used to determine the existence of subconscious resistance to a project *before* it is begun. If there is, deal with it before getting under way. Autoquestioning can also be used to determine whether a particular failure was subconsciously motivated, or if it was the product of uncontrollable, external circumstances. If the cause was in the subconscious, use the methods described throughout this book to eliminate it. If questioning shows the cause to have been of external origin, keep a positive attitude and move on to the next project.

Improving Study Ability

There are few people in modern society who do not need or desire to further their education from time to time. Many people have so much difficulty studying that further education, especially that required for job advancement, can be a source of misery and frustration. Studying difficulty can be caused by a single source of dysfunction, or by a combination of several. Whatever the source, dysfunctions in studying can be uncovered and removed just like any other source of dysfunction.

The first step is to uncover the subconscious block(s) to studying. As in all autoquestioning, the procedure should build slowly and gradually to the source, allowing the subconscious to answer smaller questions instead of the big, all-encompassing kinds of questions. Once the source has been discerned, question to determine whether or not conscious awareness of the source is sufficient to remove it. If it is not, formulate and apply suggestions that autoquestioning has shown to be acceptable and effective, and in the manner prescribed by the subconscious. Following are some sample questions for uncovering the source of a studying dysfunction:

Q: Do I have subconscious ideas or viewpoints that interfere with my ability to study?

Q: Were these ideas or viewpoints caused by something in my past experience?

Q: Do I have one or more imprints that cause my studying problem?

Q: More than one imprint?

Q: Is my studying dysfunction caused by one main imprint?

Q: Is my studying dysfunction caused by guilt imprints?

Q: Is identification part of the source of dysfunction?

Q: Is there one major imprint that contributes the most to my studying problem?

Q: Was this imprint caused by something I did?

Q: Was it caused by something I read?

Q: Was it caused by something I heard?

When there is a studying dysfunction, autoquestioning quite often uncovers informational imprints of a verbal nature (usually caused by comments from parents or teachers) and identification factors.

A case in point is that of the student whose autoquestioning prompted his memory of a time when his mother was upset with him about the grades on his report card. He was in the third grade at the time, and his mother had said to him, "You're just too lazy to study." It may seem strange that such a simple remark could create a problem with studying, but it must be remembered that the remark formed an imprint, so the subconscious accepted as fact the "laziness" of the student. His subconscious mind then motivated him to act lazy and avoid studying any more than was necessary to pass in school.

This student had compounded his studying problem by an identification with his father, whose academic values were negative. Right or wrong, he subconsciously believed that his dad considered anyone (male) who made good grades in school to be a sissy. This student wanted to be masculine, which under the circumstances precluded making good grades in school.

His suggestion, which proved very effective, was, "Every day in every way, I am becoming more and more industrious about studying, and as I study more and more, I am learning that I can study effectively and be masculine, too." The reference to industriousness in the suggestion was to remove the imprint of laziness, and the part about masculinity was to deal with the identification with his father.

Using self-communication to eliminate mental blocks to studying may not transform you into a genius, nor will results be achieved overnight. The gradual improvements that occur will seem normal and natural, as indeed they will be. I have taught these methods to college students, many of whom significantly raised their grade point averages in the same term in which they were taking the self-hypnosis course.

If studying blocks have applied to particular areas of study, such as mathematics, you will have a lot of catching up to do because you have probably avoided even thinking about mathematics for some time. But with the diligent application of proper procedures, the ability to effectively study will gradually develop, accompanied by greater enjoyment of studying. As you get better at something, you enjoy doing it more.

Improving Concentration and Memory

Very few people are satisfied with their memory. They go through life complaining about their poor memory without realizing that memory can be improved. It can be, and it is important for you to understand that there is nothing wrong with you or your equipment. The problem is in how you have been using that equipment. This assumes that you are not taking drugs that interfere with your mental ability, and that you have no medical problems that could influence your concentration and memory.

Assuming that you are basically normal, you can put aside any beliefs that you were born with a terrible memory or that you just don't have what it takes to be able to concentrate on anything you want to. The fact is, there just is not that much difference between the abilities of normal, healthy adults. There are, of course, some differences between people and the abilities they are born with, but those differences are minimal and can be overcome with proper application and effort. You have heard the tale about the tortoise and the hare, about how the tortoise won the race against the much faster rabbit through determination and sustained effort. You, too, can "win the race" by using the methods and techniques presented here.

There are many books on the subject of memory improvement. Most are presentations of mnemonic devices, or memory aids. (An excellent book on memory improvement, from the standpoint of mnemonic techniques, is Furst's *Stop Forgetting*.) Any technique that is based on sound principles will help *if there are no subconscious blocks to better memory*. It is with autoquestioning that we determine whether or not such subconscious blocks do exist. If they do, self-hypnosis and suggestion will clear the way for improvement in both memory and concentration.

Memory improvement is accompanied by better concentration ability, and vice versa. This is because memory and concentration are closely related. They work in tandem, so improvement in one leads to improvement in the other.

An important ingredient in good concentration and memory is relaxation. There is only a given amount of energy available to you at any given time. If much of that energy is being expended on tension and anxiety, there is just that much less energy available for positive mental functions. It is a common mistake to think that good concentration must be accompanied by tensing up, by wrinkling the brow and really poring over something in order to concentrate on it. But concentration is better when you are not tensing up.

One of the single most important considerations is what you consciously and subconsciously believe about yourself. If you could at this moment change both parts of your mind to believe that you have a fantastic memory and ability to concentrate, then you would have. Unfortunately, changing beliefs is not that easy. You have heard said often enough that "with belief you can do anything." But *it is the believing that is hard*. Most of what you will be doing as you improve your mental abilities centers on changing your beliefs about yourself and your abilities.

One of the first categories of negative beliefs you must overcome are those that have been formed in relation to your own past experiences. Just because your memory and concentration have not been good in the past does not mean that they have to be that way. If you really want to do it, you are going to completely change your ability to concentrate and remember things.

We often inherit negative beliefs about our abilities from our parents. Not genetically, but through observing them and the examples they set. For instance, if both of your parents had poor concentration and memory, then you may have formed the subconscious belief that you, too, should be limited in such abilities. Identification plays a strong role in this sort of attitude formation.

Another category of experience that contributes to self-image is that of communication with others. People, including parents and teachers, sometimes make unfortunate remarks about another's abilities. Ill-timed remarks such as "Can't you concentrate on anything?" or "You'd forget your head if it wasn't connected" can lead to the development of negative imprints about mental abilities.

Even in the absence of specific remarks, the expectations and opinions of others are communicated to us. We know from research that a teacher's opinion of a student can influence that student's schoolwork and even his or her scores on intelligence tests. So if certain key people think that a person has poor memory or concentration, that belief is likely to be communicated to the person and contribute to a negative self-image.

Cultural beliefs also contribute to a negative self-image. As a child is growing up, many of his or her beliefs about the world are adopted— without first-hand experience—from the prevailing conventional wisdom. Many of these cultural beliefs are wrong. But even if we reject them at a conscious level, being in contact with those beliefs may still have the effect of forming imprints or being part of an identification pattern. For example, everyone has heard the expression "dumb blond." While most of us know that the color of a person's hair does not have any direct relationship to intelligence, such expressions may very well have a negative influence on the subconscious beliefs of someone with blond hair.

The subconscious self-image is so important because we are motivated to conform to it. That is, we behave in conformity with what we think we are. If a person has a negative self-image relative to concentration and memory, then the subconscious will cause concentration and memory to function poorly. This will happen no matter what we consciously "think" we believe about ourselves, and that is why the negative beliefs must be changed in order to free concentration and memory to function naturally.

Guilt can also cause poor memory. It is uncommon, but the subconscious can reject the idea of having a good memory or concentration because of guilt feelings. When guilt is the source of the dysfunction, it is sometimes because the subconscious equates good memory with boasting or showing-off behavior.

To create a better mental reality, begin avoiding all negative references to yourself and your ability to concentrate and remember. Every time you make a statement such as "I have a terrible memory" you are contributing to the very condition you want to change. It always sounds easy to just decide to no longer say negative things about oneself. But the habits of a lifetime can be highly resistant to change, and we are so accustomed to making certain kinds of remarks that they often slip out without our being aware of them. So enlist the help of others with the procedure described earlier (getting others to "twiddle" you when you make a negative self-reference).

One way to get around the negative reference problem and still be realistic is by putting problems in the past tense. If you are in a conversation and the topic of memory or concentration comes up, it is perfectly permissible to say that you *used* to have a terrible memory, or that *in the past* you have had trouble concentrating. Follow this with a comment about how you are getting better. Don't tell people you have a great memory or ability to concentrate until it is true (if then). In the meantime, content yourself with statements such as "I used to have a terrible memory, but it is getting better."

Form a positive image of yourself being the way you intend to be. Use your imagination to picture yourself remembering things in ways and situations that have been a problem for you in the past. Imagine yourself sitting down to take a test and the answers are coming to you quickly and easily, and you are feeling very relaxed and calm. Or see yourself encountering someone on the street whom you have not seen for years, and the person's name comes to you easily and quickly.

For concentration, form a picture of yourself as a person who is able to block out distractions and concentrate on whatever you choose. Imagine yourself in situations where other people are complimenting you on your good memory and concentration. They can be strangers or people known to you, parents, teachers from your past, or anyone whose opinion you value. It is also beneficial to imagine that you are overhearing conversation between other people who are praising your abilities. Just imagine that you accidentally overhear the conversation, and that the people doing the talking don't know that you can hear them.

Being interested in a subject is one of the easiest ways to assure easy concentration and recall. Very few people have the superhuman strength (or desire to punish themselves) necessary to spend long periods of time concentrating on something that is boring and uninteresting. On the other hand, any subject or project that is interesting, fun, and meaningful is relatively easy to concentrate on.

Getting interested in a subject may seem impossible at first, but developing an ability to make almost anything interesting is in itself a worthwhile skill. To do this, formulate suggestions that the subject matter is important to you, that it is interesting and valuable, and that knowing about the subject will be fun. Also develop suggestions that you will develop more insight into ways that the subject matter is relevant to you and your life.

Form a "want" list of specific behaviors by writing a list of the things you want to be able to do. Just saying that you want better concentration and memory is all well and good, but it is not enough. You need to know more specifically just exactly what "good concentration" and "good memory" really mean. Ask yourself now, what are you going to be doing when you are concentrating the way you want to? Is your mind going to stick to the task at hand? Is the time going to pass quickly? Are you going to be thinking of relevant questions as you concentrate? Are you going to be getting more and more interested in the subject of your concentration as you get further into it? Use these ideas and any others that are pertinent to your own concepts of concentration to spell out specifically what concentration means to you.

Now do the same thing with memory. Just what does "having a good memory" mean to you in behavioral terms? Does it mean being introduced to several people at once and remembering their names and faces? Does it mean being less likely to forget errands or appointments? As in the case of concentration, write down the list of behaviors that mean "good memory" to you.

Once you have completed your want list of behaviors for better concentration and memory, you can easily convert the list into suggestions. With a few minor changes, an "I want" statement can be converted to an "I am" or "I am becoming" suggestion. As an example, let's say that you included the following statement in your "want" list:

"I want to be able to hear a person's name once and remember it."

Now you can convert this "want" statement to a suggestion by using the general format for a formal suggestion presented in the previous chapter:

"Every day, in every way, I am getting better and better at remembering a person's name after hearing it just once."

Most people find that the regular practice of deep relaxation and self-hypnosis results in a spontaneous improvement in memory and concentration. The procedures themselves are exercises in concentration, and greater mental relaxation is a natural by-product of increased self-esteem and lower levels of anxiety. Self-communication procedures lower anxiety levels and free the mind to concentrate more positively on external events, rather than expending so much energy in analyzing every situation for threatening content.

Improving Personal Health

The subconscious mind exerts a tremendous influence on the physical functions of the body, at times controlling them completely. Because of this, beliefs and attitudes can be as influential as viruses, bacteria or physical traumas. People in voodoo cultures sometimes die simply because they believe themselves to be cursed. When autopsies have been performed on such victims, no biological pathology has been found. The victims should not have died, but they did because they believed they would. Faith healers sometimes demonstrate phenomena that are currently unexplainable in medical terms, and hospital psychiatric wards house patients who have complex and painful symptoms with no discernible organic cause. Physicians with years of clinical practice find that some patients are cured solely because they believe in the healing abilities of their doctors.

Curing an illness or healing an injury is not something done *to* you, but something that occurs *within* you. Medical treatment can seldom be said to actually "cure" anyone. Drugs, physical manipulations (such as setting a broken bone), surgery, and medical advice are helpful and often necessary in allowing the body to heal. But technically speaking, the body (including the mind) must ultimately heal itself.

Medical researchers are finding that suggestion can cure or alleviate many pathological conditions. Benign tumors have disappeared with the application of nothing more than suggestion, and malignant breast tumors in women have been reduced to one-fourth their original size as a result of suggestion. I have been involved in several situations in which the positive results of hypnotic suggestions given to seriously ill patients have left hospital staff members scratching their heads in amazement.

As important as mental factors are to health, you must not make the mistake of thinking that the methods presented in this book can take the place of medical treatment. To withhold from oneself the advantages of modern medical science is foolish at best, suicide at worst. When a disease or other pathological condition exists, self-communication techniques should be thought of as an aid to medical treatment.

The application of proper suggestions can enhance and hasten the beneficial effects of medical treatment. Such suggestions may be of a general nature when there exist no subconscious blocks to healing. When such blocks are found to exist through autoquestioning, suggestions can be formulated for eliminating those blocks.

One of the most important concepts related to good health has to do with personal responsibility. You are participating in your own health or illness at all times, and there is a direct relationship between your awareness of this concept and the overall state of your health. Do not make the mistake of thinking that the mind and body are two separate entities, as if they were two unconnected levels of existence. Mind and body are inextricably joined together in their functioning and cannot be considered totally independent of one another. Each influences the other, sometimes in ways that seem mysterious and beyond comprehension.

The effectiveness of belief, or suggestion, is illustrated in cases involving placebos. A *placebo* is a relatively inert ingredient, such as sugar, put into a capsule and dressed up to look like medicine. Or it might be something like a saline solution, which has virtually no effect on the body, injected with a hypodermic needle. Whatever its form, the basic idea of a placebo is that the recipient believes he is receiving something that will have an effect on him. If the expected effect does occur, it can be attributed to the recipient's belief, not to any inherent qualities of the placebo itself.

Drug addicts on methadone maintenance programs have received saline solutions instead of methadone and experienced no withdrawal symptoms until they discovered they were not receiving methadone. Patients have experienced a complete disappearance of severe pain when given a placebo which they believed to be a powerful pain killer. Research participants have had fewer colds when they received a placebo they were told was vitamin C.

Psychosomatic control is another area in which we can see the powerful interaction between mind and body. People have learned to voluntarily control such functions as heart rate, muscle tension, sweatgland activity, skin temperature, and a wide range of internal physical states. These are all things that were once considered to be beyond the range of voluntary control.

Many more examples could be cited that illustrate the interconnection between mind and body, but what has been presented should be sufficient to convince you that you can significantly influence the state of your health. Self-hypnotic suggestion and autoquestioning are proven methods for doing this. They are not intended to minimize the role of the physician or other health professionals engaged in medical treatment. These methods can be used in conjunction with medical treatment when such treatment is necessary, and they can be used to decrease the need for such treatment by helping you become, and stay, healthier.

Any of the sources of dysfunction can contribute to the onset of pathological conditions, with guilt in strong contention as the number one source. It is highly unlikely that the subconscious orders a particular disease in the same way that one would order a shirt from a mail order house. It is more likely that the subconscious allows the normal powers of resistance, the immunological system, to be lowered. The result of this is that the host organism catches the first appropriate disease that comes along.

Negative ideas and beliefs about health can be as contagious as bacteria or a virus. For example, many people *know* they are going to catch at least one or two bad colds every year and the flu at least once. And sure enough, they do. I know a number of people who used to be like this, but who broke the pattern by changing their beliefs. Some of them have not had a cold or a bout with the flu for years.

Sometimes there are subconscious reasons for getting sick that have no direct relationship to health per se. Illness can bring attention and sympathy from others, and a minor illness such as a bad cold or the flu can provide an excuse to stay in bed and rest for a few days. Getting sick can obviously be a form of self-punishment, and it can also be a way of punishing someone else. It can also be a way of avoiding success.

To help overcome the many reasons for being sick, it is helpful to begin with a list of reasons for being healthy. This might sound silly at first, but it is often surprisingly difficult to think of very many specific reasons for being healthy. Writing this list of reasons will require some thinking and effort, but it is important. Your reasons must be your own, and they must be attuned to your own interests, values and life situation. Write as many reasons as you can think of, and make up your mind that there are no good reasons for not being healthy.

The deep relaxation you will be practicing in conjunction with self-hypnosis is itself a powerful aid to health. It combats stress, which has been found to be a culprit in many illnesses, and it has been shown that the regular practice of deep relaxation has a good effect on the immunological system.

Both verbal and nonverbal suggestions are effective in health improvement. However, experience has shown that nonverbal suggestion—imagery—tends to be somewhat more effective than verbal suggestions. Before we consider suggestive images, here are some verbal suggestions that have proved very effective for surgical experiences. Patients who are preparing for surgery can help themselves immensely by applying the proper suggestions. The application of suggestions should begin as soon as it is known that surgery is necessary, and should be continued through the post-operative period of recuperation. Each situation has its own requirements, which can be determined through common sense and autoquestioning, but the following suggestions will give you the basic idea:

"I will relax while I am in the hospital, and will enjoy the attention I receive there."

"I will experience very little discomfort before, during, and after surgery."

"Bleeding will be minimal."

"Shots and other medical procedures will not hurt or disturb me."

"I have confidence in my doctors and medical staff, and in my own recuperative powers."

"The surgical operation will create very little shock to my physical systems."

"Every day, in every way, I am becoming healthier and healthier."

"I will not be upset by, or pay any attention to, remarks or comments made during surgery."

These are very general suggestions. More specific suggggestiions can be tailored to fit the exact circumstances, but the suggestions should include the concepts of relaxation, rapid recovery and healing, elevated pain thresholds, reduced shock to the system, and reduced bleeding. The verbal suggestions can be reinforced with appropriate imagery.

Imagery suggestions must have positive expectations. Construct your mental images in such a way that they represent the condition that you want to exist. Images can use symbolic representations of bodily parts and processes. This eliminates the necessity of detailed medical, physical or biological knowledge. And you can incorporate movement or change in your image model.

Let us say, for instance, that you "feel a cold coming on." You will first need a symbolic representation of the cold that is trying to get started, and a symbol for the processes in your body that can repel it. Imagine the invader (the cold) as being a weak little gremlin that is trying to get in, but is being kept out by a troop of alert, fast and strong cavalry soldiers (your immunological system). As they repel the unsuccessful invader they are keeping your nose dry, your throat clear, and your entire body functioning normally and healthily.

For dealing with something such as a wart, imagine that it is a weak little plant trying to grow in your skin. There are numerous little workers building a brick wall around the bottom of the wart, sealing it off from the rest of your system. Since the wart can only feed on your system, the brick wall is isolating it. Without nourishment it will wither and die, leaving the skin smooth and healthy where the wart was. Actually imagine the wart withering and dying because its roots cannot get through the brick wall. It is also helpful to imagine the skin (where the wart is) being smooth and normal—"wartless."

For dealing with high blood pressure, imagine that your heart is a large, well lubricated pump that is pumping fluid (blood) through a network of pipes (veins and arteries). See the pump operating smoothly and efficiently, and the fluid moving through the pipes in a natural flow without resistance. Above the pump is a large gauge which shows the pressure (blood pressure). Each time you practice this imagery, imagine that the pressure is a little lower.

If you are facing something as serious as, say, cancer, develop a model in which there are several vigorous knights in armor. They are mounted on horseback and riding through your system, spearing cancer cells with their lances and throwing them aside to be eliminated from the body in urine and feces. As in all other cases, this is not a substitute for medication or other medical treatment; it is one of your ways of participating in your treatment.

These are just a few of the examples that could be given, but they should give you a feel for constructing and using image suggestions. You will be able to construct any number of variations for your own applications. If you have a problem whose nature you do not understand, ask your physician or dentist to give you a simple explanation of what is going on. All you need are the basic concepts so you can develop a model for your image suggestions.

There are several criteria to keep in mind when you construct image suggestions. If you are combatting a particular problem, always envision the invader or source of the problem as being weak and confused, and the treatment or defender of your system as being strong and powerful. The defender should be aggressive and eager to do battle with the invader, and so vast as to overwhelm any and all invaders. Always include a method of getting the defeated invaders out of your system, such as being flusheddd from your body through your normal elimination processes. Toward the end of each image, see yourself being healthy and whole, reaching your goals in life.

If you are in good health with no specific problems to deal with, you will want to work with images for staying that way. See yourself radiating good health and energy, moving smoothly, with all limbs functioning naturally and easily. Picture your heart as a well-oiled pump, pumping slowly and easily without effort. Imagine your lungs, throat and nasal passage clear of any obstructions or foreign elements, working efficiently and healthily. Work in this way with any parts of your body you want to pay special attention to.

You will recall that formal, verbal suggestions can be applied by repeating them a specific number of times just before starting your self-hypnosis practice. The transcript that follows is included here to give you an example of how you can apply your image suggestions. It is from the "image rehearsal" section of my *Better Health* hypnotic induction tape. Assume that you have completed your deep relaxation and deepening procedures, and are now in the image rehearsal stage of your self-hypnotic induction:

Now continue to drift even more deeply into the relaxation and picture yourself on a beautiful, high mountain peak. You are safe and serene on your mountain peak, because this is your "peak of health." You are on the highest peak, and there is a beautiful panorama of nature around you in every direction. You feel at one with nature, with all of your bodily systems functioning in a natural and healthy way. Your oneness with nature makes you feel healthy and whole.

There is a small spring flowing from your mountain peak. This is the wellspring of health and happiness, and you take a sip of water from it. As you swallow the pleasant tasting water, you can feel the essence of wholeness and health flowing into your body. You can feel the warm glow of health coursing throughout your body . . . your body and mind are absorbing the healthy essence from the spring water, just like a sponge. It is giving your body the strength to heal and cure anything that is not right.

Continue to enjoy your "peak of health," and picture yourself being healthy and well, free of disease, and full of energy and healthy vitality.

Now picture yourself doing well in life, reaching your goals and enjoying your success. This is one of your many reasons for being and staying healthy.

Now imagine each of your family members, one at a time. Each of them is healthy and well, and your relationships with them and all of the people around you are wholesome and meaningful. This is another of your many reasons for being and staying healthy and well.

As you continue to enjoy your relaxation on your peak of health, think about all of the other reasons you have for being healthy. Think about each one with the intention of staying healthy for these reasons.

Continue to enjoy your relaxation on your peak of health and think about how you are participating in your good health. Think about how your health is your own responsibility, and feel good about how you accept that responsibility. You are a responsible and worthwhile person, and you are enjoying participating in your own health. You are resolving to like yourself better and better every day. As part of this, you are becoming better and better at expressing your emotions, instead of bottling them up inside of you. Every day you are becoming—emotionally and physically— healthier and healthier.

Continue to enjoy your deep relaxation on your peak of health, and practice your own healthy images . . . Continue with this until it is time to terminate the session.

Now it is time to end this practice session. All of the positive, healthy images and thoughts you have practiced in this session are your reality . . . the positive, healthy images are your reality.

When I count to three you will return to functional alertness. You will feel relaxed and mentally alert, filled with new health and vitality.

Starting up now, one . . . becoming more alert, two . . . three, open your eyes, move your legs and arms, and feel the increased health and vitality.

As you go through these exercises, remember not to try to make anything happen, and don't try to keep anything from happening. These exercises are, in one sense, just like taking medicine. Just one dose may not have a noticeable effect, but regularly taking the medicine—in this case, practicing self-hypnosis and suggestion application—has a cumulative effect that brings about the desired results.

Try to get in from one to three practice sessions a day, depending on your needs. If you are in good health with no particular problems on which you need to work, you may only need to work with better health suggestions once a week or so. This assumes that you are practicing your self-hypnosis on a daily basis but applying other kinds of suggestions when not dealing with health-related suggestions. If you enter a period of increased stress, of if you suspect that you have been exposed to something contagious, increase your frequency of health-related practice.

Overcoming Shyness

Shyness is very common, widespread, and universal. Over 40 percent of the general population of America claims to suffer from shyness, either occasionally or most of the time. A common misconception about shyness is that women are more shy than men. This does not seem to be the case; research has found that shyness exists about evenly in men and women.

Shyness means different things to different people. Generally speaking, to be shy is to be afraid of people, usually because for some reason they are emotionally threatening. You are no doubt well aware of your own responses to this kind of threat from others. The typical symptoms include a racing pulse, a pounding heart, a noticeable increase in perspiration, butterflies in the stomach, blushing, and so on. These are all symptoms of emotional arousal and indicate that the biological system is getting ready to run or fight. The shy person usually has little choice but to run, either escaping into silence or from the situation altogether. This kind of flight contributes further to the diminishment of self-esteem, which was low to begin with.

Everyone feels fear in some situations, of course, but the shy person is one who repeatedly fails to express himself. He or she may be frightened by strangers, authority figures, members of the opposite sex who represent potential intimate encounters, and so on. Asking someone to dance is difficult, and speaking up in a group may be too terrifying to even consider. The shy person also finds it difficult to be spontaneous most of the time, and may even become embarrassed when alone while recalling some past mistake or social gaff.

It is as if the shy person has within herself both a prisoner and a guard. The prisoner part of the self wants to interact, to be spontaneous and have fun with others, and to have friends. But the guard part of her says "no, that is too dangerous or frightening," and the prisoner usually complies with the dictates of the guard.

Life itself provides countless models of this prisoner-guard relationship. Parents, teachers, authorities of all types, all must—at least at times—play the role of guard to keep children or other adults in line. Shy people are those who have strongly internalized the "guard" role which keeps many of their social desires and needs safely locked up inside of them.

There are five basic reasons for shyness, any one of which can produce shyness, and they can exist in various combinations. The first one is a *fear of people*. More specifically, this is a fear that others will see our weaknesses and inadequacies, and that they will judge us harshly and ridicule those weaknesses. If this actually happens it is a painful experience for any human being and can easily lead to the avoidance of situations in which it is possible.

The second reason is *low self-confidence and a poor self-image*. This is strongly related to the first reason. If a person does not believe she is weak and inadequate, she will not be unduly fearful of exposure.

A *lack of social skills* can also contribute to shyness. Some people do not know how to initiate or maintain a conversation, or how to deal with even mildly awkward situations. However, it is probable in many cases that this lack of social skills is the product of shyness, not its cause.

Another reason for shyness is *labeling*. Parents, teachers, relatives and playmates can often be cruel and insensitive to the needs of a growing, developing child. The child who is going through what would otherwise be a temporary stage of shyness may be the butt of unkind treatment and receive the label "shy." Most children go through shy stages in their development, get labeled "shy" for a while, then grow out of it. But for some the label sticks. It has been demonstrated time and again that attaching a label to a person tends to shape that person's behavior in a way that conforms to the label.

The fifth and final reason has to do with *conflicts between subconscious needs*. All humans have the need, or a combination of needs, for contact with other humans, and for love and support from others. But we also have a need to avoid pain. If early experiences of being in contact with others are painful enough, conflict develops between the need to avoid pain and the associative needs. The need for social contact will drive the person to associate with others, but the need to avoid pain seriously qualifies and limits that association.

For the most part, what has been presented so far refers to *public shyness*. This is the kind of observable, obvious timidity that we ordinarily think of when talking about shyness. However, there is another kind of shyness that is less obvious from the standpoint of observable behavior. Called *private shyness,* it is externally hidden by extraverted, aggressive or overbearing behavior. Not all extraverts are hiding private shyness, but it is sometimes the case.

Whether shyness is private or public, situational or general, it can be conquered. But there is one final point to be made before considering how to overcome shyness. Shy people tend to spend entirely too much time and effort analyzing their every behavior and thought. This overemphasis of self-analysis is always of the conscious sort and needs to be brought under control as a first step in overcoming shyness. Anyone suffering from shyness has to stop taking himself so seriously and quit being overly concerned about *why* he did such-and-such or *why* he said what he said. Autoquestioning to determine the sources of this personal and social dysfunction is necessary and acceptable, but the constant, conscious analysis has to go.

From this point on I will assume that you, the reader, are suffering from shyness that you want to overcome. To change, you will make changes in two areas. First, you will change the way you think about yourself and about your shyness. Second, you will make changes in your behavior.

The autoquestioning methods for inquiring into sources of shyness are similar to all of the applications presented earlier. You are looking for imprints or identification factors, probably dating back to your early childhood, that contribute to your shyness. When you have obtained enough information about the causative factors, formulate suggestions for application any time, but especially during your self-hypnosis practice. The formal suggestions can be patterned after earlier examples in this text, tailored according to what you learn in your autoquestioning.

To form image suggestions, begin by constructing a positive mental image of yourself as you want to be. This ideal image of yourself will be a blueprint for the changes you want to occur. It can take many forms and shapes, but the underlying theme will always be *yourself as you want to be*. Due to the nature of shyness, your image suggestions will, for the most part, necessitate movement and action. This puts them into the category of image rehearsal as discussed earlier. For example:

> Imagine yourself arriving at a large party or other social gathering. You don't know anyone present. As you enter, a group of people near the door turn to look at you and one of them asks, "Who are you?" You turn to that person, make good eye contact, calmly introduce yourself, and are almost immediately engaged in warm, friendly conversation with the whole group.

In this kind of image rehearsal you orchestrate the images in your imagination to rehearse how you want to behave. Here is another example:

> Imagine yourself in a classroom in which you are one of the students. A question occurs to you, so you raise your hand and ask it. Your voice is calm and firm, you do not feel any anxiety, and you go through the whole procedure as easily and calmly as saying hello to your best friend.

Be sure to include positive reinforcement from others in some of your image rehearsals. Imagine that others—such as parents, teachers from your past, or contemporaries whose opinions you value—are complimenting you for not being shy and for being so natural, spontaneous and outgoing in your behavior.

You undoubtedly have certain things that are your biggest problems related to shyness. Make a list of those situations or types of people that are most frightening to you and construct image rehearsals in which they are not a problem. Be honest with yourself as you list your scary things, and don't leave any of them out when you make up imaginary situations in which you conquer them.

If you have any difficulty in knowing how you want to behave in social situations, you probably need to do some observing. You may feel that you have already spent too much of your life watching instead of acting, but if you have trouble constructing the behaviors you want for yourself, try being more specific in your observations. When you see someone getting along the way you would like to, observe him closely and try to catalog the details of his behavior. What does he do with his eyes (where does he look when he is talking, when he is listening)? How often and when does he smile or laugh? What does he do with his hands? How does he stand or sit? And so on. You will notice, if you haven't already, that everyone has a little different style of interacting. This makes watching others a rich source of communication techniques. But make sure you do not allow your observations to be an excuse for not participating in social exchanges.

Another thing you will want to do is make a "want" list of specific behaviors. The procedure for doing this, for forming suggestions from the "want" list, and for including suggestions in a self-hypnotic induction are all spelled out in detail in the parts of this chapter dealing with concentration and memory and better health. Refer back to that material as a guideline for rounding out your program to overcome shyness. Here are some samples of formal suggestions that may prove helpful to you:

"I am more than adequate and equal."

"I am intelligent, attractive, and worthwhile."

"Every day, in every way, I am getting better and better at relating to others."

"Every day, in every way, I am finding it easier and easier to be outgoing and friendly."

"Every day I am talking to more and more people and enjoying it."

"I am free to be the person I consciously want to be."

Tenacity and perseverance are required to achieve any real degree of success at anything. Stick with your program of self-improvement, and do not be afraid to make changes on the basis of newly acquired knowledge about yourself. If blocks to acceptance are removed, and the subconscious is allowed to accept suggestions, there is no way the mind can resist a properly formulated suggestion if it is repeated often enough and long enough.

In other words, *you can do it with self-hypnosis!* The techniques required for success have all been presented in this book. No secrets have been withheld. Thousands of people just like you have achieved success and self-improvement using these methods. And some of the earlier practitioners did not have the advantage of all of the techniques presented in this book. So use these techniques and let your light shine through.

Weight control

6

INTRODUCTION

With this weight control method you are going to control your eating and condition your body to become slender and healthy. If you follow these instructions and practice regularly you will reach your goals more easily than you ever dreamed possible.

There is ample evidence that an awareness of the power of suggestion has existed since the dawning of civilization. Over the last century this ancient knowledge has been researched, updated, tested, and verified through practical use. In essence, what we now know is the culmination of over three thousand years of knowledge and experience.

By following the methods and techniques presented here, you can gain immense benefits from that vast history. These are powerful methods that can change your attitudes and values about overeating and being overweight.

It is your mind, not your stomach, that drives you to overeat. Your mind also has a profound effect on your bodily processes, processes that can determine whether your body burns food as energy, passes it out of the body as waste, or turns it into fat cells. By changing your mind, you will change both your eating habits and your bodily processes. You will achieve this change within yourself by regularly practicing the exercises and procedures outlined in this book.

Medical Considerations

As your attitudes and feelings about food begin to change, you will find yourself eating differently from the way you have eaten in the past. This makes the state of your health, and the foods you should or should not eat, important considerations. These can only be determined by your physician. You should have a medical examination and consult with your doctor before starting any kind of weight loss program.

Knowledge of Foods

Different foods have different nutritional values. You should learn the carbohydrate, protein, and caloric values of foods and follow your doctor's advice in the selection of foods that you intend to eat. You will find basic information about foods, as well as where to find further information, in the pages that follow.

Relaxed Attitude

Let yourself lose weight! Don't be overly anxious and wear out your scales watching for every lost ounce. The more relaxed your attitude about your weight, the quicker these procedures will be effective. It is assumed that you have read the previous chapters of this book and know that you must avoid triggering the Law of Reversed Effect. If it happened that you were so eager to get started losing weight that you started at this chapter without reading the earlier parts of this book, stop. Go back and read from the beginning because this chapter requires the knowledge presented in earlier chapters.

Time Factors

You are eager, you want to get rid of your extra weight, and you want to do it yesterday (I've been there myself, so I know how you feel). You are just going to have to cool it. Give your mental exercises time to work. The time required varies with each person. For some people, weight loss begins immediately and is quite dramatic. For others it takes longer. Sometimes several weeks elapse before the effects become noticeable. As compensation, keep this in mind: The slower the weight loss, the more permanent it tends to be.

The Psychosonic Rhythm

(These instructions apply only if you have my hypnotic weight control tape. If you do not, skip to the next heading, "When to Practice.")

The background rhythm on the tape is scientifically based on a great deal of research. It contributes significantly to the success of the tape. Some people like the rhythm immediately, whereas others have to accustom themselves to it. Don't be alarmed if the rhythm seems to recur in your thoughts when you are not listening to the tape; this is desirable.

Side 1 of the tape contains both the rhythm and verbal suggestions for weight control. You should start listening to Side 1 and continue using that side of the tape until it feels natural to switch to Side 2.

Side 2 contains only the rhythm. There are no instructions or suggestions on Side 2. Begin to use Side 2 only when you are sufficiently practiced with Side 1 to "think" your way through the hypnotic induction (with Side 2, you are practicing *self*-hypnosis). Even after you are regularly practicing self-hypnosis with Side 2, use Side 1 once in a while to get the benefits of hetero-hypnosis.

The approximately two-minute period at the end of Side 1 is the time for image rehearsal. Use that period as you are instructed on the tape and in this book—it is important. You will be cheating yourself if you leave image rehearsal out of your practice.

When to Practice

The instructions presented earlier about when to practice apply equally to self-hypnotic weight control. The best time of day or night to practice varies from person to person. (Remember to wait at least an hour after eating before practicing self-hypnosis. This does not apply to autoquestioning or other forms of suggestion application, just deep relaxation and self-hypnosis.) You may have to experiment to determine the best time for your practice. Generally, the time that feels right, is right. Practicing once a day is adequate, three times a day is maximum. For many people, practicing just before going to sleep at night is best, while others prefer early morning or the middle of the day. Experience will tell you which is best for you.

Keep An Open Mind

Pay particular attention to Parts 3 and 4 as you read this chapter. The exercises in Parts 3 and 4, in conjunction with your self-hypnosis practice, will make it easy for you to stick to your eating decisions. Parts 1 and

2 of this chapter will give you insight into the "why" of overeating, and information about food values and eating habits.

Never lose sight of the fact that you must reduce your eating if you are going to reduce your weight. Anyone who tells you that you can lose weight and continue to eat a lot of fattening glop is pulling your leg. The weight control method presented here does not determine for you what you can or cannot eat—you must do that for yourself.

There are plenty of diets around, and most of them work if you stick to them. Which is precisely the problem for most overweight people: They can't stick to any diet for very long! That is where this method comes in. It will make it easy for you to stick to any eating program you consciously decide on. Follow the instructions and practice regularly, and you will find it easy to eat sensibly for the rest of your life.

I want you to lose weight, and I would like to hear from you when you do. As I am writing this, I have a letter on my desk that I received this morning. It is from a lady who has lost fifteen pounds in what she refers to as "no time at all." She finished her letter with: "Thanks so much for understanding and helping people who have a hard time losing weight."

Believe me, I do understand, and I want *you* to experience the freedom from overeating that I and several thousand others have discovered through this method. (I originally developed the method for my own weight problem. With it I dropped from just under 250 pounds to my present weight of 170.)

I know from personal experience the pain and penalties of being overweight. For years I was a slave to food, constantly growing more and more desperate because I was unable to stop overeating. As my girth expanded, I became more frustrated and unhappy. Although I was trained in psychology, none of the methods I had learned was doing any good in the area of weight control—for myself or anyone else.

In desperation, I began to search for answers outside the normal realms of academic, experimental, and clinical psychology. As I searched, I began to get insights from anthropology, sociology, and religion. I even profited from such unlikely subjects as history and philosophy. Once I began to open my mind to the truth, I found that the secret to weight control (and other forms of self-control) was really no secret at all. Many of the great people of history knew the secret of inner control and tried to spread the word. Their teachings were often ignored or misunderstood.

All too often our vision is narrowed by quasi-religious thinking, a form of fact-oriented mind set that blinds us to any idea that does not fit within our narrow sphere of preconditioned "knowledge." The self-appointed guardians of the truth—and I must confess I was one of them for a long time—scoff at anything that cannot be measured with gauges or dials. They blithely ignore the fact that many known qualities of humans cannot be measured, yet those qualities exist just as surely as you and I exist. Not many would argue that love, anger, faith, creativity, imagination, or happiness—to name just a few—do not exist. They do exist, even though they cannot be measured. So, too, are there other unmeasurable qualities in our lives that are extremely useful, sometimes even necessary. If these qualities (I will be more specific later) seem mysterious, it is only because we do not yet understand how they work.

I am telling you all this because, if you have not already, I want you to open your mind to greater possibilities within yourself, greater possibilities perhaps than you have ever considered before. The fact that you have not been able to do something in the past (like lose weight and keep it off) does not mean that you *can*not do it. It only means that you *have* not done it. I think you know that. Otherwise, you would not be reading this now. If you do find yourself burdened by negative thoughts about your ability to change, that simply indicates that you have some *un*learning to do.

Unlearning is not much more difficult than learning if it is approached properly. Everyone has had some experience of learning to do something improperly. When it was pointed out that we were doing it improperly (whatever "it" happened to be), and how to do it correctly, we unlearned the improper method and learned the correct way of doing it. Then the task became much easier, perhaps possibly for the first time. The same is true of weight control specifically, and of dealing with ourselves generally.

Most people try to lose weight with the wrong methods. Those incorrect methods must be unlearned and replaced by correct methods which make weight control much easier and more natural. Our American system of education teaches us (sometimes) how to deal with *things,* but we learn nothing in school about how to control ourselves. Thus it turns out that we can earn enough degrees and diplomas to plaster a wall but remain functionally illiterate about the techniques of inner control.

The techniques of inner control that you will be practicing may seem strange at first. They may even seem weak. Remember, we are taught to manipulate things and are accustomed to manipulating material, tangible objects. The dynamics of the subconscious mind are different, so when we first start working with the techniques of inner control, the initial impression may be that they are weak and ineffective. After all, how can anything work without buttons, switches, levers, or pills? If you don't plug it into a wall outlet or put gas in it, what makes it go?

Let me assure you that these methods and techniques of inner control are far from weak and ineffective. If you will apply yourself to learn the concepts presented here, if you will put forth the effort to use these methods, and if you will stick with it for at least six weeks, you are going to discover an inner force that is far stronger and more powerful than most external, material forces. The human mind may seem like a small thing (especially at those times when we have trouble remembering what day it is), but it is powerful.

Examples of this small-but-powerful principle abound in nature. Consider the atom, for example. Atoms are definitely in the category of Small Things. Too small to be seen with the most powerful electron microscopes, an atom's diminutive size cannot even be imagined by the human mind. Yet, by splitting just one atom, a force of inconceivable magnitude is released. The atom bomb is one example of the nuclear fission that results from the splitting of atoms.

In a different kind of way, the inner forces of the human mind are equally powerful. Once we know how to "split the atom"—when we can release the immense forces within us—we are harnessing a power that makes virtually anything possible. It is that power which makes permanent, relatively easy weight control within the reach of anyone who is willing to learn and apply these techniques.

PART 1: THE MIND— CONSCIOUS AND SUBCONSCIOUS FUNDAMENTALS

The subconscious is the most powerful part of the mind. It is from the subconscious that all self-control comes. Because the subconscious can function on its own, without conscious awareness, we often have subconscious beliefs, desires, and motivations that run counter to conscious beliefs or desires. Eating is a case in point. We may want very strongly (consciously) to stop overeating and lose weight. But if we subconsciously want or need to overeat, no amount of consciously directed attempts at control will stop us from overeating.

Imprints That Cause Overeating

Since eating is our major area of interest here, let me give some examples of imprints related to eating and how they create problems. Obviously, eating is an activity that we begin shortly after birth and continue for

171

the rest of our lives. All of us usually eat several times a day and this frequency increases the likelihood that eating-related imprints will be formed. Eating is also one of the few things we absolutely have to do, and we have built-in biological mechanisms to insure that we do eat when we need to (when we can). These mechanisms are so strong they will make it impossible to think about anything but food if we get hungry enough. So it is not too surprising that eating and food are the subjects of so many subconscious imprints.

Most overeaters have problem imprints that belong in one or more of the following categories: love, attention, reward, compensation, guilt, or fear. Remember, these imprints are in the subconscious area of the mind. One is not likely to be consciously aware of their existence except through indirect evidence. So don't mislead yourself with thoughts such as, "Shoot, I don't have none of them things, I just eat 'cause I like food." It is really these negative imprints that provide the answer to why some people like food so much that they are willing to make their lives miserable for it.

Love-related imprints

Every human being needs love, whether he or she will admit it or not. For most of us, the first and strongest experience of loving and being loved was with our mothers. And what did Mother do first and most often (besides change diapers!) when we were tiny? She fed us. So it is, or was, not unnatural to subconsciously develop a connection between the act of eating and love.

This is why, later in life, we often eat when we feel the need for love. If the eating is prompted by a subconscious, love-related imprint, we are not likely to be consciously aware that what we are really needing is love. And it is a fact that *you can never get enough of what you don't really want*. In the case of a love-related imprint, it is not the food that is wanted, but love. The distinction is never clear to the subconscious, so you keep eating and eating. You are trying to get a satisfaction that you will never achieve from food because it is love that you really want.

Attention-related imprints

The need for attention is closely related to that of love and exists in all of us. If we don't get enough of it in the normally acceptable ways, we'll get it in some other way. Like overeating and getting fat. The tricky part here is that negative attention is better than no attention for most people. Both the act of overeating and the state of being overweight can get plenty of attention. We consciously know that it is undesirable attention, but we may subconsciously feel that it is better than no attention at all.

Not only does being overweight get attention, the act of eating is itself a form of attention. Eating can be an attempt to re-create the feelings of security and receiving attention that we experienced as infants when we were fed. It is this imprint—eating is attention and security—that motivates many overweights to pig-out when they are feeling insecure.

Reward-related imprints

Unfortunately, we live in a society that likes to reward good behavior or performance with food. When you were a child you probably got things such as ice cream cones for good behavior or as compensation for having undergone some ordeal. (When I was about five I had a tonsillectomy and was allowed to eat all the ice cream I wanted. For a couple of years afterward I kept hoping my tonsils would grow back so I could do it again. I was not very bright.)

We all have lots of experiences in which we are rewarded with food. If you did what your mother told you to do, you got a cookie (or five or ten). We eventually form reward-related imprints that make food mandatory if we do something good. This can lead to ironic situations at times, such as when we have not eaten much all day so we reward ourselves in the evening by putting away three days' worth of groceries before going to bed. I have done that more times than I care to remember.

The opposite of reward—punishment—gets associated with the absence of food. No one ever gets sent to his room *with* supper. It is always without it. You probably never got a cookie after school for tracking mud into the house. And you have never heard of an "awards *fast.*" Anyone who gets an award can also count on a banquet. One thing that has always amazed me is the relative paucity of instances in which people use withdrawal from food as punishment for subconscious guilt. It does happen, and it may be a motivating factor in anorexia (a pathological loss of appetite), but it is certainly not as common as subconsciously motivated overeating.

Compensation-related imprints

As mentioned above, compensation imprints are similar to reward imprints. The difference is that they are activated when things go wrong instead of when we do something good. Childhood accidents, illnesses, and mishaps almost always lead to goodies. A cookie here for a skinned knee, an ice cream cone there for a bruised shin, and so on. So now, if we have a bad day at the office or a run-in with a friend, we compensate ourselves with lots of food. Especially goodies. Treats!

Guilt-related imprints

Guilt-related imprints can function in either of two ways. The most obvious is when we punish ourselves by being fat. (And that is punishment!) A more subtle manifestation of this type of imprint is the need-to-please syndrome that gets triggered when we feel guilty. Most of us have had the experience many times over of being told to "Clean up your plate." (I still have this vision of several Chinese kids starving because I once threw away some mashed potatoes. I tried to make up for it later.) Through experiences such as these we learn we can please the most important people in our lives, our parents, by eating more than we really want. Eating-to-please is motivated by a complicated subconscious process that drives us to do something pleasing to others when we feel guilty about something (we are not likely to be consciously aware of the guilt). So we "clean up our plates." And the refrigerator and cupboards, while we're at it.

Fear-related imprints

There are so many ways that fear imprints can lead to overeating that it would be impossible to list them all here. Three of the more common types of fear-related imprints should give you a general understanding of how they work.

One very common fear-type of imprint has to do with sex and marital fidelity. A fat person is much less likely to be appealing to members of the opposite sex. Whether it is actually true or not, you may be subconsciously afraid that you could not resist temptation if others found you too attractive. So fat is safe and contributes to the preservation of your domestic relationships.

This is closely related to the frequently occurring situation in which a person tries to keep a mate overweight. For example, if a husband is insecure, it will be in his best interest to keep his wife fat so he won't have to worry so much about competition.

Another type of fear-related imprint has to do with health. An imprint can be formed by hearing a simple statement such as, "My, what a fat, healthy baby." If such a statement forms an imprint, there are really two imprints that get formed. The first is that fat is healthy. The second is that "unfat" is unhealthy. Because one of the strongest drives in the subconscious is the protection of the individual, this can be a very strong imprint that tells us to be fat in order to avoid being unhealthy.

A third kind of fear-related imprint has to do with social acceptance. Few things are more terrifying to human beings than isolation and social rejection. It is true that most of us are not unduly upset by an occasional rejection, perhaps even preferring it from some individuals or groups. But total or large-scale rejection is a frightening prospect. Now, one of the best ways to gain social acceptance and avoid rejection is to be good-natured and jovial. Which means *jolly*. Which goes with *fat*, right? So we again have a double imprint situation: If you are fat you are jolly and have lots of friends. If you are *not* fat you are *not* jolly and *not* liked.

Communicating with the Subconscious

By now you should be sufficiently aware of the complexities of the mind and be able to appreciate why superficial approaches to weight control do not work. Futile procedures, such as merely counting calories or consciously deciding you are going to cut down on your eating, do not get at the source of the problem. The real secret to successful, permanent weight control is *communication with the subconscious*. Or, as I have been referring to it throughout this book, self-communication.

The unlearning discussed earlier must take place at the subconscious level. Merely being consciously aware of a need or desire is not sufficient. Special techniques must be used to communicate the desired message to the subconscious level of the mind. Once you begin to communicate effectively with your subconscious—when you begin to gain subconscious acceptance of your conscious goals—you will find your whole attitude toward food changing. You will have the kind of inner control that makes it easy to say no to any food or drink because it will also be what you subconsciously want to do.

You learned about autoquestioning in Chapter 3 and suggestion in Chapter 4. Further methods and techniques of the self-communication process are presented in Part 3 of this chapter. But Part 2 comes first. In Part 2 you will read about supplementary methods that are taken, in some cases, from behavior modification theory. Other methods are tricks of the trade that will be beneficial to you, especially in the beginning when you are first learning self-communication.

You will learn how to count calories, or you may choose to count carbohydrates. Either way, you are going to eat less to lose weight. This business of eating less is much easier to monitor and control if you follow one of these two ways of evaluating food and measuring how much you eat: count calories or count grams of carbohydrate. Most people must do one or the other to lose weight because it is the only way to know how fattening a particular food is, and how much of it you want to eat.

The methods you will learn about in Part 3 will make it easy for you to stick to any diet you choose. My job is to show you how to develop subconscious agreement and make it easy for you to change your eating patterns and habits. The actual diet you choose is up to you. You are free to choose one that appeals most to you, or that conforms to the advice of your doctor.

If you already know about calories and carbohydrates, it will still be a good idea to read Part 2. Some of the "tricks of the trade" I mentioned above are scattered around in Part 2.

Part 2: FOOD AND EATING BEHAVIOR— SITUATIONAL CONTROL OF EATING

Too many people allow themselves to be convinced that they are overweight because they are weak or lack self-control. Often treated as second-class citizens, overweight people are the brunt of jokes, are denied certain kinds of jobs, and are sometimes openly embarrassed in public. This same negative attitude is sometimes found in medical clinics, where a doctor's viewpoint is that all a person has to do to lose weight is follow his doctor's advice. It never seems to occur to such people that the advice itself might be faulty or inadequate.

It is unfair to hold the overeater totally responsible for his or her eating. Research has shown that the *what, when, where,* and *how much* of eating are strongly influenced by situational control. *Situational control* means that some eating behavior is prompted by influences that exist in the situation and outside the person. Some of these external influences are out in the open and some are hidden. TV commercials that make foods extremely appealing and parental admonitions to "clean up your plate" are examples of out-in-the-open influences.

Hidden influences are more difficult to uncover, and they are all the more powerful for being hidden. Consider the forces at work in a husband-and-wife situation. What a husband eats is often controlled largely by the wife who cooks his food. Wives often want their husbands to be fat, and vice versa. (If one partner is fat and the other slender, it makes too much of a contrast for the obese partner to tolerate.) To deal with this kind of situation it is imperative that these matters be discussed with a spouse or roommate in order to clear the air. Otherwise, a great deal of resistance can come from him or her.

Here are some other hidden, external forces that prompt overeating:

A family cook who likes to cook and who feels slighted if everything is not eaten.

Business lunches where the guest is expected to take advantage of the host's hospitality, or the host is expected to keep up with the guest.

Grocery shopping when hungry or without a shopping list. Too much food is purchased, and it is too expensive to throw away.

A very active social life that brings one into frequent contact with lots of hors d'oeuvres and rich snacks.

This is just a partial list of the many possible external influences that can prompt overeating. You will have to sensitize yourself to their hidden nature and be on the alert for them in your own environment and lifestyle.

Diet Failures

The average overweight person goes on one-and-a-half diets per year and makes over fifteen major attempts to lose weight between the ages of twenty-one and fifty. Most of these attempts fail. One reason for so much failure is the reliance on prescription drugs. Although drugs will depress appetite, they cannot be used indefinitely. When use of the weight control drugs is eventually terminated, all weight that has been lost is regained. It frequently happens that, within a short time after terminating weight-controlling drugs, the person gains back more weight than was lost.

Other programs fail because they depend on fad diets of grapefruit, steak, fish, milk, cabbage, or funny foods of some sort. Not only are these diets nutritionally unsound, they also get very boring in a short time. They do not fit the normal pattern of the dieter's life.

Fasting also leads to failure. You may be able to eat nothing for two, four, even six days or longer. But research has shown that, even when people have fasted for two weeks, all of the weight lost is quickly regained when eating is resumed. This is because the body is a balanced system that will not tolerate getting out of balance by too much too quickly. So any rapid change in one direction quickly leads to a change in the other direction. The idea of fast weight loss may be appealing, but it just will not work permanently! At least, not for a normal, healthy adult. Ordinarily, the only exception to this rule occurs in cases of *alternate reality* phenomena, which will be discussed in Part 4 of this chapter.

To be effective, a weight control program must influence the subconscious factors that motivate eating behavior, and it must gradually change lifestyle in a permanent way.

Categories of Eating Behavior

Eating can be broken down into three categories of events. First, there are the *antecedents* of eating. These are conditions that occur, or exist, before you actually eat. Where you are, what you are doing, how you feel, whom you are with, and so on, just before you eat. You can significantly affect what and how much you eat by becoming aware of these antecedents and how they affect your eating.

Second, there is the *behavior* of eating. Of primary interest in this respect is how fast you eat, how long you take for meals, and what you are doing while you eat.

The third category is the *consequences* of eating. These are the events that follow eating, and they can be as important as the first two categories. By observing your own eating patterns for a while, and keeping the antecedents, behavior and consequences of eating in mind, you will discover cause-and-effect relationships that are important to controlled eating. Some of these relationships you will want to change. There are at least nine different steps you can take to do this.

Nine Steps For Changing Eating Behavior

STEP ONE. Try to buy only nonfattening foods. If you do buy fattening foods, keep them out of sight and out of reach. And make sure that they are of a type that need some preparation before eating.

STEP TWO. Always eat in the same room, and in that room only. Eat in only one place in that room, and do not do anything else while you are eating. If you want to watch TV, just watch TV; if you are eating, just eat. But don't do both at the same time.

STEP THREE. Never shop for groceries when you are hungry. Make a shopping list before you go, and stick to it. It has been demonstrated that most fattening foods are purchased on impulse. Also avoid preparing your shopping list when you are hungry.

STEP FOUR. Watch for your own periods of weakness. Everyone has particular times during the day when overeating is more likely. When you are aware of these periods, they are easier to avoid or resist.

STEP FIVE. Get others to help you. Spouse, fellow workers, roommates, friends—all can help you in a simple but important way. Tell them you are changing the way you eat and ask them to tell you whenever they see you stop eating at the right time. You do not want them to tell you when you overeat, but when you do not overeat; you want praise, not punishment. And ask them to refrain from ever urging you to eat, or to eat more.

STEP SIX. Know something about the foods you eat. Overeaters eat less when they know how much they are eating, and how fattening the food is. The best source of this kind of information about foods that I have found is a paperback book by Barbara Kraus entitled *Calories and Carbohydrates*. It is a dictionary of 7,500 brand names and basic foods with their caloric and carbohydrate values. Signet is the publisher (be sure to get the latest edition because it is frequently updated).

STEP SEVEN. Eat your meals slowly and deliberately. If you have a tendency to eat fast, wolfing down your meals, try eating for a minute or two and then stopping for a minute. After a couple of days of this practice you will find yourself developing stronger feelings of control over your eating behavior. Another gambit is to put down your fork between bites, not picking it up again until you have swallowed everything in your mouth. Take twenty minutes or more for each meal (eating more *slowly,* not more food). It takes this long for your brain to get the message from your stomach that you have eaten enough.

STEP EIGHT. Devise a reward system for following every step listed here. It is very important that you tie your reward system to following these steps, *not* to weight loss. One way to do this is to develop a point system in which you get so many points for following each step. When you have accumulated a predetermined number of points, you can "spend" them on something you want. The most productive system is one in which your family and friends help you, perhaps even participating in this nine step program. As an example, you might "buy" three hours of baby sitting for a certain number of points. (Be sure to talk this over in advance with all the people who might be involved—spouse, fellow workers, friends, etc.) Or you might allow yourself to buy something you have been wanting when you accumulate a certain number of points. Just be sure that your reward is not food.

STEP NINE. Make all possible efforts to avoid hunger, boredom, depression, loneliness, anger, and fatigue. These are the six most troublesome moods for overeaters.

Problem Moods for Overeaters

Hunger. Hunger is both a physiological state and an emotional mood. Physical hunger is not a real problem for overeaters. In fact, many overweight people never give themselves a chance to experience true, physical hunger because they never go long enough without eating.

Hunger as a mood is a very real problem. Eat three regularly planned meals a day, preventing yourself from getting too hungry. Use common sense to avoid getting into a hungry mood because, as you know, once the mood strikes, you will go through a lot of vittles.

Boredom, Depression, and Loneliness. These are three moods that always create serious problems for overeaters. There are several ways to deal with them. For one thing, always keep close at hand a list of friends you can phone. Don't meet them for coffee or lunch, though. Instead, take a walk with them or do something active.

Another way of dealing with these moods is to always have something interesting to read. A hobby is also a good thing to have, and there is always housework or puttering around in the garage. When one of these three problem moods begins to set in, do something that is interesting to you. If these tactics fail, you may have to engage in autoquestioning and suggestion to deal with frequently occurring problem moods.

Anger. Avoid getting angry if you can. If you do get angry, find the least expensive way of expressing it. (Pounding the seat of an overstuffed chair with a tennis racket can help. Be sure there is no one sitting in it.) Stay as far away from food as possible when you are angry to avoid expressing your anger through eating.

Fatigue. It is important that you not allow yourself to become too tired or fatigued. Eating is much harder to control when you are tired. Get regular hours of sleep, making sure you get enough to keep you feeling good.

Nutrition

Recent surveys have shown that many Americans are not eating well. The Department of Agriculture has found that only one-half of the families studied had diets that could be rated as "good." Even families in the highest income levels had "poor" diets. In these studies, a "poor" diet had nothing to do with the quantity of food people ate. The problem is one of poor food choices and poor eating patterns.

There are over sixty million overweight Americans with poor eating patterns. Because our bodies can tell us *when* we are hungry, but not *what* to eat, we must develop a knowledge of the nutritional values of the foods we eat. This is the only way to know which foods are best for our needs, and which ones are either too fattening or do us no good at all.

Good nutrition requires a proper balance of the food elements needed for good health. There are forty to forty-five of these elements (experts do not agree on the exact number). Water is included. Each of these elements is needed for good health. A deficiency in any one of them can lead to sickness or even death. Deficiencies can also lead to a craving for food because the body is trying to tell you that something is needed. Unfortunately, the subconscious cannot usually be specific about which food should be eaten. ("Eat one-half of a medium-sized banana, we're low on potassium.")

This is why, if you are going on a diet, you must do one of two things: Either educate yourself about the nutritive values of various foods and how much of the nutriments you need for good health, or follow a balanced diet prescribed by your physician or use a diet that has been developed by medical experts. To help in this respect, I personally like to take vitamin supplements, such as a good "daily" vitamin with additional C, minerals, balanced B, and E. But this is up to you. The point is, the quality of what you eat is your responsibility, and it is an important one. It is very difficult to restrain yourself from eating if the body is not getting everything it needs. And even if you could do this, you would pay a price down the road in poor health.

As to how much you should eat, the best answer is *no more than you must to meet your nutritional needs*. To lose weight, you have to eat less than your energy demands. This makes you use up some of your stored fat for some of your energy requirements.

The Low-Carbohydrate Approach to Weight Loss

Many people are unable to lose weight on a calorie-counting diet, even when they live on as little as 800 or 900 calories a day for months. It has been found that such people have a metabolic resistance to losing

181

weight. For them, lowering carbohydrate intake is much easier and more effective than counting calories for losing weight.

For those persons who find calorie-counting an inefficient method of weight loss—and you may be one of them, as I am—a low-carbohydrate diet is usually the answer. On a low-carbohydrate diet, weight loss depends on the reduction of carbohydrates. Calories are, for the most part, ignored.

One particularly attractive aspect of this kind of dieting approach is that there are some foods, such as lean beef and baked or broiled chicken, that do not have any carbohydrates. So you can eat all you want of them and still lose weight!

For more information on low-carbohydrate dieting, I recommend *Dr. Atkins' Diet Revolution* by Robert C. Atkins, M.D.

A low-carbohydrate diet is my personal preference over calorie-counting methods. I am one of those people who has a low tolerance for carbohydrates. With the exercises in Part 3, I and many others have found it easy to restrict carbohydrate intake and still eat enough to never experience hunger.

It is important for you to understand that those of us who are overweight, or who used to be overweight, must *control our eating from now on*. Weight control must become a way of life. While this may sound ominous at first, let me assure you that it is a far-from-unhappy way of life, and it is far more preferable than being fat.

Being fat is not just inconvenient or unattractive, it is unhealthy. Overweight can lead to a host of medical problems, it can take years off your life, and bouts of depression, anxiety, and lowered self-esteem are not uncommon.

No matter which program you intend to use to lose weight—counting calories or grams of carbohydrate—see a doctor first. Get a thorough examination and discuss your plans with your physician.

Charting for Eating Awareness

One of the first things you will want to get for yourself is a carbohydrate or calorie counter. This term refers to any of several books that give the values of specific foods in calories and/or grams of carbohydrate. Most people prefer a counter that gives the values for foods by brand name. There is often a wide variation in the carbohydrate or calorie content of different brands of the same food.

If you are counting grams of carbohydrate, the most handy book to carry with you is Dell Publishing's *Carbohydrate Gram Counter*. The book I like to keep around home is Kraus's *Calories and Carbohydrates* mentioned earlier. The most complete book of all is published by the U.S. Department of Agriculture. It gives the carbohydrate content of several thousand foods and beverages and is very inexpensive. The one I have is fairly old (No.8). It cost me $1.50. If you want one, write to the Superintendent of Documents, U.S. Government Printing Office, Washington, DC 20402 and ask for the latest edition of their *Composition of Foods, Agriculture Handbook*. It will take several weeks to get it; the Superintendent of Documents is either very busy or very slow.

It is important for you to get a new look at the way you eat. If you are going to count carbohydrates, you want to become carbohydrate-conscious. The same thing applies to calories, if that is what you will be counting. (A few people seem to do best by counting protein, but that is not common.) The best way to develop this awareness is to chart your eating for several days or a week. Follow these three steps in charting your eating:

1. Eat just as you normally do. Don't try to cut down, and don't go on any unusual binges. Just eat normally.
2. Keep a written record of everything that goes into your mouth. Carry something with you to write your eating record in. Write it down as soon as you eat it. If you wait until later, you will forget.
3. Don't worry about calories or carbohydrates, just write down what you eat and how much you eat (you will usually just have to guess at the quantities). At the end of the day, look up the calories or grams of carbohydrate for everything you ate and total it for the day. To get the grams of carbohydrate, use one of the books mentioned earlier that gives grams of carbohydrate for foods and drinks.

Keep your eating awareness charts neat and orderly so you can understand them and refer back to them if you need to. There is a two-day chart in Figure 6–1 to give you an idea of how to do this.

You will probably be surprised to find that you are eating very large quantities of carbohydrate—200, 300, or even 400 grams of carbohydrate is not unusual. Here is an example of my own chart for a typical day when I first started. You will see why I weighed a lot at the time.

DAILY EATING AWARENESS CHART

DATE:		DATE:	
WHAT EATEN:	VALUE:	WHAT EATEN:	VALUE:
DAY'S TOTAL:		DAY'S TOTAL:	

FIGURE 6-1 Daily Eating Awareness Charts for recording daily intake of calories or carbohydrates

Meal	*Grams of Carbohydrate*
BREAKFAST	
4 ounces grapefruit juice	16.1
1 cup cornflakes	24.7
1 cup whole milk	11.8
1 tablespoon sugar	12.1
2 slices buttered toast	28.0

LUNCH

4-ounce cheeseburger on bun	21.2
1 tablespoon catsup	4.5
1 tablespoon mustard	1.7
3 ounces french fries	30.5
12-ounce cola drink	37.0

DINNER

8-ounce hamburger steak	0.0
baked potato	21.0
½-cup green beans	3.7
2 slices Vienna bread	25.4
1 piece coconut cream pie	27.7

EVENING SNACK

4 cups popped popcorn	21.2
12-ounce cola drink	37.0
TOTAL	323.6

Isn't that amazing? On the surface it does not look like an unusual way to eat. Yet it totalled up to a whopping 323.6 grams of carbohydrate for the day, and I have since established that I gain weight with any regular, daily intake that exceeds about 60 grams of carbohydrate. I had eaten this way for years, never realizing that I was so heavily overloading myself with carbohydrates. A few days of keeping a record like this really opened my eyes. Try it and see what you can find out about your own eating.

Food Choices List

The last step in getting ready for a diet is to prepare a list of acceptable food choices. Do this by referring to your counter to select foods that are low in calories or carbohydrates, depending on which you are counting. Then use your list to plan your daily menu.

Whatever you decide to limit your calories or carbohydrate intake to, you will have several daily choices that you can select from your list of food choices. Deciding on which foods to eat is relatively simple. The real problems, in the experience of most dieters, come from trying to stick to the decisions that are made about which foods to eat. The temptation to slip back into the old patterns of eating, to have "just one more treat," are often too great to resist. All too often the whole diet goes out the window with the first really strong temptation.

The purpose of the mental exercises in Part 3 is to remove temptation before it occurs by changing subconscious motivations. By following these exercises you will avert failure because you will bring the subconscious into alignment with what you consciously know you have to do. The alternative to these methods is "willpower," which we all know is a myth. You have already failed with that method. So make up your mind that you are going to faithfully do these mental exercises. Don't fudge on them (pun intended)—practice them diligently and start letting your subconscious take the misery out of weight control.

PART 3:
SELF-COMMUNICATION PROCEDURES

Weight problems can be related to a need to be overweight, a need to eat, or a combination of these two. The imprints and identification factors that are most common have been presented in Part 1 of this chapter. If the major problem is directly related to *food and eating,* there is a subconscious connection between food and/or eating and love, attention, reward, compensation, and so on. If the major problem is one of *needing to be overweight,* there is a subconscious connection between being overweight and such states as being healthy, jolly, happy, having friends, or being safely unattractive. Identifying with overeaters can also be a source of dysfunction.

You will want to engage in autoquestioning to learn as much as you can about your own sources of the eating dysfunction. Refer back to Chapter 3 if you need to refresh your memory about autoquestioning procedures and strategies. Use the information in Part 1 of this chapter for ideas to pursue in your questioning. Don't be surprised if you come up with some causes of overeating that have not been mentioned here. We all have unique histories, so no one has had exactly the same experiences as you. Whatever you learn about your own sources of subconscious dysfunction, use that information to formulate your verbal and image suggestions. These suggestions can be applied any time; the more time you can spend on your suggestions, the more effective they will be. As described earlier, your formal suggestions can be applied just before starting your self-hypnotic induction. Image suggestions, or image rehearsals, can be applied during the scene visualization part of your self-hypnotic induction.

Practicing Self-Hypnosis

To change your problem imprints and bring the subconscious into agreement with your conscious agreement to lose weight and keep it off, you will be using the basic self-hypnosis procedures that should, by now, be familiar to you. What follows will provide a review of the method and practice of self-hypnosis, with particular application to weight control.

Self-hypnosis, when properly done, will develop a positive channel of communication with the subconscious part of your mind. Once you have gone beyond the first six weeks or so of practicing self-hypnosis in which you use the longer tensing and releasing method of deep relaxation, your total practice periods should not require more than about ten minutes. Your skill will improve as you practice, which means that it will not take as long later to do your self-hypnotic practice and suggestion application as it does in the first few weeks.

There is usually a brief period of confusion in the beginning. You won't be sure if you are doing the exercises correctly, if they are working, and so on. This period passes quickly as you become more familiar with the process of self-communication. It will be helpful if you can frequently refer back to this text to brush up on the instructions for doing the exercises correctly.

Don't try to make anything happen with these exercises. You have to let them work for you. You should not try to make them work by "force of will." Just as you cannot make yourself go to sleep or force yourself to remember something you have temporarily forgotten, you cannot *make* these exercises be effective. The most you can do is follow the directions and *let* them be effective. If you try too hard your efforts will get in the way.

Don't expect overnight miracles. This process of change must be natural to be permanent, and that takes time. You want permanent, natural change, not some flash-in-the-pan, quickie process that does not last.

Try to practice at the same time every day. This is not always possible, of course, but try to stick to a fairly regular time for your daily practice. If you must vary your schedule, do so. It is better to practice at an off time, even if it must be very brief, than to not practice at all. Do try to avoid practicing within an hour after eating. These exercises call for deep relaxation, and relaxation is very difficult immediately after eating.

Pick a time of day to practice when you feel most alert. If you are a morning person who feels more alert and alive in the morning, try to do your exercise then. If you are more of a night person, schedule your practice for later in the day or in the evening.

Some people find these exercises invigorating and refreshing. This can make it difficult to go to sleep for some time after practicing. If you find this to be the case, move the practice time back far enough to allow yourself plenty of time before trying to go to sleep for the night.

If, on the other hand, you have trouble staying awake during the practice, there are several ways to remedy this problem. One is to practice at a different time of the day. Many people have difficulty staying awake at certain times of the day, such as in the middle of the afternoon. Such times are obviously not the best for practicing.

If changing the time of day does not solve the problem of falling asleep, change the position in which you practice. Most people prefer to practice lying down, but falling asleep during practice may indicate a need to practice sitting up. If that doesn't work, practice standing up! Practice this way for a while, then go back to practicing in a more comfortable position. Once you break the habit of going to sleep when you practice, you can practice in any position you want.

Take steps to assure that you will be as free from distractions as possible when you practice. You should be alone, and turn off the TV or radio (or put either of them between stations for the masking sounds of "white noise"). If you have children, arrange for a spouse or someone else to watch them while you practice; you won't do much good if you are either anticipating an interruption at any time, or worrying about what the kids are up to while you are practicing. Be sure to explain to your family members or roommates that, unless it is for something very important, you wish not to be disturbed while you practice. If you do get interrupted during your practice, begin at the beginning when you get back to it.

Begin your practice by lying down and getting comfortable. Do not have anything in your mouth such as chewing gum or dentures (unless you normally sleep with them in). Lie on your back with your legs straight and your arms at your side or with your hands on your stomach. Do not cross your legs because that can eventually get uncomfortable, forcing you to move.

Try to put everything, especially anything unpleasant, out of your mind. This is not the time to concern yourself with worries and problems. This takes some practice, and no one can ever *totally* clear the mind of all thoughts. Just get in the habit of reserving this time of day for a carefree practice with no problems allowed. If problems or unpleasant thoughts do intrude themselves into your practice time, gently push them aside. Just think to yourself, "This is not the time to think about that, so that thought can go away." Then bring your attention back to your practice.

Refer back to Chapters 1 and 2 for deep relaxation and self-hypnosis techniques. The methods will be the same for weight control. Pay particular attention to the instructions regarding the use of imagination. This weight control exercise will call for the use of different image rehearsals during the scene visualization period of the induction.

When you get to the scene visualization, imagine yourself as you want to be. Make the image as detailed and perfect as you can imagine it. See yourself in the kind of clothing you want to be able to wear, looking trim and slender. Keep thinking to yourself, "This is the way I am becoming!"

Imagine looking at yourself in a mirror, seeing yourself in a bathing suit, healthy and good-looking. Notice that there are no folds of loose flesh, no bulging fat. You are trim and slender, with just the right shape and appearance. Or imagine yourself watching a home movie or videotape of yourself on a screen set up in your home. You are the main subject of the movie, which shows various situations in which you are in different clothing from scene to scene. Each scene shows you looking the way you want to look: trim, slender, and healthy. The final scene is one in which you are gesturing, beckoning to yourself to "join yourself." You are inviting yourself to "come be me like this."

Add other elements that are appropriate to your own situation. If you have found through autoquestioning that one of your sources of dysfunction is identification with someone who was or is overweight, get that person into your image rehearsal. Imagine that person being slender and eating (or *not* eating) the way you want to. This can be very difficult at first because you are accustomed to seeing the person only as he or she really is. But with practice you will be able to change your image of that person.

You should include formal suggestions and image rehearsals that are intended to change any negative imprints you have uncovered. If, for example, you have found that you subconsciously equate being fat with being healthy, emphasize the new relationship between health and slenderness. If you have found that you are overweight for safety reasons, such as a jealous husband, talk the matter over with him. If discussing the issue does not make you feel better, you may have to develop some assertiveness and independence before you can achieve slenderness. It is very difficult to live your life for someone else and yourself at the same time. At any rate, work on formal and image suggestions that counter the negative imprint.

Supplement your exercises throughout the day by becoming more aware of the physiques and figures of other people. Every time you see a person who looks the way you want to look, think, "That's the way I am becoming." Each time you notice a person who is overweight, think, "I don't want to look like that."

Your actual self-hypnotic exercise should be devoted entirely to weight control, which can include the enhancement of self-image. I am often asked, "How many things can I work on at once?" The answer is simple: Work on one thing at a time until you have it under control. Pick what is most important to you, and work on it until you are making significant progress toward the achievement of that goal. Sometimes you can combine things in a natural way, especially if they are interrelated anyway. Concentration and memory go together, as do assertiveness, self-reliance, self-esteem, self-image and self-confidence. But smoking and weight control are in categories of their own. So if you want to work on weight control, do it to the exclusion of any other projects until you are well on your way to success (and don't quit then, but you can add another goal or two).

Induction Script

The following transcript is provided to give you an idea of how your self-hypnotic induction should go. It is a portion of the script from my Weight Control tape. The transcript begins after the deep relaxation and deepening stages, when you should be in your scene visualization:

> Your attitudes and ideas about food are changing. Gradually, definitely, your attitudes and beliefs about food and eating are changing for the better. You are becoming less and less interested in food in general. All desires to overeat are going away. Every day, you think less and less about food and eating.
>
> You enjoy food in moderate quantities, but anything more than you need for good health and nutrition does not interest you. You are feeling better and better as you eat less and less. You are eating less because you want less. You want less. Every day you want less and less. The time you used to think about food is being directed into healthier, more productive channels. Every day, in every way, you are becoming more and more satisfied with less and less food.
>
> You eat for health and nutrition only. Eating is not a substitute for anything else. You may have problems from time to time, but you will not try to solve or forget about these problems by eating. If you are upset, disappointed

or emotionally distraught about anything, you will not think of eating or drinking to solve your problems. Eating is for nutrition only. You can, and you will, solve your problems without eating or drinking.

You will not think of food or drink as a reward. When things go well, it is easy to resist eating. Not wanting to overeat makes you feel even better.

You will not compensate for disappointments by eating. Food does not make you feel any better in times of disappointment. You find it easy to resist overeating, even in times of disappointment.

Food is not a substitute for love or attention. You will not try to fill your need for love and attention by eating. Food may have been associated with love and attention when you were younger. But you are an adult now. So you do not associate food with love. Every day, in every way, it is easier and easier to avoid overeating.

You will not eat just because you are bored. When you are bored or apathetic, you will direct your energy toward other activities besides eating. Any time you begin to feel bored, your inner mind will direct you to activities that take your mind away from eating.

Energy is both physical and mental. You have more energy as you eat less. More productive, more rewarding activities are taking the place of eating. Eating is becoming less and less important as an activity in your life. Because you are eating less, you are becoming more interested in the quality of your food and drink. Your inner mind directs you to be more interested in the quality of the food you eat and in the beverages you drink. When you are thirsty, for example, water appeals to you more than anything else. You are becoming more and more interested in the nutritional qualities of the food you eat. You want only foods that contribute to your good health and nutrition.

Your inner mind is directing your body to make good use of the food you eat. Because you are becoming more energetic, more of the food you eat is being used for energy. Your body takes what it needs for energy, good health, and nutrition, and passes the rest out of your system. Your inner mind is instructing your body to get rid of excess food. You will not store it as fat. Any fat that does exist is being burned for energy.

Your body is making more effective use of the food you eat, and you are becoming more and more energetic and healthier. You feel this happening day by day, and you enjoy it. You have more energy, and you get more done. Every day you are becoming more and more aware of the fullness of life and you are enjoying life more and more. You are becoming less and less interested in food.

Sweets, such as candy and pastries, are not desirable to you. You do not crave them because they do not contribute to your good health. You find it easier and easier to resist fattening foods of any kind. You feel more positively toward yourself each time you resist eating such foods. Pastries, candy, sweets of any kind, just don't tempt you as they used to. You are liking yourself better and better, and eating less and less.

Now picture yourself as you want to be. This is how you are becoming.

See yourself, trim and healthy, in a bathing suit or in any way that appeals to you. See other people, such as friends and relatives, admiring you and complimenting you on your trimness and good health. Enjoy your good appearance, and know that it is good. Your inner mind is developing stronger and stronger desire for the achievement of this condition that you are now picturing in your mind. Every day, in every way, your desire to be trim and healthy is growing.

Hold this image in your mind. You will think about it several times a day. Any time you are tempted to eat when you should not, or to eat or drink the wrong things, think of this image of yourself. And imagine you can hear the rhythm you are listening to now. [The Psychosonic Rhythm described earlier in this chapter.] As you do this, the temptation will go away. You will be able to resist the temptation, and you will feel good about it.

Now continue to see yourself as you want to be, doing the things that you want to do. Imagine as much detail as possible. This is your blueprint, your model. The way you imagine yourself is the real you that is gradually emerging. You are not daydreaming, you are practicing.

This is a fairly lengthy section of the transcript, but I wanted you to get a good feeling for the kinds of suggestions and images that are helpful. I cannot tell you which of the suggestions or images in this transcript are the most effective (it probably varies from individual to individual). The original research for this transcript was conducted with several hundred students at the college where I was teaching. Since the whole tape was used, I cannot identify specific aspects of it that are particularly effective.

In looking over the tape transcript while typing this, I noticed several things—wordings—that I would like to change. But I don't dare do that because it works the way it is—several thousand users have proved its effectiveness. I have learned not to muck around with something that works.

So my advice to you is to try to get as much of the transcript into your own practice session as you can. I don't think you need to memorize it, but it probably would not hurt to read it over several times.

Daily Image Rehearsals

There are many things you can profitably put into your scene visualization and image rehearsal. Since there are too many possibilities—all of them good, some perhaps necessary—to put them all into one practice, it is helpful to use different image rehearsals for each day of the week. What follows are six such image rehearsals (you can rest on Sunday if you like or, if you are Jewish, change the Saturday exercise to Sunday and rest on Saturday):

MONDAY'S EXERCISE:
DYNAMIC SELF-CONTROL

Imagine yourself seated at a table piled high with rich foods and desserts. You are eating only small portions of the foods that are good for you and avoiding the fattening foods.

You see and feel yourself having no trouble avoiding the undesirable foods because you just don't want to eat them. Keep thinking to yourself, "This is the way I am." You push yourself away from the table without any dessert, because you don't want any.

Imagine yourself at a party where fattening snacks are being offered to you. You are rejecting them, not even eating one small one, because you *choose* not to. You do not feel deprived, nor do you feel even slightly tempted by them because you decided beforehand that you would not eat any. You are proud of yourself as you turn away from the fattening snacks.

Imagine yourself doing—enjoying—activities that give you more exercise. You are walking up a flight of stairs rather than taking an elevator. You are walking short distances, rather than riding. You are playing tennis or bowling, or any other activity that appeals to you. You are doing these things and thoroughly enjoying them because you have decided on the amount of exercise you want to get and you have the discipline to carry through with your plans.

Throughout the day, take note of each time you exhibit discipline and give yourself a pat on the back. If you do something that is weak and displeases you, do not get mad at yourself. Simply resolve to do better the next time. Start with smaller expectations of yourself and gradually work up to tougher ones.

TUESDAY'S EXERCISE:
ALIGNING INNER FORCES

Imagine the forces within you coming into alignment with your conscious goals. As you develop more faith in your inner force it will magnetically attract success in the things you want to do and achieve. Imagine your subconscious mind leading you to make correct decisions and motivating you to behave in ways that contribute to the achievement of your goals.

Imagine a small but powerful generator within you that drives you to achieve your goals. As it hums and whirs within you, you want to do the things you know you should do. And you don't want to do the things you know you should not do.

Visualize a large, powerful airplane that can take you anywhere you want to go. The plane is your subconscious mind and you, the pilot, represent your conscious mind. Imagine the joy of flying, effortlessly darting in and out of the clouds, banking to the left, to the right—the plane responds to your every command.

Now picture two compasses, each with its needle that points north. One of the compasses is your conscious mind, the other is your subconscious mind. Initially, the two needles are not in agreement. The conscious compass is pointing to the north, but the subconsciouis compass is pointing in some other direction, let's say, east. Now you are moving the conscious compass needle to point east, in the same direction as the subconscious needle. It moves slowly, taking eight to ten seconds to point in the same direction as the subconscious needle. When you have the conscious needle aligned with the subconscious needle, you find that the two needles are now synchronized and move together. As you move the conscious needle first one way and then the other, the subconscious needle moves with it precisely and exactly in time. You move the conscious needle to north, and the subconscious needle moves with it to also point north.

WEDNESDAY'S EXERCISE:
SOCIAL FEEDBACK

Imagine yourself surrounded by a group of friends and relatives. These friends and relatives should be people whose opinions you respect. There should be at least six or seven persons in the group, and even more is better.

See and hear each person commenting on your weight loss and how good you look. Don't pass anyone by, having each of them speak to you in turn. Don't hold back on the praise they are giving you. Typical comments might be: "Wow, you've really lost a lot of weight." "You look terrific." "You look so healthy and vibrant." "I sure admire your discipline."

You can change the membership of this imaginary social-feedback group from time to time. Remember to restrict the membership of your imaginary group to persons whom you like and respect, and whom you want to respect you. The members need not necessarily be persons who are still alive. For example, if one or both of your parents are deceased, you can still imagine them in your group. You can also include people whom you have never actually known, such as historical figures or famous personalities.

Change the setting from time to time. You might imagine yourself walking along a beach in a bathing suit (be sure to notice the admiring looks from others). Another time you might be walking down a busy street where people stop to turn around and give you an admiring look. You can be at a party, at the office or on the job, at a club meeting, bowling—in any situation that you want to imagine. Just remember that in each situation you are getting heaps of praise and admiration (but *no envy*) for your weight loss and the way you look.

The main purpose of this exercise is for you to experience, through your imagination, the approbation, commendation, and praise of others for losing weight. Social acceptance and approval are very important to all of us and they are particularly influential in the process of losing weight. So let your imagination run free in this exercise.

THURSDAY'S EXERCISE:
DISINTEREST IN FOOD AND EATING

Try to recall a time when you were really bored with what you were doing. Recapture the feeling of boredom as strongly as you can. Then, replace the event that originally bored you with the act of eating. The purpose here is to associate feelings of tedium and boredom with food and eating.

Imagine yourself at a table piled high with foods that would normally be very appealing to you. As you begin to eat, your interest in eating the food wanes very quickly. After a few bites, you tire of eating and want to do something else besides eat. You can imagine yourself really enjoying the first few bites, but apathy toward food and eating sets in quickly after those first few enjoyable bites. Imagine yourself feeling indifferent toward food and eating.

As you imagine this scene, feel good about your lack of concern for food and eating. Feel thrilled about your feelings of monotony and dullness related to eating, especially overeating.

Imagine that, when it comes to food, you feel detached and indifferent. After you have eaten a small amount you are anxious to get up from the table. You want to resume, or get started on, some other activity that is more interesting to you. The activity can be anything that you find interesting and exciting: reading, conversation (try to hold conversation to a minimum while eating), hobbies, watching television, anything that appeals to you but that does not include food.

Imagine yourself standing on a sandy beach. Write the phrase "Interest in food and eating" on a piece of paper and put it into a bottle. Throw the bottle out to sea and watch it float into the distance, disappearing forever. Write the phrase in the sand and watch the waves gradually obliterate it.

FRIDAY'S EXERCISE:
ORGANIC AWARENESS

Listen for your heartbeat. It may be difficult to perceive at first, and you may not actually hear your heart beating. But you will begin to be aware of your heartbeat pulsing through your body. Think positive, healthy thoughts as you practice this exercise. Think about how your heart is pumping healthily and regularly. Imagine the whole process as your heart pumps healthy, red blood to all parts of your body, carrying oxygen to every cell.

Move from the awareness of your heartbeat to an imagined awareness of the functioning of all of your body parts, especially your stomach. Imagine that each time you eat you feel the food going down to your stomach, and how it feels when it is in your stomach.

Imagine yourself becoming more aware of your bodily needs for energy, and how your stomach sends messages such as: "You've had enough" when you have eaten enough to satisfy your energy and health needs.

Now move the awareness into your mouth. Imagine that you are eating something and being aware—more aware than you have ever been before—of each bite, of each movement of the chewing process. Feel the saliva in your mouth as you eat, and be aware of how many times you chew before swallowing.

In your imagination, see yourself unable to put anything into your mouth without being extremely aware of what you are doing. You are aware of each bite, of each drink, of each and every swallow.

Apply this same process of awareness of eating throughout your day. Remind yourself from time to time to be especially aware of anything you eat and drink. Your awareness of eating will be best if you avoid doing anything else while eating. This precludes watching TV, conversation, reading, and so on, anytime you are eating or drinking anything.

SATURDAY'S EXERCISE:
SLENDERNESS REWARDS

Imagine yourself at an awards ceremony where you are the guest of honor. You are in a large auditorium filled with people, most of whom you know or have known in your lifetime. You are seated on the stage in the seat of honor. There are several other people seated on the stage. One by one, each of these other people gets up and gives a short speech that praises your virtues. Each speaker gives you lavish but realistic praise, addressing such points as your super self-control, your great energy and stamina, your winning personality, and any other qualities for which you enjoy (or would enjoy) being praised.

You are the final speaker, telling the audience how you lost weight and attained your magnificent appearance. Go into great detail about how you avoid the wrong kinds of foods, how you practice every night at building self-control, how you educated yourself on the foods you eat, how you apply suggestions, and so on. In your speech, actually review all of the steps you are taking in your weight control program.

As you speak, see yourself trim and slender, full of energy and healthy vitality. Feel yourself thoroughly imbued with a natural enthusiasm that completely captivates your audience.

At the end of your speech, you receive an award for your achievements in self-improvement, followed by a standing ovation from the audience.

PART 4: DREAM YOUR FAT AWAY

Dreams can be a powerful, highly effective weapon in the battle of the bulge. They have the advantage of requiring very little of your waking time, and they put to work a time that is normally not considered constructive (other than for getting rest).

Earlier I warned you not to expect overnight miracles in your weight control program. I said they were not likely to happen, and if they did, you could expect the effects to be short-lived. Those are still valid statements, but the results of dreaming can be the exception. A dream can literally change your life overnight.

You will recall that earlier in this book I talked about alternate reality dreams. These are dreams that either represent or transmit a subconscious view of reality that is more impactful on the subconscious than is reality itself. It seems to be a general rule that the subconscious is far more responsive to dreamed realities—alternate realities—than to genuine reality.

An experience of my own illustrates how this phenomenon can work in weight control. When I was at my heaviest, I had a habit of eating a bowl of cereal every night before going to bed. The cereal had to have two tablespoons of sugar in it and a cup of whole milk. It was also necessary for me to have two slices of buttered toast with the cereal.

This had become a nightly ritual that I found impossible to stop. I kept telling myself that it was ridiculous to eat all of those empty calories and carbohydrates at bedtime. (Incidentally, in case you don't already know it, bedtime is the worst possible time to eat anything.) But I just kept on doing it, finding some excuse or pretext every night to do it again. That bedtime snack (meal!) was reward for having had a good day, compensation for a bad day, or a way of ending a humdrum day with a little well-deserved pleasure.

At that time, I had been working on my weight control program for some time. (The concepts were similar to those presented here, except they were much cruder, less comprehensive, and took longer to be effective.) But no matter what I did, I could not stop myself from eating that cursed cereal every night and hating myself immediately afterward for doing it. I was having a lot of trouble with subconscious resistance to changes in attitude toward food and eating.

Then one night I had a dream. In the dream I was eating my bowl of cereal. Everything was the same as it usually was, with one important exception: Instead of sugar, the cereal had two tablespoons of powdered cleanser in it! The kind that contains chlorine. Now, I have never been particularly thrilled by the thought of eating powdered cleanser, and I have a special aversion to the smell (and no doubt the taste) of chlorine. It was not a nice dream.

I have not eaten cereal since having that dream, and that has been several years. Not only that, but my attitude toward food in general changed after that dream. It was as if cereal epitomized all of my bad eating habits. That one, simple dream marked the turning point in my attitude toward food and eating.

I still enjoy eating, to be sure, but in much smaller quantities. And the foods that I now enjoy are of a much different nature: high in protein, low in carbohydrates, and very little refined sugar. As unpleasant as that dream was at the time, I am tickled pink that I had it. That alternate reality dream either marked the point of subconscious acceptance, or it produced subconscious acceptance, of the idea that cereal-eating at any time (as well as other forms of eating abuse) was undesirable.

I have verified, through autoquestioning, that it really was this dream that marked the turning point in my eating, and that the dream was the product of the kinds of procedures you are learning about here.

Generating alternate reality dreams is really a process of autoquestioning, self-hypnosis, and suggestion. But you can increase the probability of having alternate reality dreams by following the procedures presented in Chapter 5 for prompting and analyzing dreams.

In order to lose weight, you must eat less than enough to meet your energy requirements. This forces the body to use stored fat for energy. To keep the fat off, once you have achieved your ideal weight, you must maintain a balance between the amount of food you eat and the energy you burn.

Both of these objectives require that you keep track of how much you are eating, either by counting calories or grams of carbohydrate. Either way, you will have to maintain an awareness of the foods you eat for the rest of your life. Like the alcoholic, you must admit that you are a "foodoholic." Never lose sight of the fact that you can gain weight by overeating, and that you will overeat if you start ignoring your subconscious motivations.

The exercises and practices presented here will make it much easier for you to lose weight and keep it off. But you must practice them regularly if they are to be effective. That they *are* effective has been proved by people of all ages, sizes, and walks of life. You are never too fat to regain control of your girth, and you are never too old.

The control of overweight is well worth the effort that it requires. There is no question that being overweight is unhealthy. You will live longer by controlling your weight, and the quality of your life will be immeasurably better. The difference between slenderness and obesity can be the difference between misery and happiness.

No one else can do it for you. You must be the one to take charge of your life and control your weight. These techniques will make that task as easy as possible, but they still require some effort.

Make the effort! You'll never be sorry you did.

7

Quitting smoking

This is a method for quitting smoking without willpower and without all of the deleterious side effects so commonly related to giving up cigarettes. Called the Biocentrix Method, it is the result of many years of practice and research, much of it my own, some of it taken from research in clinics and laboratories across the country. That this method does work has been proved many times over by smokers from all walks of life. Whether you have been smoking for a long or short time, whether you smoke a lot or very little, this method will work for you if you want it to, and if you give it a chance to work.

All I can do is show you how to use this method. You will do most of the work yourself. It will not be difficult, and *it does not require willpower*. If you follow this method and do what you are supposed to do, you will quit smoking easily and with relatively little effort. With this method you will become a *nonsmoker,* not just an abstainer from smoking. There is a big difference between these two conditions.

The *abstainer* is one who always carries with him or her the desire to smoke, sometimes for years after quitting. For the abstainer, the seed of failure is perpetually lurking within the subconscious mind, ready to pounce at the slightest excuse and thrust him or her back into full-blown smoking. This seed of potential failure exists because the abstainer has made a *conscious* decision to quit smoking, but has never brought the *subconscious* into agreement with that decision.

The abstainer is edgy and grouchy, especially for the first few weeks after throwing away his cigarettes and vowing to quit. He is likely to gain weight and be generally miserable. In short, the abstainer is in about the same boat as the willing smoker who happens to be out of cigarettes, and life can be pretty miserable for him.

The picture is quite different for the *nonsmoker*. Becoming a nonsmoker means bringing the subconscious into alignment with conscious desires. When this condition of conscious-subconscious alignment occurs, there is no sense of forcefully "abstaining" from smoking or of depriving oneself of something that is desired. The desire to smoke is gone, and it does not return.

It is very easy to do something if there is subconscious agreement about it. Or, to put this in more appropriate terms relative to smoking, it is very easy to *not* do something you subconsciously don't want to do.

If you have tried to quit smoking in the past, only to give up and resume smoking after a few days or weeks (or even years), that simply means you were going about it in the wrong way. Most failures at quitting smoking occur because the smoker concentrated her efforts on an isolated segment of herself: her smoking behavior. Simply throwing away your cigarettes and consciously resolving never to smoke again is absurd because smoking is a symptom of a deeply rooted dysfunction. If you have read the earlier parts of this book, you know why trying to change a dysfunction with "willpower" is a losing proposition. If you have not read the earlier parts, do so now. Otherwise, this chapter will not make much sense to you.

Before we go any further, permit me to digress for a moment to clear up what can be a troublesome issue. I know how it feels to be told by someone who has never smoked that it is easy to quit. I started inhaling cigarette smoke when I was six years old, and I did not smoke my last cigarette until I was thirty-two. That's about twenty-six years of smoking, if my arithmetic is correct. At the time I quit, I was smoking between two and three packs a day. And I remember how I used to respond to someone who had never smoked telling me to "just quit."

Be assured that I know what it is like to try to quit smoking with "willpower." I know because I tried it, and failed, plenty of times. Like Samuel (Mark Twain) Clemens' quip of a century ago, I could also say: "Quitting smoking's no problem, I've done it hundreds of times."

A variant of the "never smoked" person is the ex-smoker who quit with what he thinks was "willpower." Few people are more self-righteous and insufferable than some of these ex-smokers. Sometimes it seems that these people have dedicated their lives to making smokers—who can't quit like they did—feel weak and inadequate: "What the hell, aincha got no willpower? Just quit, like I did."

I once had a friend (now *ex*-friend) in college who was like that. He was a smoker who had developed a cough that he was unable to get rid of. When he went to the campus clinic for treatment, the doctor told him he should quit smoking. So he did, just like that! And, of course, he never tired of telling others about his tremendous "willpower."

How do we explain these cases in which some people are seemingly able to quit smoking with "willpower?" (I keep putting "willpower" in quotation marks because it does not really exist. See my earlier comments under "The Myth of Willpower" in the Introduction to this book.) The explanation of this phenomenon has to do with the dynamics of the subconscious mind. Specifically, with the ways in which subconscious imprints and identification factors can be changed. It is possible for a person to spontaneously have an alternate reality dream, to subconsciously respond to another person's remarks (such as the physician telling my friend to quit smoking), or to respond to any other source of information in a way that changes the subconscious viewpoint. Autoquestioning, self-hypnosis, and suggestion are not the only ways in which subconscious fixed ideas are changed. These methods just happen to be the best methods of *controlled* or *directed* change.

With this method of directed change, you will be paying less attention to smoking itself, concentrating instead on techniques for changing the source of your smoking dysfunction. You will learn how the subconscious part of your mind drives you to smoke, and what you really get from smoking. Armed with this information you will be able to apply suggestions that will change the subconscious motivations so you can become a permanent nonsmoker. This will not require any "willpower," just discipline that you will be able to develop if you do not already possess it.

You can start with the discipline right now. Resolve that you are going to follow the instructions presented here for at least six weeks. This should be pretty easy for you because all you will have to do is some autoquestioning, suggestion application, and self-hypnosis practice. You are already interested in doing this or you would not be reading this now.

The exercises for quitting smoking are not much different from what you have already been introduced to in the earlier chapters of this book, and at no time will you be required to quit smoking "cold turkey." Six weeks is necessary because you may not be able to tell if anything is happening for the first couple of weeks. However, I should mention that some people have started this program and quit smoking almost immediately, experiencing no further desire to smoke.

There are four major ingredients in this program for quitting smoking:

behavior modification, autoquestioning, suggestion application (which includes deep relaxation and self-hypnosis), and alternate reality dreams. Except for the behavior modification techniques, the basics of these ingredients have already been covered in earlier chapters. You may want to refer back to them from time to time to refresh your memory. In this chapter we will be concerned only with the specific modes of application for quitting smoking.

BEHAVIOR MODIFICATION

As the term implies, the object here is to modify your behavior relative to smoking. It has been my experience that behavior modification is a poor method for quitting smoking when it is used by itself. However, many of the practices taken from this theory are helpful when used in conjunction with self-communication techniques.

Generally speaking, you will want to take steps to (a) make yourself more aware of what you are doing each and every time you smoke, and (b) begin to break down some of the connections between stimulus (such as talking on the telephone or eating) and response (smoking).

Begin by changing the location in which you keep your cigarettes. If you have for years carried a pack in your shirt pocket or purse, don't keep them there any more. Put them somewhere else or carry them in your hand. If you have to look for them when you want to smoke, all the better. That is the idea: Make yourself aware of what you are doing when you smoke. The same holds true for your matches or lighter. Start keeping them in a different place from where you customarily keep them.

Become more aware of *when* you tend to smoke the most. You may find (or already know) that talking on the telephone is a time when you always smoke. The phone rings, and the first thing you do is grab your cigarettes before answering it. What would happen if you decided to wait until *after* a telephone conversation to smoke? For one thing, you would probably spend less time on the phone. Observe yourself closely for several days to become as knowledgeable as you can about your smoking patterns.

You will probably discover that you smoke a lot more in social situations than when you are alone. You are almost always in a social situation when you drink (unless you have a drinking problem), for example, and most smokers cannot imagine having a drink without smoking. Start making mental notes about these and other kinds of situations that increase your desire to smoke. You may learn some surprising things about your behavior.

How about those times when you are angry? upset? lonely? doing nothing in particular, or very active? Pay attention to your smoking behavior and see if you can, with relative ease, change some of your patterns. Don't try to force yourself into anything that you strongly resist. But if it is fairly easy, change as many smoking patterns as you can. You may find, for example, that you can wait twenty or thirty minutes to smoke after a meal, instead of firing up immediately. If it doesn't cause too much distress, do it.

How often do you smoke? Carry pencil and paper around with you and note the exact time that you light each cigarette. If you find that you light up a cigarette, say, on the average of every thirty minutes, resolve to wait a little longer between smokes, for example, do not allow yourself to light up another cigarette until at least forty-five minutes have elapsed since the lighting of the last one. Initially, postponing a smoke is much easier than the thought of never smoking again.

Start designating times that, and places where, you will not smoke. If the first thing you do upon awakening in the morning is reach for a cigarette, try waiting until after breakfast. You can help yourself (and the rest of us) by resolving not to smoke in public places. With practice, you can continue to extend the list of places and times that you do not smoke.

Make it a policy never to show others that you are needing to smoke. If it is not yet time to smoke according to your self-imposed schedule, or if you are in a place that you have designated as a no-smoking location, don't let anyone else know if you are beginning to need a cigarette. Keeping this anxiety to yourself in both word and gesture prevents you from verbally and behaviorally reinforcing your smoking habit. And never again make such statements as, "I just can't seem to quit smoking." Keep your statements to others, and your thoughts, positive and in line with your desired goals.

It is also helpful to make a list of all the reasons for not smoking. If you are honest with yourself, you ought to be able to come up with at least thirty or forty. Write your reasons on a sheet of paper and look at it occasionally. If you keep thinking about it, you will probably be adding to this list for several days. The following list is by no means exhaustive, but it will give you some ideas for starters:

Reasons for Not Smoking

Cigarettes are expensive. The money could be put to better use.

Sometimes burn holes in clothing or furniture. Fire hazard.

Deleterious to health. Causes heart and lung diseases. *Cancer.*

Purchasing and carrying cigarettes and something with which to light them is inconvenient.

Is an imposition on people who do not smoke.

Creates tobacco breath, makes me smell like a used ashtray.

Is a dependency that limits my freedom.

AUTOQUESTIONING

You get something from smoking that you subconsciously consider very important, and it is this subconscious gratification that keeps you smoking. You can forget about the typical, conscious rationalizations for smoking: it is a habit, it calms your nerves, it helps you think, and so on. It is true that nicotine is addictive, but it is a mild addiction that, in itself, is relatively easy to overcome. The really powerful reasons for smoking reside in the subconscious mind. You are probably going to be surprised when you begin to learn some of your subconscious reasons for smoking.

You will want to engage in autoquestioning about your smoking for the same reasons with which you are already familiar: to develop insight, and to glean information upon which you can base your suggestion formulation. It is unfortunate that insight is less common when questioning the sources of smoking, probably because many people's source of dysfunction is rooted in identification factors. You will recall that insight is less likely to occur when a source of dysfunction is related to identification.

This makes identification a good category to begin your autoquestioning. The following categories of identification and imprint sources will provide you with some clues and tips for your autoquestioning.

Parents

As usual, parents are likely suspects as objects of identification, especially if either or both of your parents smoked. If you do learn that your smoking is related to identification with a smoking parent, try to determine more specifically what you subconsciously think your parent's attitudes and beliefs were about smoking. Did he or she (or both) think smoking was masculine?

If you are male you can undoubtedly see how a concern for being masculine could apply to you. If you are female, you might think that masculinity factors would not apply to you. This is not necessarily true. It is quite possible that a woman would smoke to be masculine. After all, men have, in many respects, had a better deal in what has traditionally been predominantly a man's world. So it should not be surprising to learn that a woman might want to share in the good life.

If your mother smoked, did she make smoking look feminine and graceful? To reverse the concept of masculinity, if you are a woman you may easily accept femininity as a motivating force. But it can also be a force for a man because we all, males and females, have androgynous qualities. That is, we all have both female and male characteristics. A male might subconsciously identify with certain female qualities in order to, say, counterbalance an overweening emphasis on masculinity. Or the stereotypic feminine characteristics of sensitivity and softness might be more appealing than the loutish, masculine characteristics.

Continuing with your parents' attitudes and beliefs about smoking, did they make smoking look very "adult"? Children are always looking for ways to accelerate their achievement of adulthood. Were there certain "sharing" behaviors your parents engaged in, such as lighting or smoking each other's cigarettes? Shared behaviors such as smoking could easily be perceived as "togetherness" factors.

Significant Others

Who else in your life could have been the source of individual identification? Grandparents and other relatives are good possibilities, as well as friends and neighbors. Do not forget teachers and other adults associated with your early school years. This questioning concerning significant others is essentially the same as that for parents.

Role Identification

There are numerous types of roles with which you could identify, and which could contribute to a smoking dysfunction. One of the most frequent culprits is the *archetypal* role. A common archetype related to smoking dysfunctions is that of "adult." Children usually want more than anything else to grow up and be adults. Small children like to dress up in their parents' clothing and act out adult roles, and most of the play activities of children are enactments of adult roles. Youngsters watch their parents and other adults, and they are bound to see a lot of smoking going on. It is small wonder that smoking becomes associated with adult status.

Smoking and other adult activities are not logically perceived by a child as the prerogatives of adulthood, but rather as activities that *make* one an adult. Thus it is subconsciously logical for a child to smoke as soon as possible in order to hasten the much cherished adult status.

Conscious logic would allow the cessation of acts such as smoking once adult status was secure. But subconscious logic does not follow this line. From the subconscious standpoint, it is necessary to continue smoking in order to continue being an adult because it is the *activity* that constitutes adulthood.

Another individual role identification that can often be isolated as a source of smoking dysfunction is that of the *culture hero*. Culture hero roles are harder to agree on now than it was a few decades ago, but they are still potent forces. The John Wayne role is probably the best example of a Hollywood-spawned culture hero; other examples could be drawn from politics and television. If an individual identifies with any of these roles and views smoking as an integral part of the role, then that individual will be motivated to smoke.

Observe others closely when they are smoking. If you are astute in your observations, you will begin to see role enactments in the ways people smoke. I once developed twenty-seven different smoking behavior categories after a few weeks of watching how people took out cigarettes, how they lit them, how they held them while smoking, and so on. People do a lot of posturing, especially "adult" posturing, when they smoke. After a while, watching smokers gets to be funny. Try it.

Group Identification

It is a revealing fact that most people who smoke started doing it when they were adolescents, roughly between the ages of twelve and sixteen. Peer group pressures are tremendous during that period and can lead to smoking simply to be accepted by the group. The thought of being isolated from one's peers is often more frightening than anything else during adolescence. So if smoking is the thing to do, then smoking it will be.

Here again, the subconscious will maintain an ongoing belief—for a lifetime, in most cases—that smoking is necessary to avoid that most frightening of human maladies: loneliness. Not only will one smoke to earn social acceptance, but it is a natural extension of this logic (*subconscious* logic, remember) to believe that loneliness, when it does occur, can be alleviated by a cigarette. Cigarettes become "pals."

Another phenomenon of group identification is rebellion. This belongs in the category of group identification because one who rebels almost always does so as a member of one group rebelling against another. A typical example is that of children rebelling against parents. It is almost always the case that rebelling groups have, in one way or another, less power than those against whom they are rebelling. Practically anything that violates the dictates or values of the more powerful group will serve rebelliousness. Parents, the group with more power, have almost universally tried to prevent children from smoking. So . . . they smoke.

The main point here is that *rebellion can be a form of inverse identification*. As such, it can be a source of smoking dysfunctions. In questioning yourself for rebellion factors, run through the same list of suspects that you used when checking on individual identification.

Information Imprints

Review the material on information imprints in Chapter 3 if necessary, then question yourself for information imprints that might be causing or contributing to your smoking dysfunction. Information imprints are not as likely to be as rich in source material as identification imprints, but you should check to make sure before moving on to the area of guilt imprints. If you do discover that one or more information imprints are involved, pursue your questioning until you have either achieved insight, or until you are reasonably convinced that insight will not be possible.

Guilt

Guilt, like information imprints, is not as likely to be a source of dysfunction as is identification. But guilt does sometimes contribute to the need to smoke, so check it out. Keep in mind that guilt imprints can result from your own acts, or they can be related to things for which you are not really guilty.

Guilt *for* smoking is becoming more common. This is usually a conscious guilt, a product of the more recent mood of the country. It has become "in" to be healthy, with an emphasis on physical exercise and fitness. We hear frequent admonitions in government-sponsored messages that smoking may be harmful to health. Toothpaste manufacturers promote products that "remove ugly tobacco stains." No-smoking sections on commercial airplanes are government mandated. More and more restaurants and other public places are segregating smokers and nonsmokers. Public awareness of the dangers and undesirability of smoking has never been higher.

The conscious guilt that arises from all of this may or may not create subconscious imprints. Whether or not you have subconscious guilt for smoking is of little or no consequence. You are in the process of quitting smoking and, when you have quit, the subconscious guilt will become a dead issue.

If you do discover that you have subconscious guilt factors for smoking, do not try to use them in your quitting smoking program. That is likely to create more problems than it cures, so stick with the positive aspects of your campaign and ignore any subconscious guilt for smoking. Be sure you understand the distinction between guilt *for* smoking and guilt that *causes* smoking.

SUGGESTION APPLICATION

You will recall from Chapter 4 on suggestion that it is desirable to formulate suggestions in positive terms whenever possible. For quitting smoking suggestions, this general rule usually has to be violated. To my knowledge, there is no positive English word that means "nonsmoker." Euphemisms such as "healthy" can be used, but such words lack the specific meaning wanted in a suggestion. This means that you will undoubtedly have to formulate suggestions with negative words.

Use image rehearsal and all three types of suggestions: formal suggestions applied just before your self-hypnosis exercise; informal (elaborated) suggestions and image rehearsal during your scene visualization; and waking suggestions at other times. You will recall that *waking* suggestions are not suggestions to "wake up"—they are suggestions applied in nonhypnotic or "waking" states.

Formulate two sets of suggestions, one to deal with the sources of dysfunction, the other to directly affect your smoking. Source-suggestions should be formulated to eliminate the sources of dysfunction uncovered in your autoquestioning. If, for example, you learn that the main subconscious reason for your smoking is a need for group acceptance, your suggestions might look something like this:

"I can be a nonsmoker and still be socially accepted."
"The less I smoke, the more friends I have."
"Nonsmokers are acceptable to any group."

If your source of dysfunction is a subconscious connection between smoking and being an adult, you might formulate suggestions along the following lines:

"It is not necessary to smoke to be an adult."

"I can be an adult without being a smoker."

"Smoking is childish; I am an adult, so I don't need to smoke."

When you have your suggestion(s) formulated—remember to use auto-questioning to check for subconscious acceptance—add the concepts of security and calmness to your suggestions. This is necessary because humans tend to put something in their mouths when they are feeling anxious or insecure. This is called *oral gratification,* and smoking is one of the primary ways of achieving it. By increasing your sense of security, and decreasing your anxiety level, you reduce the chances of smoking for oral gratification. By adding security and calmness concepts to the last suggestion presented above, we get:

"Smoking is childish. I am a secure, calm, and relaxed adult, I do not need to smoke."

The second set of suggestions should directly address smoking behavior. Do this by formulating at least one suggestion that increases satisfaction while decreasing the number of cigarettes smoked. Here is the basic suggestion format:

"Every day, in every way, I am finding _____ cigarettes a day to be more than enough."

To fill in the blank in the suggestion, determine how many cigarettes a day you are now smoking. This should be an *average* daily number, obtained by keeping a record for a week or two. When you know your average daily numer of cigarettes smoked, divide that number by six and subtract the result from your daily average. To illustrate this formula, let's say that you now smoke an average of two packs a day, or forty cigarettes.

$$40/6 = 7 \text{ (rounded off)}$$
$$40 - 7 = 33$$

The result is thirty-three, so you would put "33" into the blank in the suggestion. Work with this suggestion and continue to keep a record of how many cigarettes you smoke each day. When you find yourself smoking *fewer* than thirty-three cigarettes a day (note that the suggestion includes the phrase "*more* than enough"), subtract seven again, with the resulting suggestion: "Every day, in every way, I am finding *26* cigarettes a day to be more than enough." Remember, these numbers are for illustration only. Your own numbers are likely to be different.

If you were using these numbers, and you changed the suggestion every week, you would be down to smoking fewer than five cigarettes a day around the sixth week. It does not take much effort to go ahead and quit when you are down to that level. Continue to apply your suggestions at least two weeks beyond that point at which you have no more desire to smoke.

You may find that it takes more or less than six weeks to quit. It is common to find different lengths of time required for each level of the suggestion. Some shorter, some longer. Sometimes it takes five or six weeks to achieve a particular level. The worst thing you can do if this happens is get mad at yourself. After all, even if it takes you six months to quit smoking, that's not bad when you consider that you are doing it without "willpower," without feeling deprived, and without any negative side effects. And when you have finally quit, it will be permanent.

Reinforce your suggestion program with daily image rehearsals. Go back to the Daily Image Rehearsals for Weight Control in Chapter 6 and follow the patterns presented there in constructing your daily image rehearsals. The only difference is that you will make the images relevant to quitting smoking instead of losing weight.

SELF-HYPNOTIC INDUCTION

Enough instructions and examples have already been presented on the induction process for you to be able to construct your own quitting smoking induction. The steps and procedures are the same as for any other purpose: deep relaxation, deepening procedure, scene visualization, and termination. Apply your formal suggestions either before the deep relaxation or between it and the deepening procedure. Informal suggestions and image rehearsals can be applied during the scene visualization.

The induction talk for weight control in Chapter 6 can be easily modified for quitting smoking, or you can use the induction procedure presented in Chapter 2.

SLEEP AND DREAMS

The instructions for prompting alternate reality dreams presented in Chapters 5 and 6 apply equally to quitting smoking. If you have not already started with the sleep and dreaming procedures, go back and reread the relevant parts of those chapters. You want to get everything working in your favor, and alternate reality dreams can work magic for you.

You want to quit smoking, and you want to do it as quickly, painlessly, and effortlessly as possible. Application of the methods presented here will do that for you. Autoquestioning, suggestion formulation and application, self-hypnotic practice, and alternate reality dreams constitute a powerful set of tools with which you can permanently become a non-smoker.

All you have to do is follow the instructions and stick with it until you are successful. I know *you* can do it with self-hypnosis because I and thousands of others have done it.

Appendix: autoquestioning examples

The following autoquestioning examples are from actual cases. Names, dates, places, and certain other pertinent data have been changed to protect the identity of the questioners. Most of these questioning transcripts have been edited to eliminate superfluous questions, so don't feel inadequate if your own questioning is not as logical and succinct as these examples seem to be.

The examples are listed by subject, but it will be instructive for you to read them even if your particular subject of interest is not represented. Reading cases such as these can help you develop a feel for questioning strategies that will help you in your own questioning.

As you read these examples you will notice that they are not perfect. There are occasional lapses in good procedure in most of them. This should encourage you because it shows that you don't have to have letter-perfect technique to get dramatic results.

I have resisted the temptation to point out weaknesses in the questioning so that the examples will be easier to read. Most comments and summaries were written by the persons who did the questioning.

FEARS

Q: Is there another part of the mind that the conscious mind is not aware of?
A: Yes.
Q: Can I refer to this part of the mind as the subconscious?
A: Yes.
Q: Can I ask the subconscious mind for help on solving a problem?

A: Maybe.

Q: May I ask questions to help me find the solution?
A: Yes.

Q: Is there a reason behind my being afraid of small, confined spaces?
A: Yes.

Q: Does this stem from a past experience?
A: Yes.

Q: Does the reason stem from something I heard?
A: No.

Q: Something I was told?
A: No.

Q: Something I physically experienced?
A: Yes.

Q: Did I experience this more than ten years ago?
A: Yes.

Q: More than fifteen years ago?
A: Ask later.

Q: Was this experience one in which I was enclosed in a small space for a long period of time?
A: Rephrase question.

Q: Was I caught in something?
A: Yes.

Q: Was this experience between ten and fifteen years ago?
A: Yes.

Q: Was it thirteen years ago?
A: (No answer.)

Q: Does the time have something to do with the impression?
A: (No answer.)

Q: Was the experience one in which I became scared?
A: Yes.

Q: Did this experience happen at my home?
A: No.

Q: Did this experience involve another person or animal?
A: Yes.

Q: Did this experience occur in [city]?
A: No.

Q: Did it happen at a relative's house?
A: Yes.

Q: Did it happen at my grandmother's house?
A: No.

Q: At the [name]'s farm?
A: No.

Q: At the [different name]'s farm?
A: Yes.

214

Q: Was it twelve years ago?
A: Yes.

"I continued the questioning and discovered it involved something other than a piece of farm equipment. I ran out of questions and still did not have the answer, so I asked it to spell out what was involved in my experience and got PEPICONTDUI for an answer. After about ten minutes I could only guess it had something to do with a PIPE CONDUIT. My older brother says we were playing and throwing dirt clods, and I climbed into a conduit. He and my cousin wouldn't let me out until after they had hit me with dirt clods. The funny thing about it is even after he told me about it, I still don't remember the experience. He claims he remembers the experience because I got real scared after my cousin wouldn't let me out when I wanted to. I'm not a real basket case when it comes to confined spaces, however I do become uncomfortable and restless."

Q: Do I have a subconscious reason for being terrified of large bodies of water?
A: Yes.

Q: Did something happen to me that made me so afraid?
A: No.

Q: Did something happen to somebody I know or knew?
A: Yes.

Q: May I spell out what happened?
A: Yes. ("I used the spelling charts and got DEAD LAD.")

Q: Can you tell me who the dead lad is?
A: No.

Q: Can you tell me how he died?
A: Yes. ("Spelled out DROWN.")

Q: Will you tell me his name?
A: Yes. ("Spelled out SECAYO. I don't know this name.")

Q: Do you mean he fell?
A: Yes.

Q: Where did this happen? What town?
A: ("Spelled out EARTH.")

Q: May I please spell out his name?
A: No.

Q: Am I subconsciously able to remember his name?
A: ("Spelled out HORRER ALTO RALE.")

Q: Then, he fell from a high rail?
A: Yes.

Q: Where was this? A lake? A dam? A river?
A: ("Chose A RIVER.")

Q: Does my mother know about this?

A: Yes.

Q: Is it okay to call my mother and ask her the name of the dead lad?

A: No.

Q: May I spell out his name?

A: Yes. ("Spelled out JIMMY.")

Q: What is his last name?

A: ("Spelled out A FARM IS WHERE I MET POOR JIMMY.")

Q: Where is the farm located?

A: ("Spelled out JIM BESIDE A LAD, A GIRL.")

Q: Was Jim, the lad that died, a homosexual?

A: ("Spelled out "I JUST KNOW JIM GIRL.")

Q: Can you explain?

A: ("Spelled out GUNS ARE BAD—EASY.")

Q: I am more confused than ever. Please explain.

A: ("Spelled AB A BAD GIRL.")

Q: Does "AB" refer to me?

A: ("Spelled out JIM KILL AB DEAD.")

Q: Please explain.

A: ("Spelled out JIM SAME AS KILL AB.")

Q: Does that mean the Jim has taken over my subconscious?

A: ("Spelled out JIM NOW AB FUN AGAIN.")

Q: Please explain.

A: ("Spelled out EGO IMPORTANT.")

Q: Please explain.

A: ("Spelled out GIRL JILL KILL JIM BOY.")

Q: Who is Jill?

A: ("Spelled out ANNE SAME AS JIM NOW JILL.")

Q: I have not asked any of these things you have answered. Are you playing games with me?

A: Yes.

Q: Why?

A: ("Spelled out BIZARRE JOKE.")

Q: Am I punishing myself for things my subconscious feels I deserve?

A: Yes.

Q: Why?

A: ("Spelled out EGO IMPORTANT.")

Q: Then, I consider my ego too important?

A: Yes.

A: Have I punished myself enough?

A: Yes.

Q: Does this mean I have ridden myself of all my guilts and now I can stop smoking and lose weight by suggesting to myself that I can?

A: Yes.

Q: I have a feeling there is something more to say. What is it?

A: ("Spelled out ALL BUT LAKES.")

216

Q: I still fear lakes?
A: Yes.

Q: What must I do?
A: ("Spelled out WIL YOU FORGIV ME EGO IMPORTNT.")

Q: Then, I must forgive myself before I stop being afraid of lakes?
A: Yes.

"As you might know, this isn't half of the questions and answers. I included here only the main points.

"When I first began to question my subconscious, I was delighted because I felt that my subconscious is my spirit or conscience. Being able to communicate with the better part of myself was fantastic. However, sometime during the questioning, I had doubts, such as 'This is all a bunch of baloney' or 'I don't believe this is my subconscious.'

"I went back to the questioning and my subconscious must have felt that I had punished myself enough. Now, I feel great; I have stopped smoking; I have had no desire to eat all that gooey stuff I have always liked; and my memory has improved one hundred percent. The only thing I have left to test is my original fear of lakes. I can say with all conscience that this is the most fantastic thing that ever happened to me."

MISCELLANEOUS

[The following example is from a student who had a cold and scratchy throat that had been getting worse for several days. His questioning concerns this condition.]

Q: Is today Wednesday?
A: Yes. (Correct)

Q: Am I wearing a red sweater right now?
A: No. (Correct)

Q: Do I presently have the symptoms of a common cold?
A: Yes.

Q: Even though I have been taking several grams of vitamin C the last couple of days, the symptoms seem to be worsening. Am I catching a cold?
A: Yes.

Q: Is this cold endogenic? ["self-caused"]
A: Yes.

Q: Then it is possible to either subconsciously prevent myself from getting these symptoms, or clear them up once they have started. Is that correct?
A: Yes.

Q: Then this cold and its symptoms are a subconscious dysfunction?
A: Yes.

Q: I awakened earlier this morning with the feeling that I should do this questioning, that it would be very helpful. Is that feeling correct?
A: Yes.

Q: Is it all right now to talk about this dysfunction that is resulting in the cold symptoms?
A: Yes.

Q: In the past, I have made the comment that I live in continual dread of being sick at a time when I have to give a speech. Is that related in any way to this dysfunction?
A: Yes.

Q: Do I subconsciously feel that if I get sick before or far enough in advance of the speech time, then I won't have to be sick at the time of the speech?
A: Yes.

Q: Is this belief caused by an imprint?
A: Yes.

Q: Is it an identification imprint?
A: Yes.

Q: Are there any other imprints, other than the identification imprint, that bear on this dysfunction?
A: No.

Q: Is the identification factor in this imprint with one person only?
A: Yes.

Q: Is that person my mother?
A: Yes.

Q: Does my mother believe everyone has to be sick a certain amount of the time?
A: Yes.

Q: And I have internalized that belief?
A: Yes.

Q: I want to eliminate this identification factor in order to improve my health. Is there further subconscious information I could get through spelling-out that would be helpful in doing this?
A: Yes.

Q: Am I subconsciously thinking about a word or phrase that I can spell out at this time?
A: Yes.

Q: Is it one word?
A: No.

Q: Is it five or fewer words?
A: Yes.

Q: Is it two words?
A: No.

Q: Is it three words?
A: Yes.

218

"I used the method you taught us and established that the first word had three letters, the second word had four, and the third word had eight letters. Using the spelling charts, I got YOU TALK OVERMUCH."

Q: Is that phrase correct?
A: Yes.

Q: Does the "you" in the phrase refer to the conscious me?
A: Yes.

Q: Does the phrase refer to my subconscious prohibition against boasting?
A: Yes.

Q: Have I boasted about the subconscious ability to control health?
A: Yes.

Q: Was this done while explaining the subconscious to others?
A: Yes.

Q: Do I subconsciously realize that it is my job to do this? [This person worked in health care.]
A: Yes.

Q: I cannot remember overtly boasting about my subconscious powers. Is it possible that I have again become too sensitive (subconsciously) about what is and is not boasting?
A: Yes.

Q: Am I subconsciously reevaluating that position right now?
A: Yes.

Q: Will I now and in the future be able to talk about the benefits of autosuggestion and the powers and abilities of the subconscious without interpreting it as boasting?
A: Yes.

Q: As long as it is done in the spirit of helping others, can I tell of my own experiences without subconsciously interpreting it as boasting?
A: Yes.

Q: Is my subconscious position relative to the identification factor with my mother changing?
A: Yes.

Q: Do I now subconsciously agree that it is not necessary to be sick a certain amount of the time?
A: Yes.

Q: Do I place subconscious importance on being helpful to others?
A: Yes.

Q: Do I subconsciously agree that one of the best ways of being helpful is setting a good example?
A: Yes.

Q: Do I subconsciously believe that being sick sets a good example for others?
A: No.

Q: Will my subconscious, now and in the future, make every effort possible to keep me healthy?

A: Maybe.

Q: Will I subconsciously keep myself healthy if I do not boast?
A: Yes.

Q: And has the definition of boasting been subconsciously narrowed to exclude any communication that is helpful to others?
A: Yes.

Q: Am I right now marshalling my bodily defenses to eliminate this cold?
A: Yes.

Q: Will the symptoms have cleared up by morning?
A: No.

Q: Will I be better in the morning?
A: Yes.

"Two days later my cold was gone. Since this questioning I have felt much freer to discuss mental dynamics with others. I also continue to take vitamin C, not knowing whether it is the vitamin C itself, or my belief in it, that does the good. Have not had another cold since this episode."

Q: Is my sleeping problem a physical dysfunction?
A: No.

Q: Is my sleeping problem a psychological dysfunction?
A: Yes.

Q: Is there something in my subconscious causing my sleeping problem?
A: Yes.

Q: Does that something affect any other part of my life?
A: No.

Q: Is this subconscious dysfunction something that has developed in my adult life?
A: Yes.

Q: Is it anything concerning my marriage?
A: No.

Q: Is it something that has happened in the last five years?
A: Yes.

Q: Is it something resulting from guilt?
A: No.

Q: Is there a phrase that will give me an answer?
A: No.

Q: Is the dysfunction job-oriented?
A: No.

Q: Is the problem the result of one or more imprints?
A: Yes.

Q: One imprint?
A: Yes.

Q: Is that imprint a subconscious belief that I cannot sleep more than four or five hours without waking?
A: Yes.

Q: Is that subconscious belief a result of anxiety?
A: No.

Q: Is the imprint a result of habit?
A: Yes.

Q: Will conscious awareness of the imprint eliminate it?
A: No.

Q: Will a suggestion every evening that I can sleep at least seven hours erase the imprint?
A: Rephrase.

Q: Upon retiring each night, will repeated suggestions that I can sleep a full night without awakening erase the imprint?
A: Maybe.

Q: Will the use of the induction tape help erase the imprint?
A: Yes.

Q: Will continued sessions completely erase the imprint within a few weeks?
A: Yes.

SELF-CONFIDENCE

Q: Is my lack of self-confidence caused by something that happened to me before I was ten years old?
A: Yes.

Q: Before I was five?
A: Yes.

Q: Was this caused by guilt?
A: Yes.

Q: Was this caused by something that happened with a close relative?
A: Yes.

Q: Was it my mother or my father?
A: No.

Q: A grandparent?
A: Yes.

Q: Grandmother?
A: Yes.

Q: Is there a word or phrase that would help me?
A: Yes.

"Using the pendulum spelling-out method, I got U FIX WILLIAM BY LOCATIONS TELL."

Q: Is this phrase correct?

A: Yes.
Q: Is William my grandfather?
A: Yes.
Q: Did I tell my grandmother where my grandfather was?
A: Yes.
Q: I was not suposed to tell where my grandfather was. Is this correct?
A: Yes.
Q: Was my grandmother angry?
A: Yes.
Q: Was my grandfather angry?
A: No.
Q: Was I scolded by my grandmother?
A: Yes.
Q: Is this why I get upset when someone is angry?
A: Yes.
Q: Is this why I lack confidence—because I fear anger in others?
A: Yes.

SMOKING

Q: Is my smoking caused in my subconscious mind or area?
A: Yes.
Q: Is it all right, at this time, for me to know about these things?
A: Yes.
Q: Was it individual identification?
A: Yes.
Q: With my father?
A: Yes.
Q: Does guilt have anything to do with my smoking?
A: Yes.

"From my questioning, I found out one particularly interesting point. When I started smoking, my father had said to me that he could not punish me or be upset with me because he had started smoking when he was sixteen, too. It seems puzzling that what he said had any influence on my smoking. I did think that consciously I was punishing myself by continuing to smoke; however, maybe through what my father said about not punishing me, I felt as if he approved."

WEIGHT CONTROL

Q: I've just lost some weight. I'm starting to look good. Now, I find a renewed interest in eating. Do I subconsciously recognize this eating as a dysfunction?

A: Yes.

Q: Do I also subconsciously need to eat?

A: Yes.

Q: So eating is trying to give me something I need?

A: Yes.

Q: Am I eating to get love?

A: Yes.

Q: Is that the main reason I eat?

A: Yes.

Q: Do I subconsciously believe that staying overweight will keep me from being a threat to others?

A: Yes.

Q: And in that way, I feel I can have more friends?

A: Yes.

Q: Is that also why I seem to reach a certain point in achieving and then quit?

A: Yes.

Q: Do I also eat when I need love?

A: Yes.

Q: Is there a word or phrase I'm thinking of subconsciously that could give me some help in dealing with this overeating?

A: Yes.

Q: Is it one word?

A: No.

Q: How many words is it? (This questioning was done with a Ouija board.)

A: Two.

"Using the Ouija board, I found that the first word had six letters, and the second word had four letters. The following list shows the letters I obtained and the number of times I had to go through them: NZDRWM RLBT—SWOYBY DOO—WOZOTN LIFE—MOSPMP LIFE—RASCON LIFE—NOTICE LIFE."

Q: Is the phrase NOTICE LIFE correct?

A: Yes.

Q: Does NOTICE LIFE refer to the fact that I'm not fully involved in my own life?

A: Yes.

Q: Also that I haven't really taken responsibility yet for my own life?

A: Yes.

Q: Will noticing life remove overeating as a dysfunction?

A: No.

Q: Will a suggestion about noticing life remove overeating as a dysfunction?

A: Yes.

Q: So that if I take responsibility for my own life, I'll no longer need to overeat?

A: Yes.

Q: Am I thinking of one word subconsciously that could give me a clue as to what type of suggestion I should use?

A: No.

Q: A phrase?

A: Yes.

"Using the Ouija board, I found that the phrase had three words with five, three, and six letters. After going through the letters twenty-three times, I finally obtained the phrase: THANK THE HORSES."

Q: Is the phrase THANK THE HORSES correct?

A: Yes.

"This mention of horses was particularly interesting to me, because I have been having dreams in which horses would always help me out of a tight situation."

Q: Does HORSES refer to those in my dreams?

A: Yes.

Q: Do the horses in my dreams refer to my being saved by my *own* abilities?

A: Yes.

Q: So, I'm coming to my own rescue?

A: Yes.

Q: And I should thank myself?

A: Yes.

Q: And realize that I have the ability to help myself?

A: Yes.

Q: Should I direct my suggestions toward coming to the realization of my own abilities at directing my own life?

A: Yes.

Q: How about "Every day, in every way, I am more and more aware that I can control my life effectively?"

A: Yes.

Q: Will applying this suggestion enable me to overcome overeating as a dysfunction?

A: Yes.

Q: Will I then no longer need attention so badly that even my boyfriend's negative attention at my overeating is no longer necessary?

A: Yes.

Q: And if I become more aware of my own positive abilities, will that new awareness make me realize I deserve my boyfriend's respect?

A: Yes.

Q: And if I feel I deserve his (and everyone's) respect, then I'll no longer need to do things to prove he shouldn't respect me?

A: Yes.

Q: How many repetitions at a time?

A: Five.

Q: How many times a day?

A: Five.

Selected bibliography

Adler, Alfred. *Understanding Human Nature* (1927). New York: Greenberg Publisher, 1946.

Ahsen, Akhter. *Psycheye: Self-Analytic Consciousness.* New York: Brandon House, Inc., 1977.

Baudouin, C. *Suggestion and Autosuggestion.* London: George Allen & Unwin, Ltd., 1920.

Bernheim, H. *Suggestive Therapeutics.* New York: G.P. Putnam's Sons, 1902.

Bernstein, D.A. and **T.D. Borkovec.** *Progressive Relaxation Training: A Manual for the Helping Professions.* Champaign, Ill.: Research Press, 1973.

Birney, R.C., H. Burdick and **R.C. Teevan.** *Fear of Failure.* New York: Van Nostrand-Reinhold, 1969.

Coppersmith, S. *The Antecedents of Self-Esteem.* San Francisco: Freeman, 1967.

Coué, Emile. *Self-Mastery Through Conscious Autosuggestion* (1922). London: George Allen & Unwin, Ltd., 1951.

Dorcus, R.M. *Hypnosis and Its Therapeutic Applications.* New York: McGraw-Hill, 1956.

Ellenberger, H.F. *The Discovery of the Unconscious.* New York: Basic Books, 1970.

Estabrooks, G.H. *Hypnotism.* New York: E.P. Dutton, 1953.

Faraday, Ann. *Dream Power.* London: Pan Books Ltd., 1972.

————. *The Dream Game.* New York: Harper & Row, 1976.

Ferguson, Marilyn. *The Aquarian Conspiracy: Personal and Social Transformation in the 1980s.* Los Angeles: J.P. Tarcher, Inc., 1980.

Furst, Bruno. *Stop Forgetting.* Garden City, N.Y.: Doubleday & Company, 1972.

Haimowitz, M.L. and **N.R. Haimowitz.** "The Evil Eye: Fear of Success." In M. L. Haimowitz and N.R. Haimowitz (eds.). *Human Development.* New York: Thomas Y. Crowell Co., 1960, pp. 742–53.

Hamachek, Don E. *Encounters with the Self*. New York: Holt, Rinehart and Winston, Inc., 1971.

Henderson, Charles E. *Success through Self-Communication*. Denver: Biocentrix, Inc., 1973.

Henderson, C. William. *Awakening: Ways to Psycho-Spiritual Growth*. Englewood Cliffs, N.J.: Prentice-Hall, Inc., 1975.

Horney, Karen. *Self-Analysis*. New York: W.W. Norton, 1942.

Janet, P. *Psychological Healing*. Volume I. London: George Allen & Unwin, Ltd., 1925.

Jaynes, Julian. *The Origin of Consciousness in the Breakdown of the Bicameral Mind*. Boston: Houghton Mifflin Company, 1976.

Katahn, Martin. *The 200 Calorie Solution: How to Burn an Extra 200 Calories a Day and Stop Dieting*. New York: W.W. Norton & Company, 1982.

Key, Wilson Bryan. *Subliminal Seduction*. New York: Signet, 1972.

———. *Media Sexploitation*. New York: Signet, 1976.

Klinger, Eric. *Meaning and Void: Inner Experience and the Incentives in People's Lives*. Minneapolis: University of Minnesota Press, 1977.

LeCron, L.M. *The Complete Guide to Hypnosis*. Los Angeles: Nash Publishing, 1971.

———. "The Uncovering of Early Memories by Ideomotor Responses to Questioning," *The International Journal of Clinical and Experimental Hypnosis*, 1963, 11(3), 137–42.

Maltz, Maxwell. *Psycho-Cybernetics*. Englewood Cliffs, N.J.: Prentice-Hall, Inc., 1960.

Mühl, A.M. "Automatic Writing as an Indication of the Fundamental Factors Underlying the Personality," *Journal of Abnormal Psychology and Social Psychology*, 1922, 17.

———. "The Use of Automatic Writing in Determining Conflicts and Early Childhood Impressions," *Journal of Abnormal Psychology and Social Psychology*, 1923, 18(1), 1–32.

Oyle, I. *The Healing Mind*. Millbrae, CA: Celestial Arts, 1975.

Samuels, Mike and Nancy Samuels. *Seeing with the Mind's Eye*. New York: Random House, 1975.

Teevan, R.C. and P.E. McGhee. "Childhood Development of Fear of Failure Motivation," *Journal of Personality and Social Psychology*, 1972, 21(3), 345–48.

Weitzenhoffer, A.M. *General Techniques of Hypnotism*. New York: Grune & Stratton, Inc., 1957.

———. *Hypnotism: An Objective Study in Suggestibility*. New York: John Wiley & Sons, 1963.